TACACHALE

D1300459

Ripley P. Bullen Monographs in
Anthropology and History, Number 1
The Florida State Museum

TACACHALE

Essays on the Indians of Florida and Southeastern Georgia during the Historic Period

Edited by

Jerald Milanich and Samuel Proctor

A University of Florida Book

The University Presses of Florida
Gainesville / 1978

Library of Congress Cataloging in Publication Data
Main entry under title:

Tacachale: essays on the Indians of Florida and southeastern Georgia during the historic period.

   (Ripley P. Bullen monographs in anthropology and
history; no. 1)
   Papers presented in abbreviated form at a symposium
held as part of the 38th annual meeting of the Society
for American Archaeology, San Francisco, May 1973; with
one additional paper.
   "A University of Florida book."
   Includes bibliographies and index.
   1. Indians of North America—Florida—Addresses,
essays, lectures.   2.   Indians of North America—Georgia
—Addresses, essays, lectures.   3.   Acculturation—Case
studies.   I.   Milanich, Jerald T.   II.   Proctor, Samuel.
III.   Society for American Archaeology.   IV.   Series.
E78.F6T33   975.9'004'97   77-20051
ISBN 0-8130-0535-3

The University Presses of Florida is the scholarly publishing
agency for the State University System of Florida.

Copyright © 1978 by the Board of Regents
of the State of Florida

Typography by Composing Room
Grand Rapids, Michigan

Printed by Storter Printing Company, Incorporated
Gainesville, Florida

Contents

Contents

Foreword

THIS new monograph series honors Ripley P. Bullen, who passed away in December 1976. Ripley was a wonderful person who contributed much to the University of Florida, to the museum, and to our understanding of the archeology of Florida and adjacent regions. Along with scholarly pursuits, Ripley devoted a great deal of time to encouraging and educating nonprofessional archeologists. He was one of the founders of the Florida Anthropological Society and served that organization in many capacities.

It is fitting that the museum has chosen to honor Ripley and his accomplishments with a new monograph series emphasizing the publication of archeological and historical research on the southeastern United States and the Caribbean. These areas were the focus of his own research for almost three decades.

This first in the new series of Ripley P. Bullen Monographs in Anthropology and History has been partially funded by a generous grant from the Wentworth Foundation, Inc., founded by the late A. Fillmore Wentworth.

J. C. DICKINSON, JR., Director
Florida State Museum

Introduction

TACACHALE translated from the early-seventeenth-century Timucuan Indian language of northern Florida means "to light a new fire." The ritual of kindling a flame to remove or prevent some impurity was an important part of the religion of the Southeastern Indians. Often this ritual was associated with a period of transition or what anthropologists call a "life crisis" such as birth or death. Lighting a new fire was an attempt to control changes or at least to prevent unforeseen happenings at a time when the status quo was being altered. We have entitled this volume *Tacachale* in order to symbolize the efforts of the aborigines in Florida and southeastern Georgia to deal with the European presence in the New World. Unfortunately, although many changes in the aboriginal cultures took place, they could not overcome the problems posed by the Europeans. During the sixteenth and seventeenth centuries the aboriginal cultures and populations were destroyed under the brunt of Spanish, French, and English expansion into the southeastern United States. When the Spanish withdrew from Florida in 1763 only eighty-three Indians, thought to be almost all of the remaining descendants of the North Florida aborigines, accompanied them.

The Indian cultures in Florida and southeastern Georgia changed in various ways and at various rates during the two hundred years of European contact. These variations were the result of different settings for contact, including missions, military garrisons, ranches, trade networks, and the frontier town of St. Augustine. Consequently, the Florida situation affords anthropologists a comparative field situation for the study of culture change occurring as a result of contact between Western cultures (in this instance, European) and non-Western, non-white cultures (New World aborigines). The Seminole, who entered Florida over a long period of time beginning in the first quarter of the eighteenth century, also underwent rapid change due both to the adoption of Western culture traits and to cultural adjustments made in response to the successive occupation of different environmental zones over a period of several decades.

The papers in this volume were organized around this common theme—describing and interpreting the changes which occurred in the aboriginal cultures during the historic period. All of the papers, except that of William C. Sturtevant, were presented in abbreviated form at a symposium held as a part of the thirty-eighth annual meeting of the Society for American Archaeology in San Francisco in May 1973. The symposium, entitled "Historic Indians of Florida and Southeastern Georgia: Ethnohistorical-Archeological Correlations," contained a presentation on the Apalachee by L. Ross Morrell and B. Calvin Jones, who chose not to publish their paper. Sturtevant's paper, prepared especially for this volume, provides welcomed perspectives on the South Florida Indians. The paper by Samuel Proctor describes the activities of the Center for the Study of Southeastern Indians at the University of Florida and its Indian Oral History Project.

Anthropologists have long recognized the importance of incorporating information derived from historical documents into their research. The present writers are no exception. Our ability to describe and understand correctly the aboriginal cultural dynamics of the historic period is greatly enhanced when archeological data can be combined with historical information and examined through the anthropological perspective. Increasingly, anthropologists are working hand-in-hand with historians to uncover our cultural heritage. Such cooperation is evident in a diverse range of projects presently underway in Georgia and Florida, including studies of Spanish shipwrecks, the culture of plantation slaves, the locations and architecture of Second Seminole War forts, and life in sixteenth-century St. Augustine.

Today, the descendants of many Southeastern Indians still reside in areas once inhabited by their ancestors—the Seminoles in Florida, Creeks in Georgia, Alabama, and West Florida, Cherokees in North Carolina, Catawbas in South Carolina, descendants of the Powhatan Indians in Virginia, Choctaws in Mississippi and Tennessee, and remnants of various tribes in Louisiana and along the coast of South

Carolina. During the last century the lives and cultures of these people have continued to change, much as the cultures of their ancestors changed several hundred years earlier. Many have become so completely assimilated into the non-Indian cultures that surround them that they do not retain any distinctive Indian physical features. Except for a few words, the Catawbas and the Virginia Indians have lost their traditional languages. Some of the Southeastern Indians— the Miccosukees of Florida, the Mississippi Choctaws, the Pamunkeys of Virginia—are conservative, and in an effort to resist acculturation they have sought to avoid as much as possible contact with the outside world. These Indians have tried to maintain their own churches, schools, and social institutions.

The Indians of the Southeast realize how quickly knowledge about their past is fading. They are cooperating with the University of Florida's Oral History Project. By taping meaningful conversations with a representative group of Indians, particularly elderly persons in their communities, much important historical data are being saved. These tapes are transcribed, and edited, and the material is made available for use by scholars.

JERALD MILANICH
SAMUEL PROCTOR

Spanish-Indian Relationships: Synoptic History and Archeological Evidence, 1500-1763

Hale G. Smith and Mark Gottlob

THE exact date of the earliest European contact with the aboriginal peoples in Florida and southeastern Georgia is uncertain. John Cabot's 1497 voyage may have taken him into Florida waters, although the southernmost limits of his voyage are still being argued by scholars, as is the alleged expedition of Vespucci in 1497. The Council of the Indies claimed that beginning in 1510, fleets and ships had gone to Florida, and Florida is indicated on the Cantino map of 1502 (Lowery 1901:123). Thus, Florida was known to Europeans soon after, and perhaps even before, the first voyage of Columbus.[1] These early voyages of discovery, however, had little influence upon the native American groups. Not until the Spaniards came to Florida in larger numbers, establishing settlements and missions, is there any indication of culture change occurring in the aboriginal life-styles.

EARLY EXPLORATIONS, 1500-1550

In 1513, Juan Ponce de León, who had accompanied Columbus on his second voyage and who later had been governor of Puerto Rico, obtained a royal grant authorizing him to explore and settle Bimini, a fabulous island believed to contain a great treasure and a fountain of youth. The narratives of Ponce's expedition do not make clear which

---

1. The Piri Re'is map helps in supporting the hypothesis that the New World was known before 1492 (Hapgood 1966). The map dates from 1513 and shows the Atlantic coasts from France to the Caribbean and south to Antarctica. Hapgood also believes that the Piri Re'is map was derived from earlier maps.

ethnic groups he contacted. Woodbury Lowery believes that he dealt mainly with the Calusa (Lowery 1901:142, 446). Juan Ponce, however, was not the first European to encounter the Calusa since at least one of the Indians he met understood Spanish (Davis 1935:18, 20). In addition, the hostile nature of the Calusa suggests that they had already encountered the Spanish (Swanton 1946:35). Some scholars believe that during Ponce's first voyage along the east coast of Florida he met the Ais Indians, who occupied the Indian River archeological area (Rouse 1951:49).

The period from 1513 to 1526 was a time of exploration, trading, and attempted settlement of the Florida area. In 1516, Diego Miruelo undertook a trading expedition for gold along the Gulf coast, and three years later, Alonzo Alvarez de Pineda sailed along the west coast at least as far as Mobile Bay and perhaps all the way to the mouth of the Mississippi. Francisco Hernández de Córdova attempted a landing upon the southeast coast of Florida in 1517 but was repulsed (Díaz del Castillo 1938:35). In 1521, Ponce de León again tried to establish a settlement in Florida among the Calusa (Lowery 1901:158; Davis 1935:63–64; Swanton 1946:36), but after having touched the island of Tortugas, he was fatally wounded during an Indian attack upon his expedition as its members were getting settled in their new location.

By 1520, there were slave raids on the Florida Indians.[2] Lucas

2. In contrast with the Spanish colonization in other parts of the New World, the settlements in Florida never went beyond their primary status as outposts. It has been stated by W. R. Jackson (1945:77) that a primary reason for this was "the independence of character of the individual Indian, and the Spaniards could not cope with the Indian on an individual basis since they were very few compared to the number of natives they were trying to bring under subjection." It was unlikely that the hostility of the Indians was merely the result of their "independent nature." The European practice of taking slaves, which possibly occurred with the first European landing in Florida, probably led to much of the hostility.

Slaves were an important economic factor during the fifteenth and sixteenth centuries. The first recorded taking of slaves in the New World was during the first Columbus voyage. On October 14, 1592, Columbus noted in his diary: "I do not think that it (a fort) will be necessary for this people is very simple in the use of arms, as your Highness will see from seven of them that I have taken in order to bring them to you" (Helps 1885:147).

By 1499 the *encomienda*, the legal institution that required the Indians to pay tribute and allowed the use of Indians for service, was implemented by Columbus on his second voyage after he found the Indians had become hostile. Enslavement of the Indians was allowed by Queen Isabella because they were reported to be cannibals and could not be converted to Christianity. Therefore, it became an established practice to demand tribute or service, or to enslave the Indians in the New World.

The first documentation of slave-taking in Florida occurred in 1520, and it appears that the Spanish were following their already established practices in the Antilles, and in Central, Middle, and South America. The taking of Indians for slaves probably

Vasquez de Ayllón made a voyage during that year and possibly discovered the St. Johns River. A settlement was established by de Ayllón, perhaps somewhere along the South Carolina coast where the
natives were friendly and easy prey (Lowery 1901:153–57). The
friendliness of the aborigines suggests that they had not previously
encountered the Spaniards. The Florida Indians, being closer to the
Greater Antilles, undoubtedly felt the slave raids first, and their un-
friendliness was a reaction to the hostile Spanish advances.

Pánfilo de Narváez' expedition reached Florida in 1528 and, according to Swanton, landed near Johns Pass just north of Tampa Bay
in Timucua territory (Swanton 1946:37). From there the force moved
inland, proceeding to Apalachee country, where they were subject to
Indian attacks. Later, the group sailed west to Pensacola where they
also encountered hostile natives. The survivors of this expedition
eventually reached Mexico after traveling overland on foot (Núñez
Cabeza de Vaca 1904:9–54).

The Narváez expedition was the first to penetrate the interior of
Florida. During their northward march, the Spanish apparently encountered only one or two Indian villages until they came to the
Apalachee area (Swanton 1922:334). It is most likely they traveled
through the sparsely occupied and swampy coastal flatlands after leaving the central Gulf coast. In the Tampa Bay area, they went to a
village where they found "many boxes for merchandise from Castilla.
In every one of them was a corpse covered with painted deer
hides.... We also found pieces of linen and cloth, and feather head
dresses that seemed to be from New Spain, and samples of gold"
(Núñez Cabeza de Vaca 1904:12–13). According to the Indians, this
material had come from the Apalachee area.

The next major expedition into Florida was by Hernando de Soto
in 1539–40. Several narratives (Garcilaso de la Vega, Gentleman of
Elvas, Ranjel, and Biedma) describe the activities of his expedition
which landed either at Tampa Bay or at Charlotte Harbor (Brinton
1859:15–16; see Bullen, this volume). De Soto's group was composed
of six hundred men and camp followers and their livestock and provisions. Many of their supplies were either given away or buried along
their route.

They spent their first winter, 1539–40, at the town of Iniahica, near
present-day Tallahassee, and in the spring moved into Georgia. In

occurred with the first landings in Florida (Hanke 1949:19), and the hostility between
the peoples of the New World and the Old World may have had its origins even before
Columbus.

Florida, de Soto mainly encountered the Tocobaga, various Timucuan tribes, and the Apalachee. As de Soto marched through Florida
and the Southeast, he met the same general hostile resistance as had
Narváez. His enterprise ended in disaster, and from the time of its
failure until the settlement of the French on the St. Johns River, little
else was done by Spain to explore or colonize Florida.

During this period, 1500–1550, various Spanish shipwrecks occurred along the Florida coast, particularly along the southern part of
the peninsula in the Straits of Florida. As a result of attempts to rescue
the shipwrecked sailors, the Spanish undoubtedly contacted the
Tequesta and other South Florida Indians.

The main purpose of all of these early Spanish explorations was
economic—the search for gold, slaves, land, skins, and other commodities. Less important was the desire to convert the aborigines to
Christianity. The Spanish attitude toward the natives is illustrated by
Narváez' proclamation to those Indians who might prefer their own
religion or the rule of their own chief to that of the king of Spain:
"With the aid of God and my own sword, I shall march upon you; with
all means and from all sides, I shall war against you; I shall compel
you to obey the Holy Church and his Majesty; I shall seize you . . .
your property shall I take and destroy and every possible harm shall I
work you as refractory subjects" (Swanton 1939). Colonization was
held at a minimum, and little was accomplished regarding conversion
of the Indians. The explorers did not find gold in Florida, and
Spanish interest in La Florida waned.

EARLY SETTLEMENTS, 1550–1600

The latter half of the sixteenth century saw Spain once again under-
take activities in Florida. The Spanish colonies in the circum-
Caribbean were partially supplied by fleets from the mother country,
and the Plate Fleet took vast quantities of precious metal back to
Spain. The Crown was forced to extend Spanish control to the coasts
of Florida in order to protect the shipping lanes. Luis de Velasco,
Spanish viceroy of Mexico, planned to occupy Florida and develop
friendly relationships with the Indians. In September 1558, he dis-
patched Guido de Labazares to determine the best Florida site for a
projected settlement, and he reported in favor of Pensacola Bay (Winsor 1886:356–57).

Receiving this information, Tristán de Luna y Arellano began his
preparations for settlement. He sailed from Vera Cruz on June 11,

1559, with five hundred soldiers, a thousand servants and settlers, four Dominicans, and a large group of Mexican Indians (Swanton 1922:159; Lowery 1901:351–77; Priestly 1936; Winsor 1886:356–57). Their exact landing place is questionable; it could have been Pensacola Bay, Mobile Bay, Perdido Bay, or Choctawhatchee Bay. Most scholars believe that the group landed at Mobile Bay and later moved to Pensacola Bay.

Before de Luna could land his stores, a hurricane destroyed five ships, a galleon, and a bark, and blew one caravel and its cargo inland. When the storm subsided, scouting parties were sent out to explore the inland territory. In 1560, after leaving a detachment of fifty men and Negro slaves at the port, de Luna moved his main group to the Indian village of Nanipacna, where many of his people starved to death. The Spanish evidently made no attempt to cultivate the Indian fields or to raise anything for their own support (Winsor 1886:258).

At first de Luna ignored a petition to move back to Mobile, but he was forced to take this action in June 1560. Two ships arrived there to take the women, children, and sick to Havana and New Spain. A scouting party that had stopped in the Coosa area was getting along well, but the majority of de Luna's group refused to follow him there when he wished to set up a base.

Angel de Villafañe's fleet, on its way to Santa Elena, stopped at Pensacola Bay, and the remainder of de Luna's men left with him. When de Luna embarked for Havana, only fifty or sixty men were left at the settlement under the command of Biedma with orders to remain for five or six months. This expedition, as a whole, probably had little effect upon the material culture of the Indians. Its role in introducing diseases is unknown.

In 1561, after many disastrous expeditions to Florida, and only slight material gain, the area was closed to exploration by royal proclamation (Lowery 1901:376). This policy changed rapidly in 1562 after news of the French settlement in Florida reached Spain. Jean Ribault had arrived at the St. Johns River and claimed the area as French, before sailing on to South Carolina. In 1564, René de Laudonnière, with Ribault on his first expedition to Florida, returned to the St. Johns River and established Fort Caroline.

Pedro Menéndez de Avilés, seeing a threat to Spanish shipping, captured Fort Caroline, turned it into a mission, and established St. Augustine in 1565. Because Fort Caroline had been occupied for such a short period and the French had had relatively little rapport with the Indians of the area, the quantity of French materials which fell into aboriginal hands was probably very small. There is little archeological evidence of cultural materials that the French might have brought with them.

St. Augustine was basically a military outpost and frontier town, built on the earlier aboriginal village of the *Cacique* Seloy. A fort was built adjacent to the inlet, and smaller posts were established north and south of the town. Later military fortifications were established in Ais, Tocobaga, Tequesta, and Calusa territory, but they remained active only a short time.

St. Augustine became the center for a number of outlying garrisons and missions positioned to solidify Spain's hold on Florida and its aboriginal population. In 1566, the Spanish established themselves in the Guale area when Menéndez negotiated a settlement of the conflict between the Gualeans and Cusabo. To assure his control he built Fort San Pedro on Cumberland Island, Georgia. A Guale mission was established by the Jesuits in 1570, but they were recalled two years later. Franciscans arrived in the area in 1584, but in 1597, the Indians killed all but one of the missionaries and destroyed several of their missions. Other missions were also established along the Atlantic coast from St. Augustine northward to Guale.

Missionization, 1600–1700

Spanish expansion and exploration into the interior of Florida reached its peak during the seventeenth century. Mission work among the western Timucua was begun at Potano in 1606 (Geiger 1937). An Indian village (Richardson site) of the Potano period (part of the Alachua tradition 1600–1715) indicates, with other evidence from the Fox Pond and Zetrouer sites, that this group had single component Spanish-Indian villages which were established apart from areas occupied by peoples of the prehistoric Alachua tradition (Milanich 1972:35–36). Quite likely, a single, centrally located mission served several outlying villages. Such villages, some with missions, have been archeologically documented for the Timucua. Fox Pond has been tentatively dated between 1630 and 1660 and Zetrouer between 1660 and 1700 (Milanich 1972:57). The Nocoroco site in east Florida (Griffin and Smith 1949) described by Mexía (1605, 1940a, 1940b) was occupied in 1605, but the time range of occupation to either side of this date is unknown.

By 1633, all of the Timucua Indians had been brought under mission control, and the Spanish began to extend the mission chain into

Apalachee territory in northwest Florida. The Apalachee were a Muskhogean group who occupied the area from the Aucilla River on the east to the Apalachicola River on the west. Their northern boundary probably extended into present-day Georgia, with the Gulf of Mexico the southern boundary. They were primarily agriculturalists, growing maize, squash, and beans, who supplemented their diet by hunting and collecting.

The missionization was not totally altruistic; the Spaniards quickly saw that the fertile soil of northwest Florida could supply a surplus of corn sorely needed for the inhabitants of St. Augustine. Foodstuffs from the province of Apalachee were shipped by sea via St. Marks to St. Augustine or were carried overland.

The Apalachee staged a rebellion in 1647, killing three missionaries and destroying seven churches. The Spaniards quelled this violence with help from friendly Apalachee. Some leaders of the revolt were executed; others were sentenced to forced labor.

The Apalachee were later involved in the Timucua rebellion of 1656, which lasted eight months (Swanton 1922:338). This outbreak was directed against the Spanish and their policy of forcing Indians to provide labor for the Spanish farms. The rebellion was quickly put down.

The Apalachee, on the whole, became ideal mission Indians, and after 1647, the conversion of the tribe was completed. In 1655, Díaz de la Calle listed nine missions in Apalachee (Serrano y Sanz 1912:135). The later Calderón letter, written during the bishop's visit to the Florida missions in 1674–75, lists thirteen in Apalachee (Wenhold 1936). Mark F. Boyd, Hale G. Smith, and John W. Griffin (1951), working with these two lists and documents in the Lowery collection in the Library of Congress, found reference to fourteen missions in Apalachee, and the Lowery collection includes a Spanish map showing fifteen missions present. It is impossible to know how accurate these listings are, but they indicate that the number of missions had been growing in the Apalachee area since their inception.

Although the Spanish in 1679 and 1681 attempted to convert the Apalachicolas who lived on the Chattahoochee River, these were for the most part unsuccessful ventures. A single mission was established near the confluence of the Flint and the Chattahoochee rivers (Boyd 1949:2). The Spanish hoped that converting this group would make them resist English advances and that they would serve as a buffer to the Apalachee area on the west.

The English moved into the Flint-Chattahoochee area in 1685, but two Spanish expeditions from San Luis failed to engage them. The Spanish, however, received the submission of eight towns and burned Coweta, Kasita, Tuskegee, and Kolomoki (Boyd 1949:2). The Spanish in 1681, 1687, and 1688 sent out other expeditions aimed at stopping the Indians from trading with the English. In 1689, the Spanish built a blockhouse near Coweta, but the presence of the garrison and memories of earlier cruelties caused the Indians of this area to move even closer to the English.

Spanish missionary efforts in the 1600s were not restricted to northern Florida. The Guale missions were reestablished by 1601 and were maintained until the 1680s when the English, allied with Yuchi, Creek, and Cherokee peoples, attacked the missions, causing the area to be abandoned.

Missions were also established southward from St. Augustine along the Atlantic coast and, perhaps, on the lower St. Johns River. Although a minor rebellion took place in 1618 among the Santa Lucia and Jeaga (Swanton 1922:343), Governor Juan de Salinas visited the Santa Lucia and the Ais in 1622 and was well received, as was Bishop Calderón in 1675.

During the seventeenth century, the Spanish mission system reached its climax among the Florida aborigines (Boyd, Smith, and Griffin 1951). It was the time of the strongest Spanish influence on the aboriginal peoples. The systematic and intensive program of acculturation directed by the Franciscan missionaries gradually brought about many changes in the life-style of the Indians.

DESTRUCTION OF THE MISSIONS, 1700–1763

During the period immediately prior to 1704, the Georgia Indians, pressed by the English in the Carolinas, were increasing their attacks on the north Florida tribes. Swanton (1922:120) notes that Governor Zúñiga wrote on March 20, 1702, that infidel Indians had attacked the town of Santa Fe in Apalachee but were driven off after they had burned the church.

It was decided by the Spanish that a stone or coquina-rock fort be built in St. Augustine as protection from both the English and the pirates who periodically raided the town. The structure was begun in 1672 and by 1696 was completed except for some of the outer works. Fort Mosa was built north of St. Augustine to protect runaway blacks and to serve as a buffer against raids. Governor James Moore attacked St. Augustine in his invasion in 1702, but he was unable to capture the fort. Later, in 1740, James Oglethorpe besieged St. Augustine, but he also failed to take the fort.

In that same year, the Spaniards with nine hundred Apalachee Indians moved against the English and their Creek allies. When the Creeks learned about this expedition, they informed the traders who encouraged the Indians to form a defense force of five hundred men. Then, with the English traders in command, the Creeks confronted the Spanish along the banks of the Flint River. There, the Indians, by a ruse, won the skirmish (Carroll 1836).

In the winter of 1703-4, Moore—with fifty English soldiers and a thousand Creek allies—attacked and destroyed nearly all the towns in the Apalachee province. This force left Ocmulgee in December 1703, and according to a letter written by Moore to the governor of Carolina (Carroll 1836), the Ayubali mission was the first Apalachee settlement encountered. The building was burned, and twenty-five Apalachee Indians were killed. The eighty-four survivors—men, women, and children—were taken prisoner. The next morning Spanish troops from Fort San Luis arrived, but in the fighting, all were either killed or taken prisoner. Afterwards, the chief of Ibitachka, who had a strong and well-made fort, surrendered and turned over the church plate and ten horses laden with provisions.

After leaving Ibitachka, Moore marched through five fortified towns, all of which surrendered unconditionally. By this time his prisoner ranks included all the people from three towns and most of the population from four others. The people of four towns all had been killed and the inhabitants of another had fled before the English arrived, although their buildings, church, and fort were burned. The English proceeded to San Luis, captured the fort, and turned north again.

After Moore's 1704 raid, a small number of the Apalachee moved into the Mobile area and sought French protection. A few eventually resettled in the Pensacola area, and when the British took over Florida in 1763, they moved to the Vera Cruz region of Mexico (Griffen 1959:262).

The culture vacuum left in the Apalachee area was gradually filled by a new group of Indians. This new group, later to be called Seminole, was a mixed group of Hitchiti, Oconee, and other Muskhogean-speaking peoples. The Yamassee rebellion of 1715 and the resulting movement of Georgia Indians increased the number migrating into Florida who became part of the Seminoles.

Shortly after 1700, two western outposts to St. Augustine were established. San Francisco de Pupo and Picolata, built on opposite sides of the St. Johns River, were designed to blockade English movement along the river which might threaten the western flank of the town (Goggin 1951). Originally the main defenses of Florida had been oriented to the sea, but after the English attack in 1702, the Spanish attempted to strengthen their more vulnerable land side. Fort Picolata, on the river's eastern bank, was probably at the site of the Indian village of Salamatoto. The fort, attacked in 1706, was probably built prior to Fort Pupo, which is first mentioned in 1716 (Carroll 1836:144-45).

Diego Peña traveled through the Apalachee and Timucua territory in 1716, escorted by an Apalachicola cacique from the lower Chattahoochee River who wished to get into the good favor of the Spanish and come under their protection. When Peña returned to St. Augustine, he brought along several Indians, who were well received and entertained by the governor. On their return to Apalachicola, they were given presents of a length of red cloth, a blanket, and an *arroba* of powder and one of ball. The Spanish at the time were trading guns and powder to the Indians. Peña was commissioned to take three arrobas of powder and a dozen guns to present to chiefs or principal men who wished to come under Spanish protection.

In the journal of his trip, Peña noted a bull with the brand of La Chua (Alachua) and two buffalo. Cows are mentioned, although there is no indication whether they were domesticated cattle or buffalo cows. The Alachua area was, by this time, settled by Spanish ranchers (Boyd, Smith, and Griffin 1951:68), and peach and fig groves were also flourishing (Swanton 1946:297). Cattle, probably wild, were also encountered in numbers on Lake Jackson prairie in present-day Leon County (Boyd 1949). Apparently these were cattle left behind after the Apalachee exodus. Peña does not mention meeting any Indians until he approached the Ochlockonee, Chattahoochee, and Flint rivers. He proceeded northward into Georgia and notes the villages in the great bend of the Chattahoochee River and the number of warriors in each village.

The sites of Spanish settlements in the northwest Gulf coast area include Fort St. Marks, the village of St. Joseph, and Santa Rosa Pensacola. Fort St. Marks, at the confluence of the St. Marks and the Wakulla rivers in present Wakulla County, Florida, was initially constructed by the Spanish in 1672. It had a continuous occupation until 1882. The original fort was built of wood, and its guns commanded the approach from the Gulf. St. Joseph was a Spanish outpost on St.

Joseph Bay from 1701 to 1722, at which time the settlement and garrison were moved to Santa Rosa Pensacola.

The thirty-year history of the settlement called Santa Rosa Punta de Sigüenza can be described as a time of "storms and high tides" (Faye 1941:162). The western tip of Santa Rosa Island was originally named for Dr. Carlos de Sigüenza y Góngora, chief cosmographer of New Spain and professor of mathematics at the Royal University of Mexico (Manucy 1959:229). A small bastioned stockade was erected at Point Sigüenza during the war between France and Spain in 1719 (Faye 1941:158). When peace was restored the following year, Pensacola returned to Spanish control; the king ordered another fort, large enough to contain a garrison of 150 men, to be constructed on the point. In 1722, the Viceroy of Mexico chose Don Alejandro Wauchope, a Scottish soldier of fortune, as an emissary to go to Mobile and effect the transfer of Pensacola from French to Spanish jurisdiction (Ford 1939:128). Wauchope was assigned three vessels—a frigate, the *Holandesa*, and two smaller vessels—a packet boat and a *balandra*, the *Neptuno* (Ford 1939:129). Wauchope's second mission was to evacuate the post on St. Joseph Bay and to transport the occupants to Santa Rosa Island (Ford 1939:131).

Because of the swampy terrain, it was impossible to erect a fort at Punta de Sigüenza. Another site was chosen within a hundred yards of Santa Rosa Island's northern beach and three-fourths of an English mile east of the point. Cabins first were framed from cedar timbers that had been transported from Vera Cruz, Mexico; later, timbers salvaged from St. Joseph Bay were utilized (Faye 1941:161).

Wauchope had arrived in the Pensacola area November 25, 1722, and by February 13, 1723, the new settlement on Santa Rosa Island was taking shape (Griffen 1959:257). Buildings completed or under construction included "A warehouse forty feet long, twenty feet wide, and twenty feet high, from cedar boards, and nails from Vera Cruz; a powder box, made of the same material, fifteen feet long, ten wide, and five high, covered with hides; a paymaster office, of the material from Vera Cruz, twenty feet long, nine wide, and nine high; two barracks, each forty feet long, eighteen wide, and eight high, constructed of the same material, except for the roofs, which were brought in from San Joseph; a house for Captain Pedro Primo de Rivera, twenty feet long, ten wide, and ten high, made of boards from San Joseph, and nails from Vera Cruz; a powder magazine, ten feet long, eight wide, and eight tall, constructed of boards from San Joseph; twenty-four small buildings, built also of San Joseph material, roofed with bark, for the dwellings of the workmen, convicts, and other persons of the populace; eight large houses for the top officers; a bake oven for bread; and a lookout of thirty-seven cubits, built between two trees, with steps leading up to it" (Griffen 1959:225–56).

Even during the early period of the settlement, the Spanish lacked the necessary provisions for the new arrivals, and Wauchope was forced to accept food from the French in order to survive. When the settlement was ordered to cease this trade in 1723, he was forced to continue clandestine operations in order to exist (Ford 1939:141–42).

On November 3, 1752, a tropical hurricane struck the island, destroying the village and the fort. Only the storehouse and the hospital survived the three-day storm. Some residents sought refuge at the small post of San Miguel on the mainland; others attempted to build a blockhouse one-quarter mile east of the destroyed settlement. The blockhouse was constructed with the help of French supplies and provisions from Mobile (Faye 1941:163). It apparently remained until the surrender of Pensacola and Santa Rosa Island to the British in the summer of 1763 (Faye 1941:168).

European Items Introduced in the Sixteenth Century

During the period 1500–1600, European trade goods were not present in Florida in any great quantity. The Indians probably received the bulk of European materials from shipwrecks. As noted, French influence upon the aboriginal cultures was negligible. The French had remained only briefly in Florida, and they were there mainly for purposes other than trade.

The Spanish contacts during this period were also relatively light because of the Indians' reluctance to associate with them. The Spaniards had difficulty in finding food to support themselves, and the Indians withdrew rather than be forced to supply them with food.

The inventory of European artifacts from sixteenth-century aboriginal sites is not extensive. Glass beads were a favorite European trade item in the New World. Seed beads of blue, white, green, polychrome striped, and iridescent blue are noted, as well as cylindrical and chevron beads. Other glass materials include glass finger rings and looking-glass fragments.

An examination of the various types of artifacts from west coast sites of the sixteenth century reveals many differences in materials from those of the east coast sites. Iron artifacts are less numerous, perhaps indicating that west coast sites are somewhat older than those in the east or that they were receiving trade items from another source. Most metal objects are manufactured from silver, gold, or brass. Silver artifacts include pendants, tubular rolled beads, buttons, discs, and an occasional coin; brass materials include sleigh bells, hawk-bells, discs, cutlass sections, plummets, tubular beads, bracelets, and sheet brass fragments. Brass buttons and bone combs were also found.

The greatest variety of tools from this period are of iron. These include celtiform axes, knife blades, hafted axes, chisels, spikes, fish spears, adzes, boxes, pointed rods, hoes, and horseshoes. Some of these items are known from only one specimen, however. Spanish ceramics are represented by majolica from Spain and Mexico, olive jar sherds, and a tin-glazed cooking ware. French faience was present as well as Spanish, Dutch, and English pipes.

Other European-derived materials found in the 1500–1600 period sites of the west coast are all from the St. Marks Wildlife Refuge cemetery. These include the following Southern Cult materials: a copper-crested woodpecker (seahorse?) with a golden eye, an embossed copper gorget, a plain copper gorget, a copper cult tablet, an incised copper plaque with European stag depicted, a mourdant, copper beads, and two circular gold gorgets.

The few European materials acquired by the aborigines had little effect upon their material culture. The historic trade materials were, for the most part, of an ornamental nature. Tools did occur, but were represented only by a few iron artifacts.

It is assumed that a high percentage of the European trade material was of Spanish derivation. However, the brass sleigh bells from the Marsh Island site probably were of English derivation and must have come into the area by trade with a British vessel rather than being traded overland from English contacts along the east coast. Although the British did not become well established on the southeastern coast until the founding of Jamestown, occasional vessels of English registry stopped for water or trade, or to raid the Indians.

Silver is much more prevalent than gold in the sixteenth-century sites. On the east coast, the Spaniards periodically sent patrols among the coastal Indians to collect all types of metal. The paucity of gold in these sites may be due to this practice. On the northwest and west coasts, the relative scarcity of gold is probably because this area was too far away from the Florida Indians' major source, the Plate Fleet wrecks. The gold ornaments from the St. Marks Wildlife Refuge cemetery were probably brought into the northwest coast by Glades Indians (Goggin 1947:114–27).

EUROPEAN ITEMS INTRODUCED IN THE SEVENTEENTH CENTURY

During this period the mission system was the predominant stimulus for culture change in northern and eastern Florida, and relatively large amounts of European items found their way into the material culture of the Indians. Although not all of the Spanish-Indian mission sites have been located, a large enough sample has been investigated to provide considerable knowledge of the associated archeological complexes. There are numerous varieties of iron artifacts from the north Florida mission and mission-fort sites. These include, among other things, scissors, knife blades, fish spears, awls, hatchets, sword blades, pointed rods, celtiform axes, nails, shoe buckles, lance heads, spring locks, keys, slide bolts, flintlock strikers, a spur rowel, L-shaped brackets, chest handles, double and single pins, anvils, and musket barrels. Fragments of iron cannon and grenades have come from Fort San Luis at Tallahassee.

Silver artifacts were most numerous in the eastern portion of the Florida peninsula. Many types were also found at the Goodnow site in Highlands County, silver coin beads being the most common. Brass artifacts are not numerous, although there is great variety in the forms represented. There seems to be an even geographical distribution of brass materials throughout Florida. Copper artifacts, which may have been of European trade copper, consist of bead links, tubular beads, and rings. Miscellaneous metal artifacts include crosses, musket balls, beads, and finger rings, all made of lead, and a gold pendant and gold-plated clay bead. Chain mail and brigandine have also been found.

Olive jar sherds are so common during this period they might be considered its hallmark. Majolica and Mexican sherds, as well as Chinese porcelain sherds, occur in numbers. Glass fragments—mirrors, glass buttons, scrapers made of bottle glass, and Venetian vials—are present, as are various types of glass beads. Gunflints were either made of European flint or from native Floridian flint. English gunflints have come from Fort San Luis, while native stone flints were found in the northwestern Florida sites.

The remains of domestic animals—pigs, oxen, cows, and horses—occur at many seventeenth-century sites. Domestic plants are represented by remains of corncobs, peach pits, gourds, beans, peas, and garlic.

This period shows a decrease in the quantities of silver and gold objects and an increase in the number of artifacts made with various types of materials. European ceramics also occur in larger quantities. Although this was the important period for the missions in northwest Florida, few items of religious significance have been found at mission sites. The only evidence to date are rosary beads, lead crosses, a crucifix, and a piece of a marble slab which might have been a section of an altar.

EUROPEAN ARTIFACTS INTRODUCED IN THE EIGHTEENTH CENTURY

The artifact inventory from Santa Rosa Pensacola presents the most complete listing of materials for an eighteenth-century Spanish site in Florida. The site is unique because it was in existence for only a short period of time, and after its destruction by a hurricane it was not resettled. Although the trait list of European artifacts from St. Augustine may be more extensive, it is not clear which artifacts date from the eighteenth century. There is a paucity of artifactual material from Fort St. Marks since most of the archeological work has been concentrated on architectural features.

The aboriginal ceramic wares from Santa Rosa Pensacola reflect the movements of the native populations during the early eighteenth century. The majority of aboriginal sherds include those of Fort Walton, Leon-Jefferson, Alachua, San Marcos, and Seminole types (Smith 1959:128–29). Aboriginal pipe fragments are also known. European ceramics include majolica, various Spanish unglazed or glazed earthenwares (including olive jars), Mexican (Aztec IV) earthenware, French faience, Chinese porcelain, Dutch delft, German Rhenish ware, and various English types (Goggin 1947:114–25). Dutch and English kaolin pipes occur in large numbers during this period. Glassware is composed mainly of bottle fragments as well as enameled and etched tumbler, goblet, and cosmetic jar fragments. Both French and English gunflints are present. However, unlike the seventeenth-century mission sites, native gunflints did not occur.

Coins include French colonial sow and Spanish-American silver. Only ten coins were recovered from Santa Rosa Pensacola. Very few coins have been found in the Florida land sites, and the use of currency obviously was not widespread.

Iron hardware and tools include hand-wrought nails, hatchets, saw blades, wedges, adzes, and chisels. A caulking tool reflects the building or maintenance of boats or ships. Furniture hardware includes iron chest corner brackets, locks, cotter pins, padlocks, chest handles, iron strap hinges and strap bindings, and brass pull knobs. The military hardware consists of a bayonet, flintlock strikers and cocks, frizzins, spears, and sword guards. The brass gun parts were trigger guards, lock plates, butt plates, and gun barrels. Chapes also occurred.

The only agricultural-related objects were a socketed hoe and the remains of corncobs. Iron knife blades and handles, with or without bone, spoons (also of pewter), and two-tine forks were used for tableware. Iron scissor blades, with or without brass handles, and sewing thimbles composed the "sewing basket."

Personal possessions of brass include eyeglass frames, religious medallions, sleeve links, neck pendants with glass settings, finger rings, buttons (also of pewter), tinklers, belt and shoe buckles of either iron or brass, and gold-plated keys for a music box. Lead artifacts included seals from wine casks or bottles, cloth bale seals, perforated discs, sounding leads, and musket balls. Stone artifacts aside from gunflints were *manos*, basalt sharpening stones, pestles, sandstone net sinkers, and sounders. Iron fishhooks, harpoons, and lead fishline weights were also present.

The Seminoles arrived in Florida during the eighteenth century bringing with them English artifacts. The British occupation of St. Augustine, 1763–83, put an end for a time to Spanish influence in Florida. By this time most of the indigenous Indian tribes had become extinct or were so reduced in numbers that they remained only as remnant groups.

References

Boyd, Mark F.
1949.   Diego Peña's Expedition to Apalachee and Apalachicola in 1716. *Florida Historical Quarterly* 28:1–27.
Boyd, Mark F., Hale G. Smith, and John W. Griffin.
1951.   *Here They Once Stood: The Tragic End of the Apalachee Missions.* Gainesville: University of Florida Press.
Brinton, Daniel Garrison.
1859.   *Notes on the Floridian Peninsula, Its Literary History, Indian Tribes and Antiquities.* Philadelphia: J. Sabin.
Carroll, B. R.
1836.   *Historical Collections of South Carolina.* New York: Harper and Brothers.
Davis, T. Frederick.
1935.   History of Juan Ponce de León's Voyages to Florida. *Florida Historical Quarterly* 14:8–86.

Díaz (del Castillo), Bernal.
1938. *The True History of the Conquest of Mexico.* Translated by Maurice Keating, with an introduction by Arthur D. Howden Smith. New York: R. M. McBride and Company.
Faye, Stanley.
1941. Spanish Fortifications of Pensacola, 1698–1763. *Florida Historical Quarterly* 20:151–68.
Ford, Lawrence Carroll.
1939. *The Triangular Struggle for Spanish Pensacola, 1689–1739.* Washington: The Catholic University of America Press.
Geiger, Maynard J.
1937. *The Franciscan Conquest of Florida, 1573–1618.* Vol. 1 of Studies in Hispanic-American History. Washington: The Catholic University of America Press.
Goggin, John M.
1947. A Preliminary Definition of Archaeological Areas and Periods in Florida. *American Antiquity* 13:114–27.
1951. Fort Pupo: A Spanish Frontier Outpost. *Florida Historical Quarterly* 30:139–92.
Griffen, William B.
1959. Spanish Pensacola, 1700–1763. *Florida Historical Quarterly* 37:242–63.
Griffin, John W., and Hale G. Smith.
1949. Nocoroco, A Timucua Village of 1605 Now in Tomoka State Park. *Florida Historical Quarterly* 27:340–61.
Hanke, Lewis.
1949. *The Spanish Struggle for Justice in the Conquest of America.* Philadelphia: University of Pennsylvania Press.
Hapgood, Charles H.
1966. *Maps of the Ancient Sea Kings.* Philadelphia: Chilton Company.
Helps, Arthur.
1855. *The Spanish Conquest in America*, vols. 1, 2. London: J. W. Parker and Son.
Jackson, W. R.
1954. *Early Florida through Spanish Eyes.* Coral Gables: University of Miami Press.
Lowery, Woodbury.
1901. *The Spanish Settlements within the Present Limits of the United States, 1513–1561.* New York: G. P. Putnam's Sons.
Manucy, Albert C.
1959. The Founding of Pensacola—Reasons and Reality. *Florida Historical Quarterly* 37:223–41.
Mexía, Albaro.
1605. *Derrotero util y provechoso y en todo verdadero de rios, canos, lagunas, montes, poblaciones enbarcaderos, baraderos, rancherias, el qual desde la ciudad de San Agustin hasta la verra de Aiz por Albaro Mexia.* Woodbury Lowery Collection, no. 98. [Tracing in the Library of Congress. Original in the Archivo General de las Indias, Sevilla.]
1940a. *Derretero util y provechoso y en todo verdadero de rios, canos, lagunas, montes, poblaciones, embaracaderos, baraderos, rancherias el qual reza desde la ciudad de San Agustin hasta la varra de Aiz, 1605.* Lowery Florida MSS, vol. 5. [Transcription from National Park Service film by E. W. Lawson, St. Augustine, Florida.]
1940b. *Useful and Convenient Directions giving faithfully the Rivers, Channels, Lagoons, Woodlands, Settlements, Embarcation* and *Landing-Places, and Hamlets, encountered from the City of St. Augustine to the Bar of Ais.* Lowery Florida MSS, vol. 5. [Translated by Charles D. Higgs, St. Augustine, Florida.]
Milanich, Jerald T.
1972. *Excavations at the Richardson Site, Alachua County, Florida: An Early Seventeenth-Century Potano Indian Village.* Bureau of Historic Sites and Properties Bulletin 2, pp. 35–61. Tallahassee.

Núñez Cabeza de Vaca, Alvar.
   1904.   *The Journey of Alvar Núñez Cabeza de Vaca and his Companions from Florida to the Pacific, 1528-1536.* Translated by Fanny Bandelier, edited with an introduction by Adolph Francis Bandelier. New York: Allerton Book Company.
Priestley, Herbert Ingram.
   1936.   *Tristán de Luna, Conquistador of the Old South.* Glendale, Calif.: Arthur H. Clark Company.
Rouse, Irving R.
   1951.   *A Survey of Indian River Archaeology, Florida.* Yale University Publications in Anthropology, no. 44.
Serrano y Sanz, Manuel, ed.
   1912.   Documentos Relativos a la Florida. *Documentos de la Florida y la Luisiana, Siglos XVI al XVIII.* Madrid: Librería General de Victoriano Suárez.
Smith, Hale G.
   1959.   Spanish Artifacts of Florida. Manuscript, Department of Anthropology, Florida State University, Tallahassee.
Sterling, M. W.
   1935.   Smithsonian Archaeological Projects Conducted under the Federal Emergency Relief Administration 1933-34. *Smithsonian Institution Annual Report, 1934.*
Swanton, John R.
   1922.   *Early History of the Creek Indians and Their Neighbors.* Bureau of American Ethnology Bulletin 73.
   1939.   *Final Report of the United States de Soto Expedition Commission.* 76th Cong., 1st sess., H.R. 71.
   1946.   *The Indians of the Southeastern United States.* Bureau of American Ethnology Bulletin 137.
Wenhold, Lucy L.
   1936.   *A Seventeenth-Century Letter of Gabriel Díaz Vara Calderón, Bishop of Cuba, Describing the Indians and Indian Missions of Florida.* Smithsonian Miscellaneous Collections, vol. 95, no. 16.
Winsor, Justin.
   1886.   *Narrative and Critical History of America.* Boston: Houghton Mifflin Co.

The Calusa

Clifford M. Lewis

THE Calusa were the aboriginal group and culture which occupied the west coast of Florida from Charlotte Harbor south to the
Florida Keys during the historic period. They were, for the most part,
coastal dwellers. During the period of greatest contact with the
Spaniards (1566–69), the principal site of the Calusa was Mound Key,
an island in Estero Bay a few miles south of Fort Myers (Boyd
1938:188–220; Goggin and Sturtevant 1964; Lewis 1969). This location seems to accommodate all contemporary sources and the description of the Gulf coast and the "Bay of Carlos" described by the cosmographer Juan López de Velasco (1894:162–65), who located the
town on "a small island about half a league in circumference" in the
middle of a bay. Mound Key is virtually the only island in the general
area round enough to be described as having a circumference, and
the dimensions given seem to comply with modern measurements of
the island. Velasco wrote his description in the period immediately
following Spanish contact with the Calusa and most likely after con-
sulting men who had sailed that coast.

Calusa is used to designate the tribe or culture, *Calos*, the principal
town, and *Carlos*, the name of the principal chief. Only with the last
is there any difficulty. Juan Ponce de León, in connection with his
1513 voyage, used the name Carlos at a time when Charles V was not
yet on the throne (Herrera 1730: 1:248), and it apparently was a
name for Calusa chiefs long after Philip II was ruler of Spain. Solís de
Merás relates, "This cacique was called Carlos because his father was
so called, and his father gave himself that name because the Christian

19

captives had told him that Emperor Charles [V] was the greatest King of the Christians" (1964:151). Obviously either Solís or Herrera is wrong.[1] Fontaneda, writing about 1575, speaks of Carlos' father only as Senquene (1866:537). Herrera, on the other hand, writing in 1598, may have been in error.

SIXTEENTH-CENTURY SPANIARDS AMONG THE CALUSA

By 1513, forced labor in the gold and silver mines, contagious diseases, and widespread discouragement had made deep inroads into the Indian population of Hispaniola (Friede and Keene 1971, passim).[2] Montesinos and his Dominican associates were crying out in protest, even to Ferdinand, the Spanish king. After the death of the more sympathetic Isabella, however, Ferdinand gave little more than lip service to the affirmation of Indian rights. The patents that he gave to Ponce de León clearly set forth a twofold reward for Spaniards conquering lands northwest of Hispaniola: they would be given both property and the labors of the Indians to whom the lands belonged (Davis 1935:8–66).

Juan Ponce had been saddled with the dubious responsibility of discovering the legendary Fountain of Youth, so described in a story promulgated by the Arawak.[3] He was to search for it, perhaps not in Florida, but in Bimini (Andros?), an assignment he gave to a subordinate on the return trip. Juan Ponce himself explored the area on Florida's south coast from about Cape Canaveral around to the Gulf of Mexico, probably to a point between Estero Bay and Charlotte Harbor. There he fought with the Indians who came forth in a score of canoes, "some fastened together by twos" (Davis 1935). A similar, two-canoe toy was recovered from the muck at the famed Key Marco site on the southwest Florida coast, also giving evidence of the Calusa's sea-faring technology (Cushing 1897:329–448).

Following Juan Ponce, the Jesuit Father Juan Rogel was also impressed with the capabilities of Indian canoes. When things were at a

1. If Herrera is correct about the name, Goggin and Sturtevant (1964:193, fig. 2) are right in speaking of Carlos I and Carlos II. Carlos II must have had another original name, since he was not the son of Carlos I.

2. Estimates of the original population of Hispaniola run as high as eight million, which is probably too high. The Calusa are believed now by some archeologists to have occupied western Florida for more than a thousand years, much longer than the Arawak in Hispaniola, and they probably had more than ten thousand population living in a benign environment.

3. See Fontaneda's testimony concerning the Arawak on p. 26.

standstill at Estero in 1567, he proposed having Indians in a pair (*un par*) of canoes—possibly bound together—transport him to Matecumbe in Los Martires (Zubillaga 1946:291). There he hoped to establish a mission which would be a part of Menéndez' original plan for Florida (Zubillaga 1946:passim). The captain refused to accede to Rogel's request.[4] Nevertheless, the idea of the voyage must have emerged from discussion with the Indians, who indicated its possibility. There is also evidence that Indians made occasional trips to the Bahamas, and even to Cuba, to trade.[5]

A passage from Herrera's account (1730: 1:248) of Ponce's first voyage contains some interesting, though not too trustworthy, remarks: "while waiting wind to go in search of the chief Carlos, as the Indians who understood the Spaniards, who, it was believed, must be from Hispaniola or from another island of those inhabited by the Spaniards, said that they should wait, as the chief wished to send gold in order to trade."[6] If indeed the chief's name was Carlos, it was more likely a corruption of Calos, for Charles V had not yet been crowned. It would be natural for a Spanish listener to think of the common name just from the similarity of the sound. Knowing the later proclivity of Indian prisoners to seek escape when near their home, it is easy to conceive that an earlier slaver had carried this Indian to a Spanish island where he stayed long enough to learn the language of his captors. References to gold are more difficult to explain, unless gold was recovered from the wrecks in the Gulf Stream. The inferior *guanín* gold, sometimes said to have been exhibited by some of the natives, may have been obtained from the Appalachian region.[7]

In 1517, the ships of Cordoba, after bitter engagements with the Indians of Yucatán, stopped briefly on the southwest coast of Florida while en route back to Havana. The guide was the pilot Alaminos, who had been with Juan Ponce. The men obtained fresh water by digging deep wells on a broad beach. Indians soon appeared and fought from their canoes with long bows, swords, and lances. The Spanish killed twenty-three Indians not far from the same creek

4. The neglect of these Key Indians is hard to understand, considering their proximity to Cuba. The captain was wise in refusing Rogel permission to go there, however, for they probably would have killed a solitary Spaniard.
5. This has been attributed more to the residents of Tocobaga than to the Calusa.
6. There are no original accounts of the voyage of Ponce de León, and not too much credence can be attached to specific details.
7. A main goal for Spanish exploration was finding gold and silver, and they tended to believe fanciful stories concerning it. The natives of the Atlantic Coast usually told their listeners anything they wanted to hear.

which Ponce de León had once visited. Any attempt to place Ponce much north of the Caloosahatchee River is difficult since Alaminos required only a day and a half to return to Havana, in spite of the delay caused by being grounded in the shallows near Los Martires (Díaz del Castillo 1956:16). The Dominican Fray Luis Cáncer and three of his associates experienced the ferocity of the west coast Indians in 1549: they were killed almost as soon as they landed.

The adventures of de Soto at his landing point on the west coast in 1539 are of considerable interest to the ethnologist. Four accounts of his dealings with the natives have been preserved. Recent writings by Wilkinson (1947–48) make a detailed case for the Caloosahatchee River as the landing place of de Soto. Earlier commentators who were not as sensitive to the complexities of deriving the location argue for Tampa Bay. None of the de Soto documents refers to Senquene or to Carlos.

From de Soto's time until the arrival of the French on the east coast of Florida in the 1560s, Spanish ships frequently came to grief on the west coast, blown there by winds which were sometimes of hurricane force. Maps of the Gulf coast of 1700 and earlier indicate the fleets from Vera Cruz hugged that coast as closely as their draught would permit.[8] Coming south along the western shore, the fleets originally sailed around the Dry Tortugas before reaching Havana. Pedro Menéndez claimed discovery of the channel inside the Tortugas in 1566 (Barcia 1951:101). The shoreline route in the Gulf no doubt was dictated not only by currents but by fear of hurricanes, which could not be accurately predicted at that time.

René Laudonnière, writing in 1564 about Fort Caroline on the St. Johns, supplies considerable material which dovetails with later Spanish accounts. He mentions a wreck fifteen years earlier (1549?) in the Keys ("The Martyrs") near "Calos," which is shown on the Le Moyne map as the southern tip of the Florida peninsula (Lorant 1946:34–35). "King Carlos had salvaged for himself most of the riches with which these ships were laden, and through his efforts, nearly all of the crew had been saved. A number of women were also rescued; three or four were married noblewomen accompanied by their children. They were still living with this King Calos.

"When I questioned them [two Spanish survivors] further about

---

8. Pertinent maps add little to this essay, save for those that indicate routes in the Gulf of Mexico.

this King, the men told me that he was the handsomest and biggest Indian of all that region and an energetic and powerful ruler. He possessed a great store of gold and silver, which he kept in one of his villages in a pit as deep as a man is tall and as large around as a cask. The men assured me that if I would go there with a hundred soldiers, they could help me to acquire all this wealth, besides whatever else I might obtain from the natives of the country. They also told me that when the women met for dancing, they wore on their belts flat gold plates as large as *quoits* and so heavy that they interfered with their movements and that the men, too, were similarly loaded. They believed that most of this wealth came from Spanish ships, for many vessels are wrecked in that strait. What they did not obtain from the boats, they gained by trade with the other chiefs in the neighborhood."

Laudonnière next described the religious role assumed by "Calos": "The King was greatly revered by his subjects, since he had convinced them that it was his magic incantations that caused the earth to provide them with the necessities of life. To maintain this belief he shut himself up with two or three confidential companions in a certain building. There he performed these incantations, and anyone who tried to spy on what happened inside this hut was immediately put to death on the King's orders. The men related that every year at harvest time this barbarian sacrificed a victim chosen from among the shipwrecked Spaniards who were prisoners. One of my informants also told me that he had often been sent as a courier to another chief, named Oathkaqua, who lived four or five days' journey from Calos and who was a faithful ally of its King. Half way through this journey, in a great fresh-water lake called Sarrope . . . was an island five leagues wide and as many long, abounding in a great variety of fruit, especially dates, in which there was a considerable trade. There was a still bigger trade in a certain root used for making flour. From this flour excellent bread could be made, which supplied the country for fifteen leagues around. As a result the islanders were growing rich at the expense of their neighbors because they sold the root only at a very high price."

According to Laudonnière, these islanders captured the beautiful daughter of Oathkaqua, along with her retinue, as she was being taken to be married to King Carlos. The islanders prized women captured in this manner, Laudonnière's informer reported. He also noted, "King Calos lived near a river forty or fifty leagues southwest

of the promontory of Florida [Canaveral?], while Oathkaqua's village
was just north of the Cape, at a place called Canaveral, twenty-eight
degrees north of the equator" (Lorant 1946:56–60).

The two Spanish survivors were ransomed by the French from
kings named Onatheaqua and Mathiaca. Both Spaniards were naked,
bearded, and long-haired. There is a question of whether Carlos, by
turning over the captives, was seeking to extend his hegemony northwest of Canaveral. If he moved northeast of Canaveral he would have
collided with Saturiba, who was also ambitious. The Spanish eventually had to settle accounts with Saturiba.[9]

Some of the information supplied by Laudonnière and Le Moyne
may profitably be analyzed in the light of later information from
Spanish records of Calos. The distance from Calos to Canaveral—
forty or fifty leagues—is a sufficiently accurate estimate of the distance
from Mound Key to Canaveral. Actually, Le Moyne's map places
Calos too close to Los Martires, a natural mistake since most Europeans would likely underestimate the range of the Florida natives.
That King Carlos did go to the wreck with his own Indians indicates
his hegemony over the entire southwest coast. It also suggests a good
reporting service and is additional evidence that Charlotte Harbor
was not Carlos' headquarters. Vessels were passing the Tortugas at
the time and continued to do so for some two centuries. All in all,
Laudonnière's report of the events has a mark of authenticity that ties
in with what the Spaniards later reported regarding the scattering of
prisoners to various villages and also with their descriptions of the
temple activities.

Although Pedro Menéndez himself had recommended abandoning
the Florida projects in 1561, events which occurred shortly thereafter
reawakened the king's interest in a settlement in the area. At the same
time, Menéndez had a personal reason for taking on the responsibility
for putting the old plan into effect, with some modifications of his
own. In 1562, the French, under Jean Ribault, established a settlement at Port Royal, or Santa Elena, and two years later they entered
the St. Johns River and built Fort Caroline. Menéndez' personal
interest was the loss of his son, Don Juan Menéndez, when a treasure
ship foundered. Menéndez speculated that the accident might have
occurred off the west coast of Florida, although he checked points

9. Saturiba is also spelled Saturiwa. The French, lacking the letter *w*, originally
rendered the name as Saturioua. He was a dangerous politician and more friendly to
the French than to the Spanish. The Spanish did succeed in taking two of his young
subjects to Spain for indoctrination.

along the Atlantic coast also. His planned intensive search of the Gulf coast was delayed by his bloody expulsion of the French from Florida and the establishment of St. Augustine in 1565.

Menéndez was given jurisdiction for all provinces of La Florida, stretching from Texas to Newfoundland and he was directed to evangelize the natives. Previously, only four religious orders had been permitted by the Crown and the Council of the Indies to carry on missionary work in the Spanish Empire. The Jesuit order had been founded in 1540 and was working in the Indies and in Brazil. After a rupture with the Dominicans and an unexplained failure of Franciscans to arrive in Florida, Menéndez turned to the Jesuits to direct his religious plan for Florida. The king consented to that order doing missionary work in his dominions, and Jesuit officials agreed to supply men. To put his master plan for ecclesiastical and temporal control of Florida into effect, Menéndez wished first to establish beachheads— garrisoned forts at strategic points around the peninsula and the east coast as far north as the Chesapeake. He would then seek short cuts for water transport, one across southern Florida by way of Lake Okeechobee and another completely across the North American continent to finally establish the water route to China. Third, he would settle many of the garrisons with colonists, livestock, and the means to cultivate the land. A fourth aspect of his plan, and most pertinent to this study, was to put an end to the Indians' quarrels among themselves and, through gifts and pacts, bring them under Spanish control. To insure a disciplined soldiery, to provide religious worship to the settlements, and to make the Indian population docile, Menéndez would use both secular and religious clergy. He ended up, however, with only a handful of secular priests and Jesuits.[10]

The Jesuits who came to Havana and Florida appear to have supported Menéndez' plan, which was well detailed by 1567. They would set up a school in Havana for the education of the Indians, particularly the sons of important chiefs. Mission teaching stations would operate on the east and west coasts of Florida and in Los Martires— specifically Upper Matecumbe Key. To deter any Indian troubles, including the molestation of shipwreck victims, Menéndez thought he held good hostages in the sons and wives of the chiefs that he was bringing to Havana to instruct (propagandize) to prepare them to serve as mission helpers.

10. Actually Menéndez was seeking both Dominicans and Franciscans in 1566, and it is not known why the Franciscans did not arrive until 1573.

To bridge the language barrier, adolescents from Spain or the Florida colonies went to live with the tribes to acquire the native tongues quickly and naturally. Soldiers and shipwrecked persons cast among the Indians were also used as catechists and translators. In addition, Jesuit missionaries, at Menéndez' insistence, struggled to learn the Indian dialects, starting with the Calusa.

Fontaneda (1866; 1945), while a captive of Carlos, traveled widely in Florida and described in his memoirs his observations of Carlos' kingdom and the fifty subject villages he was able to count, although Fontaneda could remember the names of only half.

Fontaneda spoke of Carlos' father not as the elder Carlos, but as Senquene, who is credited with making a town for the Arawak of Cuba, who had come searching for the Fountain of Youth. The possibility of such a miraculous fountain was reportedly proclaimed by the Arawak in Hispaniola and elsewhere. Fontaneda called its stream "The River Jordan." The Arawak among the Calusa had their own village, named Abaibo. The continued existence of the Arawak in Florida was implied by Fontaneda when he wrote his narrative between the years 1571 and 1575. He maintained that both he and the Florida natives were so convinced that the magic water existed that they would bathe in any pool, no matter how small, hoping to find it. Rouse (1948:515) believes that there was travel back and forth between the islands and Florida, but such contact would be insufficient to significantly affect the culture of either region. The Arawak contact is cited here chiefly to demonstrate Calusa openness to acculturation when it proved advantageous.

Fontaneda inferred for Florida three spheres of influence, although there were more: Carlos in the south, Saturiba in the northeast, and Tocobaga in the west. As it is known, chiefly from other sources, Carlos and his successors were engaged against Tocobaga— Carlos offensively, in an expansion move, and his successor Don Felipe somewhat defensively, in the attempt to regain stolen allies.[11]

After first attempting to convert the Indians and losing many soldiers in the effort, Menéndez supported Fontaneda's proposal that all the Florida Indians be sold into slavery among the various islands of the Caribbean. The government in Spain, however, disapproved of these suggestions, including one limiting the period of slavery to twelve years to allow time for acculturation (Connor 1925, passim).

11. Our chief reliance for Hernando de Escalante Fontaneda (1866) is from *Documentos ineditos del archivo de indias, colección de Muñoz*, tomo 84, pp. 532–48.

Plans for a Gulf coast mission station became clear to Menéndez after he discovered the headquarters of the Calusa nation while exploring that area in 1566 in search of his son. He met the *cacique* Carlos, and to cement the alliance, Menéndez went through the pretense of a marriage with Carlos' sister. She was clothed in Spanish attire and christened Antonia for the ceremony (Solís de Merás 1894:106). The Jesuits accompanying Menéndez opposed the mock marriage, which cooled their ardor for his leadership. Their antagonism was heightened when he delayed, in 1571 and 1572, the search for the Jesuits missing in Virginia where they had journeyed without military protection to work among the natives.

In his first contacts with Carlos, Menéndez succeeded in winning him over as a *vasallo*, "vassal." This Spanish word defining the relation of subordinate chiefs to head chiefs probably had varying significance, determined by their distance from the head village and their amount of control. Carlos gave the Spanish many reasons to be suspicious of his professions of allegiance. His own hegemony seemed to be in a state of flux, as one might expect of an arrangement held together by force. Menéndez wanted peace, but it is not clear how he hoped to effect this arrangement: peace with one or with several chiefs reporting directly to him. He did not succeed completely in making peace with Carlos and Tocobaga, but he was successful in mending fences between Carlos and Tequesta, who were blood relations. Blood relationship was a means employed by Carlos and Tequesta to bind the remaining nations along the east coast into the alliance, but it was clear that the head of this arrangement was Carlos.

Probably early in June 1566, Menéndez, with two ships, sailed from Havana for Calos and arrived there on the third day. He left Doña Antonia and returned to Havana. The Calusa were reassured by her return but grieved for other Indians who had fallen ill and died in Cuba. Sometime after September 1566, Menéndez sent Captain Reinoso and thirty soldiers to Calos. With them was Carlos' cousin and heir, Don Pedro, who had been baptized and whom Menéndez hoped to marry to Doña Antonia. Reinoso was instructed to build a blockhouse in Carlos' village and to erect a cross in front of it. The soldiers were to take Doña Antonia and some Indians as hostages.

The Jesuits first attempted to set up a mission on the mainland in March 1567. Menéndez, with his nephew Pedro Menéndez Marqués, left Cuba with seven ships on March 1, together with Father Juan Rogel, Brother Francisco Villareal, Doña Antonia and her Indian servants, and some Tequesta Indians. After a two-day voyage,

Menéndez landed and was greeted by Carlos. The latter, in a pretense at friendship, agreed to a peace with the brother of Tequesta.

To try to negotiate peace between these two quarrelsome leaders, Menéndez and Carlos sailed on March 6 for Tocobaga. After two days, they reached Safety Harbor where Tocobaga had his temple mound. The interpreters had been instructed to listen to the conversation of the rival chiefs lest they plot against the Spanish (Barrientos 1965:130–31).

Menéndez then returned to Mound Key, where he strengthened the fort and emplaced some cannons. A total of thirty-six cabins and a place where mass could be celebrated had been or were then built within the walled enclosure. Carlos was not satisfied with the peace with Tocobaga and communicated his dissatisfaction to Doña Antonia, who began to criticize her Spanish husband.

Menéndez forbade Father Rogel to attempt conversions at that time. He then set out for Spain, stopping first at Tequesta, at the mouth of the Miami River. There he checked on the progress of the fort and the mission served by Brother Villareal, who staged a religious drama for the entertainment of the soldiers and Indians. There Menéndez took on board Tequesta's brother, Don Jaime, and two other Indians, who sailed with him to Spain. Don Jaime became a Christian, and on his return to Florida he demonstrated extraordinary patience and firmness in keeping the east coast Indians from permanent disaffection after fighting broke out between them and a Spanish garrison.

Apparently on his last visit to Carlos, Menéndez decided that until the fort was ready and Carlos had quieted down, the Jesuit and at least some of the soldiers should be moved out to an island, probably present-day Fort Myers Beach. At first, Carlos was asked to move some of their supplies through the canal in his canoes. Reportedly he planned to sink the boats in the canal, but nothing happened since the supplies were transported in Spanish ships. Father Rogel does not mention this incident, but soldiers later testified (Connor 1925, passim) that it was likely that the Indians in canoes attacked the Spaniards. Pedro Menéndez Marqués was wounded in the hand, and a spear was driven harmlessly against the breastplate of Menéndez himself. Carlos, pretending to assist the Spanish in the return to Mound Key, upset three canoes bearing ammunition and tried unsuccessfully to kill the sailors who were in them. Captain Reinoso, then in command, asked permission to execute Carlos, but Father Rogel stoutly refused. Reinoso was infuriated, and he and his associates schemed to get Rogel off the island; they convinced him to go to Havana for supplies for the starving fort at Tocobaga. While Rogel was away, the Spaniards killed Carlos and his ringleaders. After baptizing on the Epiphany in Cuba, Rogel, with Pedro Menéndez Marqués, returned with the needed supplies. At Tocobaga he was confronted with a tragedy—the slaughter of the entire garrison. Father Rogel blamed not the Indians, but the Spaniards, presuming them guilty of coward-ice and oppression. In his view the troubles of that fort were due not only to hunger and scavenging but to a lack of kindness; to obtain their wants, all were exploited "except the King and captain-general" (Zubillaga 1946:296).

To replace Carlos, the Spanish supported his "captain-general," whom Father Rogel called Don Felipe, and who had taken the lead in venerating the cross. Don Felipe immediately proposed war against Tocobaga, for besides killing the Spanish, he had also seized some villages under Carlos' suzerainty. But the confrontation with To-cobaga did not occur at that time, although the Jesuits did not oppose the action.

Both Carlos and Tequesta had used a blood relationship to build their system of allegiances, with Carlos the dominant figure in the South Florida network. Menéndez now superimposed a new headship over all the tribes. It is known what he and the other Spaniards meant by the term "vassal," but there is doubt as to how well the interpreters were able to define this term to the chiefs. There was, however, little if any obvious resistance to the arrangement. The chiefs clearly con-ceived the relationship to be the same as that of their inferior tribal rulers to them, as they used the same ceremony of rendering gifts to the superior. Thus Don Felipe, on becoming the vassal of Menéndez, performed the following acts as described by Father Rogel: "When we—Pedro Menéndez Marqués and I—went from Havana to Escampaba—thus was called the kingdom of Carlos—during June of 1567, this fellow who is now cacique [i.e., Don Felipe] determined to become a vassal [vasallo] of the King of Spain on seeing that it was suitable for the security of his kingdom and for a peaceful life, and so, he gave away his possessions. And as a symbol of his loyalty, his captains and he himself, along with the chieftains of individual vil-lages that were in that area, brought a tribute of common things given to him by his vassals, mere poverty and misery consisting of feathers and mats and fruits and other edible things, and gave them away publicly, in front of all the Spaniards and his Indians, as a vassal to the King of Spain, and in his absence to Captain Pedro Marqués" (Zubill-aga 1946:277–78).

In 1570, when Esteban de las Alas was acting governor of Florida, he ordered the abandonment of Ais and Calos. Apparently the missionaries had left the preceding year shortly after the Calusa evacuated the area. Considering the fact that Calos lay between Cuba and the Franciscan missions in northern Florida, Spanish contacts with them, or what remained of these Indians, were few during the next two centuries. Spanish ships from St. Augustine visited the Calusa in 1612 and learned that seventy villages were reporting to a chief still called Carlos, though this may have been the Spanish way of referring to the cacique. Apparently the Calusa had not yet lost their enthusiasm for empire building.[12]

There are many references in Spanish archives of the late seventeenth and early eighteenth centuries to the efforts of the bishop of Cuba to enlist volunteers for missions to the Calusa, who were now probably seeking Spanish help against invading Indians from areas north of Florida. One effort by a small group of Franciscans among the Calusa in 1697 was abortive, and the fathers were stripped and beaten. Allegedly the Indians feared or disliked the missionaries' marching in a procession attired in their long robes (Swanton 1922:343). Swanton also reports settlements of a few Choctaw in Florida among the Calusa, and he notes a linguistic resemblance between the two. His findings, which link the Calusa to the Choctaw in both language and general Muskhogean classification, are tantalizing but inconclusive.

The Calusa, who reportedly had a population of about six thousand well into the seventeenth century, gradually declined in numbers, and in the nineteenth century they had disappeared completely. A small number may have been absorbed by the Seminoles.[13]

12. Swanton (1922:343) says that the Spanish called at Calos after a punitive expedition against the chiefs of Pohoy and Tocobaga because they had attacked Christian Indians. He quotes Lowery as the source for this and for the additional information that "The same year the Indians came from beyond Calos asking for missionaries." The Calusa were still expanding, for in addition to the more than seventy towns already mentioned, there were many which paid tribute because they feared the Calusa chief. There is no evidence that missionaries responded to the appeal of the southern Indians at that time, but when they arrived in 1680, the Indians of the extreme southern section refused ministration because of their fear of the Calusa. By that time, Indians from Guale were beginning to settle among the Calusa, according to the same source.

13. James Mooney (in Hodge 1907:963) notes that the Muspa Indians, a Calusa affiliate, were living in the Pine Island area in the nineteenth century.

SOCIAL ORGANIZATION AND RELIGION

In the social organization of the Calusa, there were class distinctions and differentiation in roles. When the Adelantado asked Carlos if he wished to become a Christian, cut his hair, and go to a land of Christians as he had offered, or if he wished to have Christians brought in to teach them, Carlos withdrew more than a quarter of a league away with some of his associates, including his brother-in-law (captain-general?) and probably a group of counselors. They had a brief discussion and returned after a half hour. Carlos announced that for nine months he would not go to a Christian land or become a Christian for fear his subjects would rise in revolt and kill him. After that, though, he would accept Menéndez' offer. Obviously he was hoping that delay would solve his problem.

In fact the captain-general, later named Don Felipe, was regarded as having more power than Carlos, not because of his position, but because of his political power and leadership qualities. He was so impressive that when he succeded Carlos, Father Rogel described him as "another King of Bungo in Japan" (Zubillaga 1946:281). He was baptized in 1587.

Both the French and the Spanish disapproved of Christians having untrimmed hair. Laudonnière described the recovery of two Spanish captives originally with "Calos," whose "hair hung down to their thighs in the Indian fashion." The French cut their hair immediately, and the Spaniards saved the locks as proof of their "hardships." One man had concealed a gold coin in his hair. The Indians called the Spaniard who had been in the charge of King Onatheaqua "The Bearded" (Lorant 1946:56). This suggests that the Florida Indians either had little facial hair or customarily pulled it out.

The drive of Carlos to bring Tocobaga under his control, and presumably with him all of his tribes, was typical of the kind of empire building going on at the time among the Indians along the Atlantic Coast from Maine to Florida. For some, the training of youth was geared to warlike accomplishments. It is not known how many men made up a Calusa raiding party, but it is conceivable that a force of at least twenty-five to fifty warriors might have been required. Great distances were traveled for military purposes; the men of one or more villages were often engaged, and fighting took place over an extended period of time.

At the time of Spanish contact there is little evidence of intertribal conflict. When Don Felipe wished to retaliate against Tocobaga for

alienating some of the villages under Calusa control, he had to make
the necessary weapons. This implies that their availability was not a
constant necessity.

Women had a dignified role in the tribe. Carlos' chief lady was
given a seat of honor on ceremonial or official occasions, and she had
her own attendants. She ran the risk, however, of being set aside for a
younger, more comely successor. According to Father Rogel, Carlos
at first had married his sister, a privilege accorded only to the head
cacique, apparently to maintain an orderly succession of power without possibility of conflict.[14] After Carlos' death, Father Rogel investigated the cacique's right to power, and concluded that Carlos had
usurped the right of Don Felipe, whom the Spanish installed after
killing Carlos. Goggin and Sturtevant have described this relationship
after research into sibling marriage customs.[15] In the case of another
Florida Indian, Saturiba, there was an even more complicated situation. After casting aside his wife, his son Athore took her, and together, mother and son conceived several children (Lorant 1946:51).

Carlos had given proof, by offering his former wife in marriage to
Menéndez, that marriage was not regarded necessarily as a permanent state, at least for the chiefs. Father Alamo extended this attribu-
tion of impermanence to the whole tribe, but the other Jesuits apparently were not so sure on this point.

Father Rogel had fairly good rapport with the Indians in informal
conversations about religious matters. For a brief time, Don Felipe
encouraged his chiefs to attend instruction, but usually the women
and children came for instruction more readily than the men. Rogel

14. The account of the marriage relationship is found in the April 25, 1568, letter of
Father Rogel to his provincial, Father Portillo, who was governing the Florida Jesuits
from Peru (Zubillaga 1946:309–11).

15. My explanation of the Calusa sibling marriage tradition is essentially the same as
offered by Goggin and Sturtevant (1964). Nevertheless, there is no explanation for the
sudden appearance of the siblings who married Carlos and Felipe, who were already
married before entering the sibling relationships. Carlos replaced his older sibling wife
with a young comely girl. Felipe, though attracted to Christianity, refused to abandon
his sibling marriage. The following chart shows the relationships of the Calusa chiefs
during this period.

Stage I

Senquene's Brother	King Senquene	Senquene's Sister
(Chief priest of Idols)		and her husband,
		captain-general in
		conference at
		Menéndez' first visit

Stage II

Temporary King or Regent		Don Felipe
		At age seven or eight wears regal decoration of gold and beads
	Senquene dies about time of his daughter's marriage	At age ten to twelve marries Senquene's daughter, his first cousin

Stage III

		Don Felipe compensated when given his father's office of captain-general and given Senquene's brother's wife, Felipe's first cousin, in marriage
Regent's son, Carlos, married to Don Felipe's wife. She was first cousin to her successive husbands		
Carlos chosen as king by his father and some of the tribes		
Carlos marries an older sister, later called Antonia		
Carlos breaks sibling marriage, takes comely twenty-year-old as wife; successfully Carlos urges marriage of his discarded sibling wife, Doña Antonia, to Menéndez		

Stage IV

Carlos killed by Spanish		Don Felipe installed by Spanish in Carlos' place, now somehow with a sibling partner he refuses to give up

Stage V

		Don Felipe killed by Spanish; replaced by Sebastian's son Pedro, first cousin of Carlos

used gifts and corn supplied by Bishop Toral of Yucatán to encourage their interest, for the Indians displayed little interest in doctrine. Seeing various religious objects in Rogel's room, the natives became curious about them, and he seized the opportunity to explain their significance. The obstacle constituted by shamanism, however, was insurmountable. An important subordinate chief once fell sick. He was baptized, instructed, and fared well for a while, but he was forced by the Indians to resume his duties in the house of idols. As Father Rogel reports: "I talked to the chief Don Felipe to have him acquitted from his duties in the house of idols and not to be ordered to learn things pertaining to their ritual, because he was already Christian, and he promised to do so. And later in that same day the witch doctors were to engage in some kind of witchcraft and idol worship; as this Christian was one of them he put ornaments on in their fashion to gain admittance there and when someone told me, I sent to tell him not to do it. Regardless of that and of having asked the King myself, on that same day he went to worship idols and this is the third ruinous sign I have seen in this King establishing the presumption that he is not willing to become Christian" (Zubillaga 1946:303).

On one occasion a religious procession came from the little hills up the broad slope to where the fort stood. Rogel describes this event: "It came to the point that, as was known later, they were about to catch him outside the fort to take him to their temple and sacrifice him there, making his people understand that, in spite of their reluctance, they would make them worship the idols. And they even tried to come up to our fort to walk around with their masks, coming from the hillocks, where their houses were, to the eminence on which our fort stood. Between these there was a small valley through which they used to walk with the aforementioned display and affrontery to be seen by the people. And the women worshipped them and sang praises to them. It was before these that they tried to carry out the devotion and thus the masked idols came up from the valley to the Spanish fort while Father Rogel [he used the third person when speaking of himself] was at the door. He shouted at them, commanding them not to come up, but they, without paying attention to him, persisted in climbing up; then Father called Captain Francisco de Reinoso to have him stop their intentions. Coming out with a small spear, he [Reinoso] hit one of the forward men with the handle on the head, sending him to the ground. The Indians, on seeing their idol fallen, were angered and came out of their huts with their hatchets and boat poles. But they did not dare to climb up to the fort, for the soldiers were already armed, and thus the bringing up of the idols ceased and there was no other happening but this one in that conflict and, as far as it was known, there were not fifty Indians that would come out to fight" (Zubillaga 1946:607–8).

While instructing the Calusa in Christian doctrine, Father Rogel learned much about their traditions and their religious and cultural beliefs. "They claimed that each man has three souls; one is the pupil of the eye, another one the shadow that each one makes, and the other one is the image one sees in a mirror or in clear water, and when a man dies, they say that two of the souls leave the body, and the third one, which is the pupil of the eye, always remains in the body; and thus they go to speak with the dead of the cemetery, and to ask them advice about things that have to be done, as if they were alive; and I believe that there they get answers from the Devil; because many things that happen in other places or that come up afterwards, they know by what they hear there. They are also told to kill Christians and do other mischief; and when someone gets sick, they say that one of his souls has left and the witch-doctors go to look for it in the woods, and they say they bring it back making the same movements that people go through when they try to put an unwilling wild goat or sheep in the pen. Later they put fire at the door of the house and the windows, so that it would not dare to go out again, and they report that they put it back in the man through the top of the head by conducting some ceremonies over it. They also have another error; when a man dies, his soul enters some animal or fish; and when they kill that animal, it enters another smaller one, until little by little it comes to vanish" (Zubillaga 1946:278–81).

There are parallels between Calusa ceremonies and those of the Arawak as summarized by Rouse (1948:535–37). The chief ceremony centered about a temple; there were processions, singing, and costumes. The processions involved belief in idols called *zemis*, expressed by carvings of animals or vegetables. Despite the similarities, there were enough differences between the Calusa and Arawak to counsel against taking as evidence the presence of the Arawak near Mound Key to explain the procession described by Rogel. The two groups had significantly different beliefs about life after death. It is doubtful if an Arawak would have laughed at Rogel's explanation of immortality as did the Calusa.

Another difference was in art style. The Calusa art of Key Marco was more realistic; Arawak art tended to reflect the stylization common to South and Central America. To Rogel, Calusa masks ap-

peared repulsive. It cannot be assumed that Mound Key art objects
were exact copies of the Key Marco discoveries, but if the Arawak
came to Calos after the Key Marco art was buried in the muck, and
thus influenced Calusa art, it is quite conceivable that Mound Key art,
at least to a Spaniard, was repulsive.

When the subject was first broached, Carlos expressed a willingness,
as did almost all the pagan Indians, to have a cross erected. He was
also willing to become Christian, but he quite clearly implied that
Christianity was to be added to his other religious practices without
eliminating any native ceremonies. When he and his successor, and
doubtless the shamans, came to the full realization that the Spaniards'
religion must completely replace their own, they lost their interest in
becoming Christian, as Christianity would have robbed them of
shamanism, a powerful tool in tribal control.

The tribal rulers, including the shamans, kept the common people
in ignorance of the real significance (if there was any) of their witchcraft and ceremony, as well as their belief in a Supreme Being. That is
probably why the Calusa and Tequesta Indians were converted to
Christianity without much resistance. They had no intelligible beliefs
to abandon; only the fear of consequences suggested by the shamans
kept them in conformity, as was intimated by Rogel (Zubillaga
1946:298).

GEOGRAPHY OF THE CALUSA AREA

An understanding of geographical setting is needed to determine the
basis for acculturation. A tribe living along the seacoast, as the Calusa
did, was more amenable to acculturation, particularly Spanish culture, than were the tribes in the interior of the peninsula. It was
difficult for the Spanish to reach them.

An increasing number of writers, influenced in part by Juan López
de Velasco's *Geografía y descripción universal* (1894), have identified at
least tentatively the Bahia de Carlos with Estero Bay and Carlos' ruling
village with Mound Key (e.g., Boyd 1938; Goggin and Sturtevant
1964). López de Velasco wrote his geography between the years 1571
and 1574, according to the title, and possibly completed it in 1575,
just after the Spanish abandoned Carlos. Although Velasco was not an
eyewitness and his reporting is not without its flaws, he is very detailed
and reasonably accurate in his description of the west coast of Florida
from Tampa Bay to the Keys, making it fairly easy to fit Estero Bay
into the picture.

Along the west coast of Florida from Charlotte Harbor to Estero Bay, there is a string of islands riddled by native-made waterways and dotted with mounds of ceremonial or burial import. The present interest is with the unique circular mound in Estero Bay. Estero was not the original name of the bay opposite Fort Myers Beach, and, of course, it is not mentioned under that name by Velasco. It can be reasoned, however, that the bay he describes is modern Estero. The first reference to the island in his *Geografía* appears in a descriptive list of "Depopulated Towns and Forts": "In the year 1566 the Adelantado Pedro Menéndez made a settlement in the Bahia de Carlos, on the little island which is in the middle, with thirty-six houses constructed of thatch and wood; and this settlement lasted until the year 1571 [*sic*], when the Indians having rebelled against the Spaniards and the barracks being in danger, Pedro Menéndez Marqués, by order of the Adelantado, beheaded the cacique with twenty-two other principal Indians, and abandoned the said fort."

On the west coast, Velasco describes "The Bay of Carlos, which in the Indian language is called Escampaba, for a cacique of that name who afterwards called himself Carlos from devotion to the Emperor and this bay seems to be the same as that called Juan Ponce, because he disembarked in it in the year 1515, where he lost his people and where the Indians gave him the wound from which he died. It is at 26½ degrees. Its entrance is very narrow and full of shallows, so that one cannot enter without light craft; within, it is spacious, about four or five leagues in circuit, although completely marshy. In its center is a small island of about a half league in circumference, with other islets around it, in which the chief Carlos had his seat, now occupied by his successors. One may pass with canoes from them to the arm of the sea which goes to Tampa [Velasco's name for the Charlotte Harbor area] by some passages which are between one sea and another."

There can be little doubt that López de Velasco was describing the territory of the Jesuit mission, for Father Rogel also designates the kingdom of Carlos and Fort of San Antonio as "Escampaba." The estimate of 26½ degrees latitude is within the margin of error one should allow for early Spanish calculations. It falls at the top of the Fort Myers Beach Quadrangle of the U.S. Geological Survey, which includes Mound Key and Estero Bay. The only significant central entrance to Estero Bay, Big Carlos Pass, is relatively narrow and confronted with shallows. This is reflected in Father Rogel's letter describing a journey he made on September 22, 1568, to Calos with Governor Menéndez: "The passage which ordinarily takes but two days, took ten, and at the entrance to the harbor one of the ships almost foundered, while a great number of passengers nearly drowned during a storm which arose as they were entering the shallows" (Zubillaga 1946:336–37).

Solís de Merás (1894) describes Menéndez as exploring the coastline, while looking for his son, in a brigantine which drew only a half fathom, or three feet, of water. This was necessary because of the shoals along the coast, and it was with two brigantines that he entered a harbor and landed on a spot about two arquebus shots from Carlos' house.

There can be no doubt that the Carlos mission lay on the southwest coast of Florida. On a visit to the Jesuit fathers in Seville on December 16, 1567, Pedro Menéndez described Rogel's position as on the coast facing New Spain (Mexico) and on the route of the treasure fleet. In a letter by an unidentified Jesuit father describing Menéndez' visit, someone (perhaps Menéndez himself) drew a crude map of Florida and Cuba, putting "P. Rogel" on the west coast, and an almost illegible "Franco Villareall" in the east, with a bracket pointing to the Miami area, and with "Santa Elena" shown farther up on the east coast. The same letter indicates that Brother Villareal was 25 leagues from Cuba and 40 leagues from Father Rogel, which is an underestimate in the first case but about correct (100–200 miles) in the second. A southerly position on the west coast can be inferred from two-day journeys by Father Rogel, both to and from Havana and Carlos. The 100 miles a day required to do this would have been extremely good time. Menéndez averaged around 150 miles a day on his record sailing from Santa Elena to the Azores, but doubtless he was running with the wind and the strong Gulf Stream. On the contrary, Rogel's pilot took four days to return from Tocobaga in Safety Harbor, though Menéndez covered this distance in less than two days. Tocobaga was about 130 miles from Mound Key.

But was the home of Carlos an island and not a point? There is no hint in Merás or Barrientos, but Rogel, reporting the temporary removal of the Spanish from Calos while a wooden structure was being built, says that they established themselves "on another island" (Zubillaga 1946:306). This would imply that their former residence, Calos, was also an island. The only available suitable island nearby would have been Estero Island, now Fort Myers Beach. The remains of a huge mound are located near the middle of the island, but a cursory examination gave no indication that there was any activity on or near it in historic times. Another mound is known to have been located at

Bowditch Point at the northern end of the island. A detailed analysis
showing how the geography in and around Mound Key fits the
documentary evidence is given in a manuscript by this writer, dated
1969. The same manuscript gives a brief history of the island's ownership, and the exploitation of two huge shell middens for road construction material. One contract permitted excavation as deep as six
feet below low tide to admit boats carrying away the shell. Excavations
for the canal, still visible, indicate that shell was still being found at the
bottom of the cut. This leads to the inevitable conclusion that Mound
Key, like Key Marco, demonstrates a long period of prehistory and
possibly fulfills Cushing's speculation on thousands of years of continuous occupation. Cultural borrowings were possible, however, for
people to whom the sea was a highway.

Mound Key is an island divided almost in half by a native-built ditch
fifty feet wide. The ditch is still filled with water at high tide; it runs
fairly straight in a southwest to northeast direction. At low tide it can
be traversed on foot. Inflow of water, and probably fish, appears to
have been controlled at two places in the southeast portion. The canal
narrows to only four feet at one of these points. Much of the southeast
portion of the island is exposed, but the northeast area is almost
entirely covered with mangroves and other bushes and is difficult to
map or even traverse. At high tide the incoming water forms little
lakes studded with small mounds, and the whole is covered with mangrove swamps. This may explain Father Rogel's reference to the lakes
to which the Indians could retire, "and where the Spanish cannot go."
He speaks of the Indians going into the woods to look for the soul of a
sick man.

The presence of cover on even the occupied parts of the island is
implied in many ways. Barrientos tells of the Indians hiding in woods
along a path to waylay the Spanish. The survey maps, with five-foot
contour intervals, give an inadequate picture of the aboriginal
mounds and dikes that create a bewildering labyrinth in this area.
Today, when the tide goes out, the water remaining in the ponds
above sea level is absorbed by the earth. One of the mounds, of earth
and shell, about thirty feet across, is in the northern mangrove area
within about fifty yards of the bay. It has been pitted all over by
treasure seekers.

An aerial view of the island indicates that smaller canals spread out
like fingers in every direction from the main waterway. The highest
mound on the island—and in all Florida—is a truncate cone thirty-
one feet high, situated southeast of the island's center. The top is

roughly a circle about seventy-five feet in diameter, which was once surmounted by a twentieth-century observation tower. A Coast and Geodetic Survey marker, located on top of the mound until at least as late as 1969, could serve as a reference point for anyone wishing to map the island. The mound is bordered, especially on the south, by hillocks and plateaus from five to fifteen feet in height. Across the canal, to the northwest, is a roughly square elevation about three hundred yards wide, dotted with several inconspicuous mounds. The fort, which was probably triangular, could easily have occupied this area.

Before the turn of this century the residents of the island and of Estero did some digging in the so-called burial mounds and reported finding gold beads, a sheet of brass or copper, a small gold bar, and other pieces of contact goods. Frank Hamilton Cushing, who talked to Mrs. Johnson, the wife of the earliest settler, learned "that here on the heights, many Spanish relics have been found: Venetian beads, scraps of sheet copper, small ornaments of gold and silver, and a copper-gilt locket" (Cushing 1897:348). This information is almost identical to that given me by a ninety-year-old former resident of Estero, the late E. E. Damkohler. Cushing did not excavate Mound Key, but the archeologist Clarence B. Moore, shortly after Cushing's visit, made "persistent excavations" in the three or four feet of muck that accumulated in the canals, "resulting in the discovery of a few bits of earthenware only and a handsome implement wrought from a conch-shell, unfortunately without a handle." Correcting Cushing's exaggerated description of the principal mound, Moore (1900) gives an accurate estimate of its height—30 feet, 2.5 inches from the general level at its base. He describes the mound, which had earlier yielded European contact goods: "The burial mound in the northeast part of the island, to which we have referred, lies in a mangrove swamp. It is 65 feet across the base and about 11 feet in height. It is composed of sand and loamy material with a certain admixture of shell. We dug into this mound to a certain extent, finding nothing of particular interest. Many relics, however, of European origin, have come from it. Some of these, we believe, have been presented to the Museum of Science and Art of the University of Pennsylvania by Mr. Joseph Willcox" (Moore 1900:367).

Recent archeology on Mound Key has resulted in additional evidence of the Spanish presence. Goggin reported finding sixteenth-century olive jar sherds and a tentatively identified piece of Isabella

Polychrome majolica, a sixteenth-century ceramic ware. I visited the
island four times between 1965 and January of 1969, mainly to examine the topography and to determine how it tied in with the documents. To examine any valuable surface data which might be recovered, 150-foot squares were spotted on a map of the island. These
were based on an aerial stereo photograph made in 1958. With the
help of the map and the aerial photograph, sherds could be assigned
to the correct area when recovered, before they were turned over to
the Florida State Archeologist in Tallahassee. Equal attention was not
devoted to all squares, but the results were significant nevertheless.
Three olive jar sherds were recovered near the northwest landing,
three near the southeast landing, one near the entrance of the main
canal, five on or near the supposed temple mound, and the remainder
of more than sixty, along with a piece of majolica, in an area approximately 400 feet long and 150 feet wide on the flat eminence (Rogel's
zerro) across the canal from the supposed native dwelling mounds
(Rogel's *zerrilos*). Several of the olive jar sherds were in the range of six
to seven millimeters thick, thus qualifying for a sixteenth-century
date, according to Goggin (1964:281). The majority were above seven
millimeters and would bear a later date. Exact dating is difficult, however, since the Calusa may have been on the same island up to the
eighteenth century and could have been responsible for bringing the
thicker, later olive jars onto the island. I recovered a small chisel,
apparently dug up and discarded by a treasure hunter, on the western
slope of the "temple mound," which perhaps was one of the pieces of
iron brought to the Indians by Father Rogel.

Indian pottery is quite abundant on Mound Key. Without a working acquaintance with Florida pottery types, one can make only tentative identifications. Possibly 90 percent of the ware appears to be
Glades Plain or Glades Red. The few scattered exceptions possibly
include Plantation Pinched, Englewood Incised, Surfside Incised, Aucilla Incised, and a variety of sherds suggesting Fort Walton. The only
check-stamped sherd featured a geometrically perfect pattern of
squares one quarter of an inch in width, while another sherd had a
perfect pattern of deep, square holes. Other aboriginal artifacts included a broken projectile point, several Busycon picks or hammers, a
columella pendant, and a broken abrading implement of granite.

Although little or no evidence of contact has been discovered at Key
Marco, some forty miles south of Mound Key, the archeological discoveries made there throw some light on the culture of the Calusa,

particularly that aspect of it which led to conflict and the failure of the mission—the profession of witchcraft.[16] In 1895, residents and visitors to the island digging in the muck of an ancient water court, roughly triangular in shape, discovered by accident certain artifacts. These were brought to the attention of Frank Cushing of the Bureau of American Ethnology in Washington, who happened to be visiting at the museum of the University of Pennsylvania when Colonel C. D. Durnford, a member of the British army and one of the Key Marco explorers, came in to report the discoveries. The result of this chance encounter was the formation of a joint project of the University of Pennsylvania and the Bureau of American Ethnology for the excavation of the ancient inlet on Key Marco and for the exploration of other sites on the west coast of Florida. The Key Marco investigation produced an almost unparalleled group of finds, many associated with the shaman's trade. The finds included masks which the shamans could wear and manipulate, giving us some idea of the equipment worn in the parade which disturbed Father Rogel so much. The Key Marco equipment shows some signs of burning and of falling into the water of the pond. It was as if a bolt of lightning had struck the elevated quarters where the shaman had kept well-worn implements and was in the process of manufacturing more. Perhaps the greatest mystery of the ancient incident is why the owner or owners of these implements made no effort to recover them. Inlets remininscent of those of Mound Key are pictured in a map of Key Marco made by Wells M. Sawyer for the Pepper-Hearst expedition which was responsible for the Cushing surveys.

Two recent investigations at Key Marco serve to fill out the picture of the Glades cultures. One series of excavations under the direction of state archeologist L. Ross Morrell started in 1967 at Caxambas Point on the southwestern side of the island, where midden material was discovered which suggested cultural association with the Cushing site on the northern end of the key. Discovered also were impressions in the shell refuse of rectangular houses located at the water's edge. In 1968, excavations were conducted on the high and extensive sand hills on the southern part of the island. Radiocarbon dating substantiated earlier estimates of at least 1500 B.C. for man in southwest Florida. Survey work undertaken in 1969 resulted in documentation of fifteen sites, some probably Calusa, while aerial photographs

16. See Frank Hamilton Cushing's "Ancient Key Dwellers' Remains on the Gulf Coast of Florida" (1897).

suggest the possibility of even more (Division of Archives, History and Records Management 1970). There are indications that the early inhabitants of the island depended heavily on terrestrial life for food. This dependence was reflected in the 1965 report *The Marco Midden, Marco Island, Florida,* by John C. and Linda M. Van Beck (1964). The site they excavated is only 850 feet east of the Cushing site. They estimated that the midden site ranges in age from Glades IIa through Glades IIIa, or from A.D. 800 to 1500, stopping just short of the current estimate of IIIb for the Cushing find.[17]

There are two reasons for not making the Cushing site contemporaneous with historic Mound Key: the absence of evidence of Spanish contact and the absence of the bow and arrow, which were used with skill at Carlos' village and which seemed to be the principal weapon. The atlatl, rather than the bow and arrow, was found in the muck. Bone fragments indicated that meat played a greater part in the diet at Key Marco than at Mound Key, though the author found the skeletons of deer on Mound Key from modern times, as well as an abundance of racoon and other animals on or near the island. Signs of native habitation are found at Coconut and other places on the mainland not far from Big Carlos Pass. It is difficult to believe that islanders, at times when the mullet were spawning and edible game were to be found nearby, would not take advantage of their archery skills and shoot animals while they were migrating in search of food. A Spanish captive wearing a deerskin was found by Menéndez, some indication that these animals had not been hunted out. In fact, biologists claim that the area a short distance inland was richer in wildlife than any area to the north and was virtually a tropical paradise.[18] This position, however, in no way detracts from the accomplishments of the Calusa as a nonagricultural people.

ACCULTURATION

In examining the influence that European and Calusa had on each other, one is tempted to dismiss the subject as of little significance, since most of the written accounts on this subject cover a period of only four years, 1566–69. Yet the Jesuit correspondence for these years pertaining to the La Florida effort embraces 643 pages, of which

17. This represents a general shift downward several hundred years from Goggin's earlier estimate for the Glades IIIa period (Goggin 1964:113).

18. Frank Craighead (1971) describes the abundance of wildlife in the Glades area in the five thousand years before the coming of the Europeans.

more than half deals directly or indirectly with the Calusa mission. In addition, Solís de Merás and Barrientos, whose accounts are contemporary and almost identical, each devotes more than twenty-five pages to happenings and observations involving Spanish contact with the Calusa.

Several documents from the Spanish archives reflect problems being faced by the Calusa in the seventeenth and eighteenth centuries: invasions by northern tribes and the willingness of a small percentage of the Calusa to become Christian and to move to Cuba. Much more, however, can be learned about the Calusa from the Jesuit documents and from Solís de Merás, for they deal with personalities, internal struggles within the tribe, and a host of other details.

In assessing the effects of interaction between the two groups, one should examine the influence of the Spanish on the Indians. As one might expect, the effects on external behavior were the most notable and easiest to achieve. The Calusa readily consumed Menéndez' gifts of bread (cornbread?) and honey. Carlos and his two chief women quickly accepted and wore the clothing he gave them. The women did not even object to wearing petticoats, and Doña Antonia exhibited no reluctance in donning complete Spanish attire for her trip to Cuba and, as far as we know, for the rest of her life. This behavior is not too surprising; other Indians of southern Florida eagerly seized what clothing they could from people forced ashore in wrecks, as Jonathan Dickinson's narrative relates.

The Indians were most receptive to Spanish musical instruments and Spanish singing. Europeans thought Carlos was discerning when he had his own singers stop in order to listen to their performance, which was so well received that the instrumentalists had to give a lengthy rendition. The antics of "a very small dwarf—a great singer and dancer—whom he [Menéndez] always took with him" seemed to please the crowd, as did the confections—wine and marmalade—which the Adelantado served on a table set with tablecloth, plates, and napkins.

Little is known of the influence of the Spanish captives in teaching the Indians their language. Children born to a Spanish mother and Indian father were probably bilingual. Indian men, women, and children taken to Cuba were taught to speak Spanish as part of the plan to promote the Catholic religion when they returned to Florida. Many Spanish men and women captured in the shipwrecks demonstrated that they had not forgotten the language, and they were able to act as interpreters. Marriage was doubtless also a vehicle for acculturation.

There is no evidence of marriage between Spanish men and Indian women, but many Spanish women married Indian men.

The Spanish, starting with Menéndez, traditionally took Indian leaders to Cuba and even to Spain for political and cultural indoctrination, with varying degrees of success. Although Carlos resisted going to Cuba, Felipe did agree to go. Indian fathers seemed willing to let their children travel by sea from Florida, even to far-distant Spain. The Spanish experienced varying degrees of success in their efforts to Christianize the Indians. It is likely that the more than 200 Spanish being held captive must have exercised some influence over the Calusa. Judging from the captive who shouted for help from his canoe, religion was uppermost in his mind, as he cried, "Spaniards, brothers, Christians!" He also took from his deerskin clothing a cross and a letter from his fellow captives. The Spanish, he said, were slaves. He was described as "naked and painted like an Indian" (Barcia 1951:101). Perhaps, as in the case of some earlier captives farther north, the paint was a concession made for survival. Repeated statements indicate that the Calusa were open to new cults, particularly those believed compatible with the existing order of things. New rites must not hinder social control based on the shamans' power. The most prominent shaman was the chief witch doctor, an office held either by the head cacique or someone almost equally powerful.

It is remarkable that Menéndez was able to reduce Carlos, and later Felipe, to the position of vassal so easily, especially in view of the temper tantrums displayed by Carlos on his visit to Tocobaga. Perhaps Carlos was playing a game to see how many gifts he could acquire before striking. There is no way of knowing the real mind of Felipe when he finally decided to destroy his idols. One is more certain of the deep Christian convictions of two women taken to Cuba, one of whom was forced to go through a long preparation for admission into the Church. The outstanding example was Doña Antonia, who was misled by Menéndez into thinking he was truly her husband and was moved back and forth to Cuba. She died in Cuba after a last confession to Father Rogel.

Menéndez tried to bring peace to all the warring combinations of tribes, of which there were at least five and probably more in Florida, all engaged in expansionist activities. Various factions bid for the support of both French and Spanish in pursuing their goals. Menéndez' efforts to maintain the status quo were not successful. The rival leadership vied for Spanish support just as the Indians along the St.

Johns River had done in involving the French in their factional dis-
putes. Pedro Menéndez Marqués almost let the Spanish be com-
promised against Tocobaga on the side of Don Felipe. The return of
three of the four Calusa chiefs, however, postponed the conflict,
which had both Indians and Spanish forces poised for an invasion.
The conflict between French and Spanish, both Christian nations,
confused the Florida Indians, with Menéndez trying to make them
understand his distinction of "good Christians" and "bad Christians."

There is little information on the Indian effect on Spanish behavior
patterns. Long hair and scanty attire were endured rather than chosen by male captives. It is not known whether Spanish men put paint
on their faces by choice or by command. Probably all of the surviving
captives conversed in the Indian tongue. Fontaneda claimed to speak
four Indian languages, but some of these may have been variations of
the Muskhogean, although there is no proof that the Calusa spoke a
Muskhogean-related dialect.

Doubtless the major effect the Indians had on Spanish behavior patterns was through marriage to white women. Some who had borne
children to Indian men decided to remain with the tribe, and
Menéndez respected their wishes. Others, who went to Cuba, left
their children with great reluctance, and some of these, perhaps all,
returned to Calos for a visit or perhaps to stay. There is no indication
that they remained or returned because of love for their husbands.
Carlos had apparently given or traded some of his captives, both men
and women, to interior tribes. At Menéndez' request, he made an
attempt to recover these people, and he was at least partly successful.
It is likely that over the years, through death and / or intermarriage,
the whites lost their identity. Menéndez could account for fewer than
20 of the original 250 captives. Testimony of officers and soldiers
varied, but it is unlikely that many of the captives were sacrificed during beheading ceremonies. Reports of losses in this manner vary from
one a year to several a year. Testimony taken includes reports of
observing a pile of fifty skulls, but these could have been from Indian
victims also. In a letter dated November 10, 1568, Father Rogel
speaks of Don Felipe and his supporters dancing about with the heads
of four of the fifteen chiefs he had slain after learning of their
planned rebellion against his rule. Rogel foresaw the possibility of his
being honored in like manner. Reports of cannabilism were circulated
by Spaniards, but Father Rogel stoutly defended the Indians against
these allegations.

It is believed that the entrenchment of shamanism in the native power structure, coupled with Don Felipe's sibling marriage, were the chief causes of the failure of the Spanish missions. Sibling marriage was not a necessity, as Carlos demonstrated by his divorce, but in Felipe's case, he only promised that he would give up the relationship. Christianity was certainly a threat to shamanism, and the ruler could not help but oppose it, for it weakened his power.

There was still another weakness in the Calusa structure; the danger developing from the internal struggle for power, most evident in the Carlos-Felipe rivalry. While Carlos was in power, Felipe was informing the Spanish of his rival's schemes, some of which may have been the product of his own imagination. The Indian women seemed to have easy access to the barracks and often warned the Spanish of danger. This seeming disloyalty to the chief, not uncommon to American Indian women, may reflect their realistic anticipation of being captured and winding up as a wife in an enemy tribe.

After the Spanish withdrew from southwestern Florida in the 1570s, the Calusa were left almost undisturbed for more than a century. Spanish traders and fishermen, however, still made stops along the coast, and European-introduced diseases probably continued to further reduce the native population.

Throughout the first half of the eighteenth century the English and their Indian allies raided into southern Florida, ultimately destroying or scattering the remaining Calusa. Some joined other Indians in the Miami area by the 1740s (see Sturtevant, this volume) while others possibly lived in small isolated groups elsewhere in South Florida. It is not known for certain whether or not any of the Calusa population survived to merge with the entering Seminoles.

References

Barcia Carballido y Zúñiga, Andrés González de.
    1951. *Chronological History of the Continent of Florida*. Translated by Anthony Kerrigan from the original Spanish edition of 1723. Gainesville: University of Florida Press.
Barrientos, Bartolomé.
    1965. *Pedro Menéndez de Avilés*. Translated by Anthony Kerrigan from the original Spanish edition of 1564. Gainesville: University of Florida Press.
Boyd, Mark F.
    1938. The Arrival of de Soto's Expedition in Florida. *Florida Historical Quarterly* 16:188-220.
Connor, Jeannette Thurber.
    1925. *Colonial Records of Spanish Florida: Letters and Reports of Governors and Secular Persons*. Vol. 1, 1570-1577. Publications, Florida State Historical Society, vol. 1, no. 5. Deland.

Craighead, Frank C.
  1971. Is Man Destroying South Florida? In *The Environmental Destruction of South Florida*, edited by William R. McCluney, pp. 5–16. Coral Gables: University of Miami Press.
Cushing, Frank Hamilton.
  1897. Exploration of Ancient Key Dwellers' Remains on the Gulf Coast of Florida. *Proceedings of the American Philosophical Society*, vol. 35, no. 153, pp. 329–448. Philadelphia.
Davis, T. Frederick.
  1935. History of Juan Ponce de León's Voyages to Florida. *Florida Historical Quarterly* 14:1–70.
Díaz (del Castillo), Bernal.
  1956. *The Discovery and Conquest of Mexico, 1517–1521*. New York: Ferrar, Straus, and Cudahy.
Division of Archives, History, and Records Management.
  1970. Key Marco Reveals Early Florida Life. *Archives and History News*, vol. 1, no. 1. Tallahassee: State of Florida, Department of State.
Fontaneda, Hernando d'Escalante.
  1866. Memoria. In *Documentos Ineditos del Archivo de Indias, Colección de Muñoz*, 84:532–48. Madrid.
  1945. *Memoir of Do. d'Escalante Fontenada Respecting Florida, Written in Spain, about the Year 1575*. Translated by Buckingham Smith, edited by David O. True. Coral Gables, Fla.: Glade House.
Friede, Juan, and Benjamin Keen, eds.
  1971. *Bartolomé de Las Casas in History; toward an Understanding of the Man and His Work*. De Kalb: Northern Illinois University Press.
Goggin, John M.
  1964. *Indian and Spanish Selected Writings*. Coral Gables: University of Miami Press.
Goggin, John M., and William C. Sturtevant.
  1964. The Calusa: A Stratified, Nonagricultural Society (with Notes on Sibling Marriage). In *Explorations in Cultural Anthropology: Essays in Honor of George Peter Murdock*, edited by Ward H. Goodenough, pp. 179–219. New York: McGraw Hill.
Herrera [y Tordesillas], Antonio de.
  1730. *Historia General de los Hechos de los Castellanos en las Islas i Terra Firma del Mar Oceano*. Madrid: Imprenta Real de Nicolas Rodriquez Franco.
Hodge, Frederick W.
  1907. *Handbook of North American Indians North of Mexico*, Part 1. Bureau of American Ethnology Bulletin no. 30.
Lewis, Clifford M.
  1969. The Spanish Jesuit Mission of 1567–1569 in Southern Florida. Manuscript in possession of the author.
Lewis, Clifford M., and Albert J. Loomie.
  1953. *The Spanish Jesuit Mission in Virginia 1570–1572*. Chapel Hill: University of North Carolina Press (for the Virginia Historical Society).
López de Velasco, Juan.
  1894. *Geografía y descripción universal de las Indias, recopilada por el cosmógrafo-cronista Juan López de Velasco desde el año de 1571 al de 1574*. Madrid: Establecimiento Tipográfico de Fortanet.
Lorant, Stefan, ed.
  1946. *The New World: The First Pictures of America*. New York: Duell, Sloan, and Pearce.
Mooney, James.
  1907. Calusa. In *Handbook of American Indians North of Mexico*, pt. 1, edited by Frederick Hodge. Bureau of American Ethnology Bulletin no. 30, pp. 195–96.

Moore, Clarence B.
  1900. Certain Antiquities of the Florida West Coast. *Journal of the Academy of Natural Sciences of Philadelphia* 11:349–94.
Rouse, Irving.
  1948. The Arawak. In *The Circum-Carribean Tribes*, vol. 4 of *Handbook of South American Indians*, edited by Julian H. Steward. Bureau of American Ethnology Bulletin no. 143, pp. 507–39.
Solís de Merás, Gonzalo.
  1894. Memorial que hizo el Doctor Gonzalo Solís de Merás, de todas las jornadas y sucesos del Adelantado Pedro Menéndez de Avilés, su cuñado, y de la conquista de la Florida y justicia que hizo en Juan Ribao y otros franceses. [Written in 1567.] In *La Florida, su conquista y colonización por Pedro Menéndez de Avilés*, by Eugenio Ruidiaz y Caravia, 1:1–350. Madrid: Hijos de J. A. Garcia.
  1964. *Pedro Menéndez de Avilés*. Facsimile of the 1923 edition, translated and edited by Jeanette Thurber Connor. Gainesville: University of Florida Press.
Swanton, John R.
  1922. *Early History of the Creek Indians and Their Neighbors*. Bureau of American Ethnology Bulletin no. 73.
Van Beck, John, and Linda M. Van Beck.
  1964. The Marco Midden, Marco Island, Florida. *Florida Anthropologist* 18:1–20.
Wilkinson, Warren H.
  1947–48. Various articles in *The American Eagle*, Estero, Florida, vol. 42, no. 29, through vol. 43, no. 5.
Zubillaga, Félix (ed.).
  1946. Monumenta Antiquae Floridae (1566–1572). *Monumenta Historica Societatis Iesu*, 69; *Monumenta Missionum Societatis Iesu*, 3. Rome.

Tocobaga Indians and the Safety Harbor Culture

Ripley P. Bullen

TOCOBAGA is a generic term for the aboriginal peoples inhabiting the Florida Gulf coast from about Tarpon Springs to Sarasota at the time of European contact. There is some archeological evidence indicating that the Tocobaga region can be extended as far south as Charlotte Harbor and north to the Aucilla River (Willey 1949:625–27; Bullen 1969:418). More research is needed, however, to portray accurately the populations of those additional areas and to determine their relationship to the historic Indians of the Tampa Bay region.

Judging from the Spanish accounts (Smith 1968; Garcilaso de la Vega 1605), the Tocobaga did not form a single, united group but consisted of small chiefdoms whose leaders frequently waged wars against each other. Often the same name is used for the province, the largest town, and the chief. The Tocobaga seem to have been the most important of these chiefdoms, which include the Mocoço and Ucita.

Territories of the Tocobaga, Mocoço, and Ucita coincide with the geographical region defined as the heartland of the archeological Safety Harbor culture (Willey 1949:475–88; Bullen and Bullen 1956: 52–54; Bullen 1969:418), and it appears certain that Safety Harbor is the archeological manifestation of the Tocobaga and other Tampa Bay area aborigines. The period of the Safety Harbor culture can be divided into two phases: an earlier pre-Columbian one and a later historic one in which European items are found in considerable quantities (Bullen 1952a). Disappearance of the Safety Harbor culture in the early eighteenth century coincides with the demise of the Tocobaga groups.

50

Safety Harbor culture is well known archeologically, although excavations have been heavily weighed toward ceremonial mounds; few village middens have been investigated. Thirteen villages with truncated, pyramidal temple mounds and adjacent plazas have been located (Bullen 1955:61) and most have been at least partially excavated. Burial mounds are also present at several of these villages. In addition to villages with temple mounds, other villages and isolated burial mounds are known (Sears 1967). The distribution of all of these sites is along the coast from southern Pasco County down to northern Sarasota County, with the heaviest concentration around Tampa Bay. Only one village site, the Parrish Mounds, has been found inland.

Information about the Tocobaga Indians is meager and is gleaned from the brief accounts of Spanish explorers, colonizers, or prisoners. The main sources are an account of the 1528 Narváez expedition (Bandelier 1922); the narratives of the 1539 de Soto expedition (Smith 1968), supplemented by that written later by Garcilaso de la Vega (1605) from interviews with the survivors; the biography of Pedro Menéndez de Avilés, founder of St. Augustine, who visited Tocobaga in 1566 (Solís de Merás 1964); and sparse data from the *Memoir of D° d'Escalante Fontaneda* (Fontaneda 1945), a prisoner of the Calusa from about 1545 to 1563. The classic account of Juan Ortiz, who had been a prisoner for twelve years and was rescued by de Soto, is included in both the de Soto narratives and that written later by Garcilaso.

Neither Narváez nor de Soto visited the town of Tocobaga, but they did pass through the main Tocobaga territory, some distance to the east of the town, on their journeys up the Florida peninsula to the center of Apalachee territory near Tallahassee. Their landing places on the Gulf coast are in doubt, but they are important to our investigation. If the *conquistadores* landed on or near the southern shore of Tampa Bay, as Swanton (1939) postulated, then all that they noted until they reached the various western Timucua tribes described the Tocobaga Indians. While Ucita, the first village de Soto occupied, was not the Terra Ceia site (Bullen 1951:36–37, 1952b; Swanton 1939, 1952, 1953), a good case can be made for Swanton's choice of the Shaws Point area as the landing place.

The case for Fort Myers or the Caloosahatchee estuary as the site of Ucita is not quite as good. In none of the Narváez and de Soto accounts is there reference to Carlos or to an important chief living to the south of Ucita or Mocoço. Carlos' son, also named Carlos, was head chief of the Calusa when he was visited by Menéndez several times in 1566 (Solís de Merás 1964). Carlos at that time was about twenty-six, and his territory extended southward from Charlotte Harbor. Even the Indians along the western and southern shores of Lake Okeechobee (Mayaimi) were said to have paid homage to him (Fontaneda 1945:28–29).

If Ucita and Mocoço were along the Caloosahatchee River, as Schell (1966) maintains, they would have been under the control of Carlos' father, who was living in 1539 when de Soto landed. Carlos' headquarters is believed to have been on Mound Key in Estero Bay south of Fort Myers (see Lewis, this volume). Menéndez, when at Carlos' headquarters, was told that two leagues from the chief's pueblo there was a river that connected with Mayaimi (Lake Okeechobee) (Solís de Merás 1964:219). Two leagues is about five and one-fourth miles, while the correct distance to the Caloosahatchee is nearly eight miles. This is too short a distance for Carlos not to have known of de Soto's expedition. Fontaneda (1945:30) stated that "We will now leave Tocobaga, Abalachi, and Mogoso, which are separate kingdoms." If "Mogoso" is the same as Mocoço, de Soto and Narváez did not debark near Fort Myers.

Furthermore, if de Soto had landed in Calusa territory, it seems strange that Fontaneda, who seems to have been there in 1545—only five years later—did not mention de Soto as having visited in that area. After locating Tocobaga, Fontaneda writes: "There are more than forty leagues of distance, following up the stream, to which Hernando de Soto thought to colonize; but he did not do so, in consequence of his death" (Fontaneda 1945:29). This vague and incorrect reference does not support a Fort Myers landing. Also, Ortiz (Smith 1968:33) wrote, "thirty leagues [Biedma says twenty and Garcilaso reduces it to sixteen leagues] distant was a chief named Paracoxi, to whom Mocoço, Ucita, and all they that dwelt along the coast paid tribute, and that . . . his land was better than theirs, being more fertile, abounded in maize." As de Soto marched to Paracoxi (Smith 1968:35–36) *beyond* Mocoço, he encountered, according to Garcilaso (1605), "grape, walnut, evergreen oaks, mulberry, plums, pines, and oaks." This more accurately describes the territory around Arcadia and Wauchula rather than that of the Caloosahatchee River.

There is good evidence that both Narváez and de Soto landed at approximately the same location. While de Soto speaks of the town of Ucita and of a neighboring *cacique*, Mocoço, who was very friendly, he never was able to talk to the chief of Ucita (Smith 1968:23–30). Garcilaso is more explicit (1605:2–12): he writes that the chief's name was "Hirrihigua" and that Narváez had ordered his nose be cut off and his mother thrown "to the dogs to be eaten." The chief's sister was Mococo's wife. If this is correct, Narváez and de Soto must have landed at approximately the same place. The presence of Ortiz, lost from a boat looking for Narváez, also supports this conclusion.

The Gentleman of Elvas (Smith 1968:23–27) describes Ucita: "The town was of seven or eight houses, built of timber, and covered with palm leaves. The chief's house stood near the beach, upon a very high mount made by hand for defence; at the other end of the town was a temple, on the top of which perched a wooden fowl with gilded eyes, and within were found some pearls of small value, injured by fire, such as the Indians pierce for beads. . . . Their bows are very perfect; the arrows are made of certain canes, like reeds, very heavy, and so stiff that one of them, when sharpened, will pass through a target. Some are pointed with the bone of a fish, sharp and like a chisel; others with some stone like a point of diamond." This weapon seems to describe a Pinellas arrow point, typical of the Safety Harbor culture; the sharpened fish bone, "like a chisel," suggests a stingray spine. The description of Ucita resembles the Safety Harbor settlement pattern. It is presumed that structures on temple mounds were for storing ceremonial paraphernalia, including bodies cleaned for later mound burial. Perhaps the cacique was also the priest and did live on the mound. It is also possible that the Gentleman of Elvas was wrong and has reversed the chief's house and the temple. I prefer to believe the temple was a charnel house where bodies of the dead were cleaned and stored. According to Ortiz (Smith 1968:30), "he was put to watch a temple, that the wolves in the nighttime, might not carry off the dead there." Garcilaso (1605) also refers to a charnel house: "These corpses were laid in wooden crypts above the ground, which served as tombs, without hinges or any other provision for fastening except some boards with which they were covered, and with stones or logs on top. Through the wretchedness of the enclosures used to house them, the bodies were carried away from these crypts by the lions."

At Parrish Mound 2, east of Tampa Bay and well within Tocobaga territory, Reichard, in January 1934, excavated the remains of a charnel house or enclosure consisting of four walls of posts set at intervals of about six inches, with a strengthened corner containing charcoal and partial cremations. Also in the mound were Safety Harbor ceramics, fragments of carved wood, some cordage, a tortoiseshell comb, blue and white glass seed beads, and a brass pendant (Willey 1949:146-52). This clearly documents charnel houses during the historic portion of the Safety Harbor period and demonstrates them as a Tocobaga trait.

As de Soto moved northward, he encountered larger villages and an abundance of corn. This was also true of Narváez. Four leagues from his first camp, Narváez' men captured four Indians who guided the Spaniards to a village and showed them maize "that was not yet fit to be gathered" (Bandelier 1922:12). Ten to twelve leagues further, the expedition "came to another village of fifteen houses, where there was a large cultivated patch of corn nearly ready for harvest, and also some that was already ripe" (Bandelier 1922:13-14). This suggests that the Tocobaga Indians planted their fields at different times so that harvesting would be spread over several months.

Citing observations from de Soto's journey, Garcilaso (1605) includes in the Tocobaga aboriginal settlement pattern a location on high land; a large mound or midden supporting ten to twenty houses for the cacique, his family, and their serving people; a quadrangular public square around which nobles and head men had their establishments; and, outside of this, the huts of the common people.

The "standard" Tocobaga settlement pattern for small or large ceremonial centers of the Safety Harbor period around Tampa Bay had a midden paralleling the shore; a rectangular temple mound with a ramp in the middle of one of its longer sides leading toward the main part of the midden; and a burial mound off to one side. The area more or less surrounded by these features—the plaza—was kept clean of rubbish (Bullen 1951, 1969). Shell deposits are sometimes found at the open sides of the plaza. A similar arrangement occurred at Crystal River during the Safety Harbor phase; this pattern closely resembles that delineated by Garcilaso.

Evidence that the Safety Harbor site was the location of the "city" of Tocobaga is provided by accounts of Menéndez' 1566 visits to Carlos' pueblo and the joint expedition by Carlos and Menéndez to Tocobaga, as well as by Fontaneda's narrative. According to Fontaneda's memoirs: "Between Avalachi [Apalachee] and Olagale is a river . . . Río de Cañas. . . . On this river, arm of the sea, and coast, are the pearls, which are got in certain oysters and conchs. They are carried to all the provinces and villages of Florida, but principally to Tocobaga, the nearest town [to the river] . . . on the right-hand side coming to Habaña" (Fontaneda 1945:29). If Old Tampa Bay is identified as the "river of canes," then the Safety Harbor site is on the right-hand side going south. Fontaneda also noted that Tocobaga is "inland on the last cape of the river" which agrees with its location along the western side of Old Tampa Bay (Fontaneda 1945:29).

Carlos' pueblo was located on Mound Key in Estero Bay about two leagues south of the mouth of the Caloosahatchee River. On his first visit to Carlos' pueblo in February 1566, Menéndez learned that "50 leagues farther from there was a very good harbor, where there were three other Christian captives in the power of Indians" (Solís de Merás 1964:143–44). On his second visit in April, he, with six brigantines, arrived from Havana "in two ordinary days, with a prosperous wind" (Solís de Merás 1964:222). He was told that the passage he sought (across Florida) was "50 leagues farther on, in a pueblo they called Tocobaga . . . where the cacique was a great enemy of Carlos" (Solís de Merás 1964:223). Fifty leagues comes to about 132 miles, while the minimum water distance from Estero Bay to the Safety Harbor site on Old Tampa Bay is about 130 miles! It is the same distance to the mouth of the Hillsborough River at Tampa, also inland on Tampa Bay. "Within three days after he [Menéndez] reached Carlos, he sailed with all 6 brigantines in the direction of Tocobaga; he took Carlos with him and 20 of his principal Indians . . . he arrived at the harbor the 2nd day, at night. The cacique lived 20 leagues inland, and one could sail up close to the side of his house by a channel of salt water: an Indian of those parts who came with Carlos, steered in such a manner toward the north, although it was at night and there was no moon, that with a prosperous wind, the Adelantado arrived one hour before daybreak near the house of Tocobaga, without being discovered, and he ordered the brigantines to anchor with great secrecy" (Solís de Merás 1964:224). This account agrees exactly with the proposition that the Safety Harbor site is Tocobaga.

Before leaving, Menéndez made a temporary peace between Carlos and Tocobaga and left thirty Christians and a captain to teach the Tocobaga Indians to become Christians. He also rescued some Europeans who were Tocobaga slaves and ten or twelve of Carlos' people, including one of his sisters. It should be noted that Menéndez discovered from time to time whites who had survived wrecks and storms and who had been enslaved by the Indians. Prisoners reported that Carlos and his father had killed more than two hundred Christians over the preceding twenty years (Solís de Merás 1964:221)! The prisoners learned the Indian language, wore only Indian loincloths, and were hewers and carriers of wood. When their rescuers arrived, they could act as interpreters. While most were happy to be rescued, the records indicated that some of the women preferred to remain with their children.

Various early accounts give information on other Tocobaga traits. Carved wooden building ornaments and wooden boxes are mentioned as well as bows and arrows. The accounts note fish, shellfish, deer, turtles, watercress, pumpkins, "cabbage from the low palmetto" (Smith 1968:37), maize, beans, and small dogs were utilized as food. Houses are described as covered with reeds or brush.

The narratives also describe patterns of social stratification. A cacique was brought on a man's back to see de Soto (litters, however, are not mentioned). Four social classes are indicated: chiefs, or caciques, headmen, warriors and ordinary people, and slaves. The slaves may have been Europeans or captured Indians. There seems to have been some movement of people from group to group, apparently for a variety of reasons. Often a chief's sister was married to another chief, perhaps to secure both favor and peace. Carlos married an older sister to Menéndez, and one of his sisters was said to be a prisoner of Tocobaga. Hirrihigua's (Ucita's chief) sister was Mocoço's wife, and Urribarracuxi (Paracoxi) was Mocoço's brother-in-law.

The Tocobaga had been exposed to European material culture even before Narváez landed. Narváez captured four Indians who took him to a village where were "found many boxes for merchandise from Castilla. In every one of them was a corpse covered with painted deer hides. . . . We also found pieces of linen and cloth, and feather head dresses that seemed to be from New Spain, and samples of gold" (Bandelier 1922:12). "There was also found pieces of shoes and canvas [*lienza*], of cloth and some iron, and enquiring of the Indians they told us by signs that they had found it in a vessel that had been lost on this coast and in that bay" (Bandelier 1922:13n4). The size of box was not given; the corpses could have been flexed and wrapped or tied with deerskins.

When Calderón broke camp to join de Soto, he gave Mocoço material which he could not take with him. The following is a list, perhaps exaggerated, from Garcilaso. From the ships: sails, tackle or rigging, rosin or pitch, tow, tallow, rope (halter or cord), panniers, trail baskets, hampers or crates, anchors, cables, iron tools, iron, steel or steel material; general supplies: cloaks or mantles, sack coats, doublets or jackets, breeches, long loose trousers, coverings for legs and feet, shoes, laced shoes, hempen sandals; arms: cuirasses, shields or bucklers, pikes or long lances, lances, and steel helmets; and 500 *quintals,* or a little over 100 pounds, of cassava bread.

Early introduction to European goods seems to have had very little effect on the inhabitants of Tocobaga. The missions at Tocobaga and at Carlos' pueblo were short lived and had hardly any effect on the inhabitants of either location. Although European items are found throughout the Tocobaga area (and, indeed, over much of Florida), these were luxury goods passed on by finders to caciques and had little impact on Tocobaga life-style.

During this acculturation period, the Tocobaga way of life seems to have been virtually untouched until the early seventeenth century, when a chain of Spanish missions was established across North Florida and European-introduced diseases became rampant. Populations must have declined rapidly. In the eighteenth century, the remnants of the Tocobaga probably merged with the Creek peoples moving southward into peninsular Florida.

REFERENCES

Bandelier, Fanny.
   1922.   *The Journey of Alvar Nuñez Cabeza de Vaca*. New York: Allerton Book Co.
Bullen, Ripley P.
   1951.   *The Terra Ceia Site, Manatee County, Florida*. Florida Anthropological Society Publication no. 3.
   1952a. *Eleven Archaeological Sites in Hillsborough County, Florida*. Florida Geological Survey, Report of Investigations no. 8.
   1952b. De Soto's Ucita and the Terra Ceia Site. *Florida Historical Quarterly* 30:317-23.
   1955.   Archeology of the Tampa Bay Area, Florida. *Florida Historical Quarterly* 34:51-63.
   1969.   Southern Limits of Timucua Territory. *Florida Historical Quarterly* 47:414-19.
Bullen, Ripley P., and Adelaide K. Bullen.
   1956.   *Excavations on Cape Haze Peninsula, Florida*. Florida State Museum Contributions, Social Sciences no. 1.
Fontaneda, Hernando d'Escalante.
   1945.   *Memoir of Dº d'Escalante Fontaneda Respecting Florida, Written in Spain, about the Year 1575*. Translated by Buckingham Smith, edited by David O. True. Coral Gables, Fla.: Glade House.
Garcilaso de la Vega.
   1605.   *La Florida*. Translated by B. B. Lewis and W. H. Wilkerson, 1963. Gainesville: Florida State Museum.
Griffin, John W., and Ripley P. Bullen.
   1950.   *The Safety Harbor Site, Pinellas County, Florida*. Florida Anthropological Society Publications no. 2.
Schell, Rolfe F.
   1966.   *De Soto Didn't Land at Tampa*. Fort Myers Beach, Fla.: Island Press.
Sears, William H.
   1967.   The Tierra Verde Burial Mound. *Florida Anthropologist* 20:25-73.
Smith, Buckingham.
   1968.   *Narratives of de Soto in the Conquest of Florida*. Original translated edition, 1866. Gainesville, Fla.: Palmetto Books.

Solís de Merás, Gonzalo.
   1964. *Pedro Menéndez de Avilés.* Facsimile of the 1923 edition, translated and
          edited by J. T. Conner. Gainesville: University of Florida Press.
Swanton, John R.
   1939. *Final Report of the United States de Soto Expedition Commission.* 76th Cong., 1st
          sess., H.R. 71.
   1952. De Soto's First Headquarters in Florida. *Florida Historical Quarterly* 30:311–16.
   1953. De Soto and Terra Ceia, Florida. *Florida Historical Quarterly* 31:196–207.
Willey, Gordon R.
   1949. *Archeology of the Florida Gulf Coast.* Smithsonian Miscellaneous Collections, vol.
          113.

The Western Timucua: Patterns of Acculturation and Change

Jerald T. Milanich

WHEN the first Europeans arrived, the Timucua were occupying the northern third of peninsular Florida (except the Gulf coast) and a small portion of southeastern Georgia. This area was bounded by the Aucilla River and the coastal flatlands environmental zone on its west side and the Atlantic Ocean to the east. The southern boundary coincided with the lower end of the north-central, pine-oak hammock zone, roughly the Marion–Lake County line. The northern limits of the Timucua cannot be ascertained. They probably did not live beyond a line drawn from Valdosta, Georgia, across the northern edge of the Okeefenokee Swamp to the mouth of the Satilla River at the north end of Cumberland Island, Georgia.

The division of the Timucua into eastern and western tribes is based both on geographical distribution and on the grouping of techno-environmental factors (Harris 1971:144–46), i.e., similarities in environment and methods of exploiting that environment. Thus, the western Timucuan tribes (the Potano, Ocale, Utina, and Yustega) were primarily adjusted to the pine-oak forests of north-central Florida west of the St. Johns River, while the eastern Timucuan groups were aligned culturally to three broad groups of habitats: the St. Johns River, its tributaries and back swamps, and the pine forest of the coastal flatlands, extending eastward to and including the coastal lagoon (Saturiwa, Acuera, Freshwater); the rivers, swamps, and forests of mainland southeastern Georgia (Cascange, Icafui, Tucururu, Yui, Yufera); and the coastal marshes and oak hammocks of Cumberland Island, Georgia, and the adjacent mainland (Tacata-

59

curu). The natural environments of the Tawasa in Alabama and the Oconi in Georgia are not well known since their exact location is in question, and no information is available on their material culture.

Although distribution of Timucuan tribes or groups of tribes roughly corresponds to specific, broad natural zones, all of the tribes utilized the resources of several of these zones, increasing the total number of floral and faunal habitats, which they exploited for subsistence. For example, the tribes dwelling along the St. Johns River frequently moved to the coastal lagoons to fish and collect shellfish and probably sent hunting parties west of the St. Johns to the deciduous forest hammocks where hunting was better than in the coastal flatlands.

John M. Goggin (1953) provided the first correlation between the Timucuan tribes and their respective geographical location and archeological complexes. He separated the tribes into eastern (Freshwater, Saturiwa, Tacatacuru, Yui, Icafui, Yufera), western (Potano, Timucua, Onatheaqua, Yustega), southeastern (Acuera, Ocale), southern (Tocobaga, Ucita, Pohoy, Mococo), and isolated (Tawasa). Nothing is known about the Onatheaqua except for a brief reference by René de Laudonnière. Later the Onatheaqua were also cited by Le Moyne (probably basing his information on Laudonnière's narrative), who marked their presumed location on his map (Lorant 1946:34–35). Later documents do not refer to such a tribe in north-central Florida, and it seems best to delete them from the list of Timucuan tribes until there is more evidence concerning their existence.

Also, it seems likely that Goggin's southern Timucua group were not Timucuan-speakers. There is no evidence, either direct or indirect, that the central Gulf coast Indians spoke Timucuan; rather, it seems that J. W. Powell (1891:123–24), in his *Linguistic Families of America North of Mexico*, inadvertently included the Tampa Bay and middle Gulf coast in his Timucuan linguistic area. Later researchers, referring to Powell, cited the area as Timucuan (Swanton 1946:193; 1952:147–50). The central Gulf coast Tocobaga culture seems to have interacted politically with the south Florida tribes, such as the Calusa (Zubillaga 1946:278, 291, 381; Fontaneda 1945:68). The Calusa in turn had political dealings with the Mayaca and Jororo (who were related to one another linguistically—Escobar 1717; Franciscans 1735), and the Ais, Jeaga, and Tequesta (see Goggin and Sturtevant 1964:187–89 for a summary of Calusa political ties and alliances). Tropical South Florida seems to have been a separate cultural and linguistic area from north-central and northeastern Florida.

While Goggin's basic division of eastern and western Timucua remains valid, although altered somewhat on the basis of documentary
evidence, this division does not reflect tribal alliances or linguistic
groupings. The Timucua were composed of at least fifteen separate
tribes who shared only a common language. At no time were the
Timucua united into one ethnic or political unit. The tribes were
cross-cut both by dialect differences and differences in material and
probably nonmaterial culture. Based on the writings of the early-
seventeenth-century Franciscan priest Francisco Pareja (Adam and
Vinson 1886:xxi, 47, 88, 119, 121; Pareja 1627:36–37) it is possible to
distinguish nine Timucua dialects: Agua Dulce (Freshwater), Icafui,
Mocamo (Agua Salada, or Saltwater), Oconi, Yufera, Tucururu,
Timucua (Utina), Potano, Santa Lucia de Acuera. Tawasa also is a
Timucuan dialect, according to John R. Swanton's analysis (1929) of a
short Tawasa vocabulary collected in 1707–8 (Bushnell 1908).

Most of the tribes can be shown through archeological evidence to
have participated in one of four material cultural traditions: Alachua
(Milanich 1971a, 1972a); St. Johns (Goggin 1949, 1952); Fort Walton
(inland)–Leon–Jefferson (Willey 1949:452–70, 488–95, 512–13, 515–
16; Smith 1948; Deagan 1972); and an unnamed Cumberland Island
archeological culture which was probably derived from the earlier
Coastal tradition Deptford and Wilmington-Savannah cultures (Milanich 1971b, 1972b, 1973). Tribal, dialect, and archeological complex
correlations are summarized in Figure 1.

The first three of these material cultural traditions can be traced
back to at least a thousand years before the historic period. This dis-
proves any generalized statements postulating relatedness between
language (or dialects) and material culture. Rather, in the case of the
Timucua, the evidence suggests a correspondence between culture
and natural environment. Dialect differences, then, must be a
phenomena of tribal formation, social endogamy, and/or territorial-
ity, especially in Florida where there are no natural barriers to human
contact. On the other hand, the separate Timucuan dialects have not
been studied, and word differences may exist which are the result of
different natural environments and different subsistence procurement systems. The effects of environmental adjustment on the formation of Timucuan dialects are unknown.

The determination of the linguistic relationships of the Timucuan
language has long posed problems. Many of the early researchers
included Timucuan within the Gulf or Muskhogean stock, basing
their conclusions more on geographical proximity of the Timucua to

Muskhogean speakers (cf. Creek) than on linguistic ties. Recent research, however, has tended to disassociate Timucua from the Gulf
stock (Haas 1958), instead suggesting either Siouian or Arawakan
relationships (Swadesh 1964; Haas 1971). Granberry (1971) believes
there are close ties between Timucuan and the Warau language. The
Warau, meaning in their own language "boat people," are found in
the Orinoco Delta on the northeast coast of Venezuela. Before the
introduction of horticulture in the twentieth century, the Warau subsisted mainly by fishing, with some hunting and gathering (Wilbert
1972:65–115). More archeological research is needed to determine
the extent of population migrations, colonization, and cultural diffusion in the Florida-circum-Caribbean area.

Fig. 1. Correlation between tribe, dialects, and material culture in
the seventeenth century

Tribe	Dialect	Archeological Culture
Yustega	Potano	Leon-Jefferson
Utina	Utina	Leon-Jefferson
Ocale	?	Potano (Alachua tradition)
Potano	Potano	Potano (Alachua tradition)
Saturiwa	Mocamo	St. Johns
Acuera	Acuera	St. Johns
Freshwater	Aqua Dulce	St. Johns
Cascange	Icafui	? (possibly Wilmington-Savannah and St. Johns)
Icafui	Icafui	? (possibly Wilmington-Savannah and St. Johns)
Tucururu	Tucururu	?
Yui (Ibi)	?	? (possibly Wilmington-Savannah and St. Johns)
Yufera	Yufera	? (possibly Wilmington-Savannah and St. Johns)
Tacatacuru	Mocamo	Derived from Wilmington-Savannah

Anthropological research among the western Timucua has been a
combination of archeological surveys and excavations and archival
use for ethnographic and linguistic information. References to these
documents can be found in Michael Gannon's *The Cross in the Sand*
(1965:191–98) and in *Francisco Pareja's 1613 Confessionario: A Documentary Source for Timucuan Ethnography* (Milanich and Sturtevant
1972:1–21). There have also been a few articles written on western
Timucua culture which include information on agriculture (Spellman
1948) and general culture traits (Ehrmann 1940; Seaberg 1955;
Swanton 1922:320–87). The last two do not differentiate specific
tribes, and most of the information probably applies more to the
eastern Timucua than to the western tribes. Brief summary descriptions of all the Timucuan tribes will appear in my forthcoming article

on the Timucua (Milanich, n.d.) in the *Handbook of North American Indians* to be published by the Smithsonian Institution.

Archeological investigations into the western Timucua have centered on the Potano. This is due to the accessibility of historic and prehistoric Potano village sites to the University of Florida, which is located at about the geographical center of Potano territory. Excavations at three seventeenth-century Potano sites have been carried out. These are Richardson, an early post-contact village near Evinston (Milanich 1972a); Fox Pond, the presumed site of the San Francisco de Potano Spanish mission (Symes and Stephens 1965); and Zetrouer, possibly a late-seventeenth-century Spanish-Indian cattle ranch near Rochelle (Seaberg 1955).

Archeological research has also been carried out at three prehistoric Potano sites. Prehistoric Potano culture correlates with the archeologically known Alachua cultural tradition. The three sites are Rocky Point (Milanich 1971a:15-25) on the northern side of Paynes Prairie; the Woodward burial mound and village on Levy Lake (Bullen 1949; Milanich 1971a:9-15); and site A-273 adjacent to Fox Pond (Milanich 1971a:7-9).

Descriptions of material culture from a presumed Utina-Spanish site on the Ichetucknee River have been published (Deagan 1972). Also, the Florida Department of State, Division of Archives, History, and Records Management, completed test excavations at two Yustega mission sites east of the Aucilla River (Jones 1972:1-2). Although archeological and ethnographic information on the western Timucua is scarce, there are sufficient data available to determine the intensity of European contact, to outline tribal regions, and to make some interpretive statements concerning aboriginal culture and the changes resulting from contact with the Spanish and French.

YUSTEGA

The Yustega, along with the Ocale, are the least known of the western Timucua. First mention of the province (a Spanish concept) of Yustega is in the de Soto expedition narrative of Luis Hernández de Biedma written in 1544 (Smith 1968:234-35). Interpretation of de Biedema's account and also that of the Gentleman of Elvas (Smith 1968:45-46) by the de Soto Commission placed the Yustega east of the Aucilla River and west of the Suwannee River (Swanton 1939:146-47, 157-59). This is roughly the area of present-day Madison and northern Taylor counties.

Physiographically, this area is similar to the Apalachee Indian province west of the Aucilla, i.e., pine forests with remnant clay hills which are old beach lines. The southern boundary of the Yustega in Taylor County marks the change from pine forest to low, coastal flatlands. The possibility exists that prehistorically the Yustega moved seasonally between these two broad natural zones, but more archeological research is needed to test this hypothesis. The Yustega region is cut by the Aucilla, Econfina, and Fenholloway rivers and their tributaries. Many lakes are also spread throughout the region, providing natural habitats for economic exploitation.

The de Soto narratives (Smith 1968:45–46, 233) refer to another province, Uzachile, or Veachile, which lay between the Yustega Indians and the Suwannee. To date, however, no additional documents have been found to lend more information on this probable Timucuan tribe, and their territory is generally subsumed within the Yustega region. Later research, either documentary or archeological, may provide the necessary evidence for a division of the Yustega region as presently defined. The town of Asile visited by de Soto (and the probable location of the later mission of San Miguel de Asile) was located within the Yustega province.

The Yustega are also mentioned in the accounts of the Frenchman René de Laudonnière, who refers to them as one of the tribes hostile to the Utina (Ningler et Confrontes 1927:154–55). One of Laudonnière's men, Groutald, reported that he had visited the Yustega and that the chief could raise an army of 3,000 to 4,000 warriors, probably an exaggeration. Groutald's report infers that the Yustega traded with the Creek tribes of the Georgia piedmont area (Ningler et Confrontes 1927:178–79). Another Frenchman, La Roche Ferriere, also had contact with the Yustega in 1564 (Ningler et Confrontes 1927: 165).

With the departure of the French from Florida in 1565, and with the establishment of garrisons and missions by the Spanish, there was continual, though light, contact between the Yustega and Spanish soldiers, traders, and traveling missionaries. But it was not until after 1633 that missions with resident priests were established among the Yustega. Presumably three of the four Yustega missions were located close to the St. Augustine–San Luis Spanish road and were built at the same time as the Apalachee missions. These three—San Pedro y San Pablo Potohiriba, Santa Helena de Machaba, and San Miguel de Asile—all appear on the 1655 list of missions found in Don Inigo Abbad y Lasierra's "Relacion de la Descubrimiento, Conquista, y Pob-

lacion de las Provincias y Costas de la Florida" (Serrano y Sanz
1912:132–33). The fourth mission, San Matheo de Tolapatafi, probably was built after the Indian rebellion of 1656, since it does not
appear on the earlier list.[1] It is known that in 1659 the Spanish sought
to rebuild the towns in Yustega destroyed by the Spanish soldiers
during the rebellion (Swanton 1922:338). Perhaps San Matheo was
established during this period. Swanton, however, lists San Matheo as
one of the mission villages participating in the rebellion (1922:338),
and it might be that the mission was not operating when the 1655 list
was drawn up. More documentary research is needed to clear up this
point.

The 1656 rebellion seems to have started among the western
Apalachee and the Yustega mission Indians (Swanton 1922:338). It is
perhaps significant that the rebellion took place roughly twenty years
after the onset of intense Spanish-Indian mission contact, the establishment of the missions having begun in 1633. Twenty years is
needed for one generation to mature to adulthood. That generation
was subjected to dual enculturation processes, the indigenous culture
of their parents and the Christianized and somewhat Hispanized culture taught by the Spanish priests (see Milanich and Sturtevant 1972
for some of the changes in the Indians' cultures which the Franciscan
priests tried to make). This type of contact situation might easily have
led to a revitalization movement and / or an overt rebellion, either of
which would have been an attempt to revive and perpetuate specific,
valued Indian culture traits at the expense of Spanish traits (Linton
1943:499; Barber 1941:667).

A letter written in 1651 by Manuel, chief of the mission village of
Asile (Manuel 1651), outlines some of the reasons for the unhappi-
ness with the Spanish. Spanish military officials tried to take Indian
land for their own use by misrepresenting the position of the Spanish
government. Also, the Indians were used as laborers on plantations
and cattle ranches without being compensated. Manuel complained
that many of the Yustega were moving into the Apalachee province so
that they did not have to work for the Spanish.[2] This population

1. Translated from the Timucuan, *tola-patafi* means "at the foot of the laurel."
2. The Spanish translation accompanying the letter refers to the Yustega Indians
who were moving into Apalachee as *cimarrones*, or "wild ones." Charles H. Fairbanks
(1957:4–6) has shown how this Spanish term was used somewhat later to refer to the
Creeks who moved southward from Georgia and Alabama into Florida during the
eighteenth century. The word underwent pronunciation changes, eventually becoming
seminole, the name popularly given by whites to the descendants of the Florida Creeks.

emigration evidently weakened the chief's political power. Manuel also noted that even though he was chief, he could not give away or sell Yustega land (although he could lend it), since the land was owned jointly by his sons and nephews and the other lesser chiefs and the principal men of the tribe. This concept of landownership was alien to the Spanish.

After the Yustaga rebellion of 1656 was subdued and the situation returned to normal, the missions entered a half century "Golden Age"; at least this is the interpretation of European and modern white historians. Bishop Gabriel Díaz Vara Calderón visited the missions in 1675 and noted their respective locations (Wenhold 1936). The four Yustega missions were spread evenly along the Spanish road two leagues (five miles) from one another. San Miguel was the west-ernmost mission, two leagues from the easternmost Apalachee mis-sion located across the Aucilla River. At the other end, the east-ernmost Yustega mission, San Pedro, was ten leagues (twenty-five miles) from the westernmost Utina mission across the Suwannee River. This settlement pattern seems to indicate that by 1675, and probably much earlier, the Yustega Indians were clustered in the western portion of the region which has been described as the Yustega province. This lends support to the de Soto documents, which indicate that the Yustega did not extend eastward to the Suwannee but were buffered on that side by the Veachile province. The mission region is referred to by Calderón as the "Ustacanian" province (Wenhold 1936:8), thus the region retained its identity as Yustega territory from the time of de Soto, nearly 150 years.

A report to the king by Governor Pablo Hita Salazar, in 1675, spreads out the locations of the missions relative to one another over a distance of seven and one-half leagues, slightly more than Calderón, but his figures still indicate a gap between the Yustega and the Utina. Salazar gives a total mission population of 940 Indians for the Yustega province (Salazar 1675).

In 1688, a letter signed by the chiefs of the four Yustega mission villages was sent to the king (Gatschet 1880:495–97). It is likely the letter was contrived by Spanish officials or priests since the contents relate only the Indians' glowing praise of the Florida governor, Don Diego de Quiroga y Lassada.

There are no reliable sixteenth- or early-seventeenth-century popu-lation figures with which to compare the census figures of the mis-sions' "Golden Age," other than the French report of a 3,000–4,000-man Yustega army. If figures from other Florida Indians are correct, there was a rapid and severe population decrease. A 1689 census lists 330 families, roughly 1,650 persons, for the four Yustega missions (Compostela 1689). That this figure is so large is probably due to an influx of Creek peoples from Georgia and Alabama to the Florida missions.

In 1690, two priests were sent to the mission of San Matheo to learn the Indian languages (Geiger 1940:43, 68, 69). However, this action was more a result of political activity within the Catholic church than it was an attempt to have the priests understand newly introduced Indian languages. The 1690 restationing of priests at the missions was widespread throughout the Santa Elena church province (Florida and Georgia).

The letters of 1651 and 1688 point out one major change in Yustega political organization resulting from European contact. Sixteenth-century documents (cf. de Soto and Laudonnière) refer to a chief of the Yustega under whom the various village chiefs and the villagers themselves seem to have been united as a tribal unit. This was a very common pattern among nearly all Southeast Indians at the time of contact. After the establishment of the missions in 1633, the only references are to chiefs of separate villages. Evidently contact with the Europeans led to a breakdown of tribal level organization and to the decline in the importance of or to the disappearance of a tribal level chief.

This change in political organization reflects several related possibilities. The mission system, which operated on the level of individual Indian villages with resident Spanish priests, tended to decentralize tribal government. The priests purposefully worked to decentralize tribal authority and to increase the importance of village chiefs; the fathers usually tried first to win over the village chiefs to Christianity in the belief that they would be instrumental in converting the rest of the population. There are also instances where the priests interfered with indigenous inheritance patterns by appointing as village chief a person of their choice rather than the rightful successor. Usually this individual was someone sympathetic to Christianity who could be maintained in power by the active support of the priests. The priests chose to work on the level of the individual village since there was no longer any strong inter-village structure. Declining populations and changed subsistence and religious patterns (the latter important in the support of a tribal level chief) had destroyed the ability of the Yustega to maintain the indigenous political form of inter-village ties and a hierarchy of chiefs. These alliances were necessary for the maintenance of tribal civil, military, and religious collective activities. Decentralization, then, led to changes in social organizations, belief systems, and the ability of the aborigines to defend themselves. Ethnocide and genocide were the results.

In some areas in Florida, e.g., the lower Atlantic coast and south-central Florida, the missions established by the Spanish among the western Timucua were extremely successful. The failure of the Spanish to maintain missions among the Ais, Mayagua (a tribe probably located on the southern portion of the St. Johns River), and other south Florida Indians was due in part to the aboriginal subsistence pattern which required seasonal movement of villagers between coastal and inland riverine environmental zones. Horticulture was either not practiced or was not very important in south Florida. The Indians in this area of Florida could not have successfully lived year-round in one environmental zone as they were urged to do by the priests. Even if horticulture was introduced by the priests, it is doubtful that the Indians could have been successful sedentary farmers. The soils in south Florida were poor and not suited for growing corn or wheat. Also, the Indians had a strong cultural tradition of seasonal hunting and gathering. On the other hand, one reason for the success of the Timucuan missions was that there was a long tradition of horticulture in north-central Florida which dated from at least one thousand years before the historic period. The Spanish priests successfully introduced new horticultural techniques and tools. Horticulture expanded, and dependable food resources became available, allowing year-round occupation at the mission villages.

Although there is no archeological evidence at this time for such a subsistence change among the western Timucuan tribes, Spanish sources documenting new crops and new horticultural techniques strongly hint at this explanation. The major change in Indian subsistence patterns must have been reflected in trait changes throughout the cultures, including increasing autonomy of individual villages resulting from economic self-sufficiency.

Destruction of the Yustega population and villages was rapid. The San Matheo and San Pedro missions were raided and evidently destroyed by the English and their Indian allies in September 1704 (Governor Zúñiga in Boyd, Smith, and Griffin 1951:68–69). The other two Yustega villages were probably also destroyed at that time. The remaining Indians not captured or killed withdrew to the vicinity of St. Augustine for protection. A 1711 census shows a total of 833 Indians living in St. Augustine with nine outlying Indian villages still occupied, none of which was in the Yustega region (Córcoles y Martínez 1711). It is likely the remaining Yustega who were living in the town or in outlying villages were simply referred to under the generic term Timucuan.

Archeological research is needed in the Yustega region in order to check correlations between archeological complexes and presumed tribal distribution and to document specific mission village sites along with changes in material culture brought about by acculturation of Spanish and non-Yustega Indian traits. Presently, the meager archeological evidence available suggests that Yustega ceramics were like those of the Apalachee Indians. Archeological evidence (other than ceramic typologies) may distinguish the Yustega material culture from that of the Apalachee. Preliminary research has located and given identities to a number of Apalachee villages and two Yustega villages, providing an ideal basis for future comparative studies.

Ocale

Other than a relatively definite location, nothing is known about the province and Indians known as Ocale (or Cale, or Etocale). The interpretation of the de Soto narratives by the de Soto Commission (Swanton 1939:144, 150, 159, 308) places the province of Ocale northeast of the Withlacoochee River near present-day Ocala. Artifact collections of tools and pottery from this area appear to belong to the same material culture tradition as those in use among the Potano.

The Ocale region, which lies west of the Ocala forest, north of the central Florida lake region, and west of the coastal flatlands, is an extension of the mixed hardwoods-pine forest found in the north-central Florida Potano region. This helps to explain the similarities between Ocale and Potano material cultures. Archeological research in the Ocala forest and in the central Florida lakes region shows that the prehistoric Indian inhabitants had a St. Johns material culture. Most likely these peoples were Timucuans, who moved inland seasonally from the St. Johns River. The Gentleman of Elvas noted (Smith 1968:36) that the Ocale were at war with the Indians who dwelt in a "land where it was continually summer." This was probably a reference to these central Florida Timucua, who during the late summer and early fall traveled inland to hunt and to gather nuts and berries.

Utina

The Utina were one of the largest Indian groups in Florida, probably ranking after the Apalachee and the Calusa. Certainly they had the largest population of any of the Timucuan tribes. From the narratives of the de Soto expedition (especially that of the Gentleman of Elvas, Smith 1968:40–44; Swanton 1939:152–58) and the knowledge of the location of the Spanish missions, the Utina region can be reconstructed as having extended from the Santa Fe River north into southern Georgia (perhaps to Valdosta), and from the Suwannee River east to the edge of the coastal flatlands, perhaps as far as the St. Johns River. This region encompasses the present-day Florida counties of Hamilton, Suwannee, Columbia, Baker, Union, Bradford, and western Duval and Clay, and Echols and southern Clinch counties in Georgia.

The western half of this region is similar to the Yustega and Apalachee provinces—pine forests with some rolling, remnant clay hills. Toward the center of the region, just west of Lake City, mixed hardwood hammocks are common, and the area resembles the Ocale and Potano provinces. The eastern portion of the region is characterized by a flat topography with long-leaf pine forests. Several rivers flow through the Utina region, most notably the Suwannee, Alapaha, New, and St. Marys, and Olustee Creek. There is also a vast network of tributaries and smaller streams feeding these rivers, and the area is dotted with hundreds of lakes, ponds, and, in the western portion, limestone sinks. Prehistorically, seasonal exploitation of this varied environment may have occurred, but again there is little evidence one way or the other, except the account of Laudonnière (Ningler et Confrontes 1927:181) stating that in the winter the Utina went into the woods. Interpretation of other French documents also leaves the impression of seasonal movement.

Earliest European contact with the Utina was by the Pánfilo de Narváez expedition in 1528 (Smith 1871). According to the narrative of Cabeza de Vaca, the expedition met Indians in what was probably the western Utina region (Smith 1871:31–32). Eleven years later the de Soto expedition traveled north and west through the heart of the region and was involved in several skirmishes and a full-scale battle with the Utina. In the latter engagement, 350–400 Indians attacked the Spaniards (Smith 1968:40–44) but were finally defeated.

The French in 1564 and 1565 under Laudonnière traded with the Utina and aided them in warfare against the Potano. Laudonnière speaks of forty kings (and villages, most likely) being vassals of the tribal chief Utina (Ningler et Confrontes 1927:154). The French documents indicate that Chief Utina's village was located near the St. Johns River upstream some twenty leagues from Fort Caroline, itself

located near the mouth of the river (Ningler et Confrontes 1927:163).
Either the water route traveled to this village was not the St. Johns,
although there is no alternative river which would have flowed inland from the presumed location of Fort Caroline, or Chief Utina was
residing in the extreme eastern portion of his territory in order to be
accessible to the French. It is also possible that Indians with a chief
named Utina with whom the French intrigued were not the mission
Indians of the tribe Utina. Utina is a Timucuan word meaning chief
or king and the usage might have been widespread through the area
in which Timucuan was spoken. The Indians in the French accounts
might have been the Freshwater Indians of the later Spanish documents.

The question of who were and who were not the Utina will be
determined only through archeological investigations which can
demonstrate whether or not the Utina material culture found in
north-central Florida (cf. Deagan's 1972 analysis of presumed Utina
materials from the Ichetucknee River) also occurs just west of the St.
Johns River.

In the early seventeenth century the Franciscans turned their missionary efforts to north-central Florida after they had established the
chain of missions along the upper Florida and Georgia Atlantic
coast. Previous to this time there was only sporadic contact between
the Potano, the Utina, and the Franciscan priests. Most notable was
Father Baltazar López, who between about 1587 and 1599 traveled
frequently from his mission station on Cumberland Island to administer to the Utina (Geiger 1940:68). Beginning in 1607, Father Martin
Prieto, founder of the Potano missions, also traveled throughout the
Utina region and in 1609 founded the San Martin de Timucua mission (also referred to as San Martin de Tomole or San Martin de
Ayacuto at various times; Oré 1936:114–15). Prieto reported in 1607
that the more than twenty Utina villages were subject to a single chief
(Swanton 1946:202).

By 1616, when Father Luís Gerónimo de Oré visited the interior
Florida missions, three other Utina missions had been established:
Santa Cruz de Tarihica, San Juan de Guacara, and Santa Isabel de
Utinahica.[3] The latter is said by Oré (1936:129–30) to have been fifty

3. Guacara evidently was the Suwannee River, making the San Juan mission the
westernmost in the Utina region. San Martin was the easternmost. *Utina-hica* translated
into English is "Utina village." The mission of San Juan de Guacara is believed to be at
Charles Spring in Suwannee County, while Santa Cruz de Tarihica was probably near
O'Brien, also in Suwannee County.

leagues north of Santa Cruz. This was either an exaggeration or the village was located far to the north along the St. Marys River, if not in southern Georgia. Distance from San Juan to San Martin was twenty-seven leagues, about sixty-seven miles. San Martin, marking the eastern end of the Utina region during the mission period, was thirty-four leagues from St. Augustine and was probably located near present-day Lake Santa Fe (distances are taken from Abbad y Lasierra in Serrano y Sanz 1912:132–33, and Calderón in Wenhold 1936). During his visit, Oré noted that at Santa Cruz (established probably in 1611 and with a population of 712 Christian Indians) men and women had learned to write in Spanish even though they were thirty to forty years of age (Oré 1936:129).

By 1655, San Augustin de Urica, Santa Maria de los Angeles de Arapaha, and San Francisco de Chuaquin had been established. They were probably built north of the Spanish road during the 1633–35 period of expansion into the Apalachee province.[4] After 1659, the Santa Catalina de Afurica (or Ajohica) mission was established. There is some confusion concerning this matter since Calderón in 1675 (Wenhold 1936) mentions both a Santa Catalina and an Ajohica mission. A later letter (Salazar 1677–78), however, notes that Ajohica was deserted by that time. Probably two missions existed in 1675 and by 1678 were joined to form one mission which is believed to have been located on the Spanish road near the Ichetucknee River. Salazar's later letter, actually a collection of reports on a visit by Sergeant Major Domingo de Leturionde through the provinces of Timucua and Apalachee in 1677–78, also states that a Spanish cattle ranch was operating between the two locations. The mission was raided in 1685 by coastal Georgia Yamassee Indians (who were slave raiders for the English) and destroyed. In 1675, only three of the Utina missions were still operating; in addition to Santa Catalina, these were Santa Cruz and San Juan. Together the three villages had a population of only 230 persons (Salazar 1675:38). A severe population decrease must have occurred, since one priest alone, Father Antonio de Cuellar, is said to have converted some 4,000 Indians in the vicinity of Tarihica during the second quarter of the seventeenth century (Geiger 1940:46). The 1656 rebellion and various European-introduced illnesses, together with the English-Indian slave raids, must have had a crushing effect on the Utina population.

---

4. *Urica* is translated as "little village"; *Arapaha* (for which the present-day Alapaha River is named) means "many houses." *Chua*, as in *Chua-quin*, is "sinkhole" or "spring."

The 1688 letter to the king, signed by four Yustega chiefs, was signed by only one of the Utina chiefs, that of the westernmost mission village, San Juan de Guacara, which was closest to the Yustegan province (Gatschet 1880:495–97). This mission was destroyed in either late 1689 or early 1690 by the English since it is listed in a 1689 census (Compostelo 1689) and it is known to have been abandoned by 1690 (Boyd, Smith, Griffin 1951:11). The 1689 census also lists the Santa Cruz de Tarihica mission. Total Indian population for the two villages is given as 50 families, roughly 250 persons. This is about the same population figure listed for 1675, suggesting the addition of non-Timucuan Indians to the mission villages, counteracting the population decline which must have continued at perhaps an accelerated pace due to increased slave raiding.

Although there is no positive ethnohistorical evidence, the Santa Cruz mission was probably destroyed with San Juan in 1689–90, ending Spanish mission activity in the Utina region. The population was removed to St. Augustine and to the Potano Santa Fe mission. In 1703, the Spanish garrison at the (former?) location of the San Martin de Timucua village was also withdrawn due to renewed English raids. The garrison, probably reasonably effective against Indian slavers because of superior armament (only seven soldiers manned it in 1703—Barcia 1951:350), was probably no match for the equally equipped but larger English forces who were reinforced by their Indian allies. In 1728, the handful of remaining Christian Utina and other Timucuan Indians was clustered in small villages around St. Augustine. By this time all the missions had been destroyed, and it is doubtful whether any non-Christian Timucua still existed in north-central Florida. The St. Augustine town of Timucua, moved to within two cannon shots of the presidio by this date, contained only fourteen Indians (the exact number of Timucua is uncertain—Geiger 1940: 134). Between September 1 and October 5, 1728, a pestilence struck the village, killing all but three Indians, one a *cacique* (Geiger 1940: 136). By the 1730s, the Utina (and the rest of the Timucua) were destroyed.

The Utina came in contact with the early Spanish exploratory expeditions in 1528 and 1539 and with the French in 1564–65. Contact was sporadic; the Europeans were mainly interested in exploitation of mineral wealth (of which there was none) and food. More intense contact leading to the acculturation of Spanish traits above merely an artifactual level began in 1587 with the visits of the Franciscan missionaries, and then in 1608 with the establishment of mission villages.

Although the earlier missions appear to have been widespread throughout the Utina region (reflecting a dispersed, seasonally sedentary pattern?), the later missions were centered in the southern and western portions of the region. This reflects a change in aboriginal settlement patterning, probably the consolidation of the population in sedentary, horticultural villages. The villages might have persisted in those areas best suited for horticulture. In the case of the Utina region, this would have been the southern and western regions. No doubt the presence of the Spanish road, over which trade was carried out, also influenced the persistence of the missions in the western and southern Utina region.

Spanish farms, perhaps styled after the farming traditions of seventeenth-century Spain, were established among the Utina as early as 1640 (Deagan 1972:40). Wheat plantations were also established by the Spanish who disliked bread made from ground Indian corn flour (Boyd, Smith, and Griffin 1951:47). Not all the plantations were successful, however, since the Indian labor force was not skilled in plantation methods nor was it adaptable to an economy designed to produce a food surplus for export.

The 1651 "Jesus Maria" letter written by Manuel, chief of Asile (which derives its name from the invocation at the top), mentions the Spanish farms and refers to cattle ranches among the Yustega. Cattle ranches were also established among the Utina using the Indians as rancheros (Manuel 1651; Salazar 1677). Other domesticated animals introduced to the Timucua were pigs, chickens, and horses (Boyd, Smith, and Griffin 1951:31, 45). From the Santa Catalina mission site, archeological investigations have yielded large numbers of peach pits and charred corncobs as well as cow bones (Deagan 1972:39). Corncobs appear in larger quantities at the later historic Timucua sites than they do at prehistoric or early-sixteenth-century historic sites. This indicates either that more corn was being grown (once charred, the corncobs deteriorate only negligibly; thus the length of time underground should not be an appreciable factor in their absence from prehistoric sites), or different techniques of storage and processing were being employed after the first quarter of the seventeenth century, allowing the retention of charred corncobs at sites. The de Soto narratives describe large fields of corn among the Timucua, suggesting the introduction of some new processing techniques during the later historic period, perhaps some sort of parching. A list of foodstuffs introduced by the Spanish includes figs, oranges, and watermelons also (Swanton 1946:294, 297). Thus, the Spanish made available to the Indians new commodities, new food processing and / or storage techniques, and perhaps new methods for increased production, such as crop rotation. The combination of these must have led to changes in Utina settlement patterning.

Other changes in Utina culture also occurred. Oré's statement that adult Indians could read and write Spanish is a notable example. These adults, said by Oré to be thirty to forty years of age, were just children when Father López began his conversion of the Utina. Thus, the adults had grown up under Spanish and Christian influences. Like the Yustega, there also seems to have been a breakdown of Utina tribal unity after the establishment of missions, and their individual chiefs and villages seemed to have gained more autonomy.

Deagan (1972), in analyzing the aboriginal ceramics from the Fig Springs–Santa Catalina mission site, notes that by the time of the establishment of the mission (ca. 1660) there was an almost complete replacement of prehistoric pottery types by types of the Leon-Jefferson historic, wooden paddle–stamped series. This same series appears by a comparable date in the Apalachee province, also replacing types in existence at the time of contact with Spanish missionaries. The origin of this stamped ware seems to have been central Georgia Muskhogean speakers, probably one or more of the Creek groups. Deagan concludes that some sort of population movement of Creeks into northern Florida occurred during the middle of the seventeenth century. Many of the Spanish documents mention the entrance of new groups into Florida, substantiating the meager archeological evidence. The effects of such contact on the Utina and other northern Florida Timucuan groups is unknown at this time. The movement of Creeks into Florida continued into the eighteenth century, and this immigration formed the backbone for the repopulation of Florida by the tribes later known collectively as the Seminole. The question of whether or not the adoption of Georgian pottery styles by Florida Indians represents diffusion of techniques or actual population mixing remains unanswered. The rapid spread and adoption of new ceramic styles in the mid-seventeenth century might have been related to a nativistic-type cultural reaction by the Indians to acculturation of Spanish traits and life-styles. This facet of aboriginal culture change among the western Timucua needs a great deal of research.

POTANO

The territory of the historic Potano Indians coincided with present-day Alachua County. Mixed hardwood and pine forests characterized the region before the development of modern-day cattle ranches, lumber industries, and farms. No major river systems are found within the Potano region, although Alachua County contains many small creeks and is dotted with lakes and limestone sinkholes, which often contain water.[5] On the north, east, and south sides of their territory the Potano shared boundaries with the Utina, Freshwater, and Ocale Indians, respectively. Their western boundary was marked by the end of the north-central Florida highlands and the beginning of the coastal flatlands. Small Potano campsites are found in this environmental zone in Gilchrist and Levy counties, indicating some utilization of the natural resources of the coastal zone. Trade with the cultures of the Gulf coast probably occurred within the coastal flatlands, which served as a natural buffer between the Timucuan tribes and the Tocobaga. The Potano were a horticultural people whose subsistence pattern, which included hunting, fishing, and collecting wild foodstuffs in addition to horticulture, was well adjusted to the various environmental habitats of north-central Florida.

Archeological investigations (Milanich 1971a, 1972a) have shown that the Potano Indians were the manifestation in the historic period of the Alachua archeological tradition. The beginning of the Alachua tradition has been put at ca. A.D. 800, and its end is marked by the destruction of the Potano culture at roughly 1700 (Milanich 1971a:47).[6] The four periods within the temporal range of the tradition are Hickory Pond period, ca. A.D. 800–1250; Alachua period, ca. A.D. 1250–1600; Potano I period, ca. A.D. 1600–1630; and Potano II period, ca. A.D. 1630–1700. The division of the Potano period into two temporal segments is a refinement of the Alachua tradition chronology presented previously (Milanich 1971a:47).

The Hickory Pond and Alachua periods are differentiated solely on the basis of changes in frequencies of pottery decorative styles. During the Hickory Pond period, more cord-marked pottery was made than corncob-impressed pottery; during the Alachua period the reverse was true.[7] Among the aboriginal inhabitants of the Southeast

5. The respective territories of the western Timucuan tribes seem to have been well defined, and certainly the boundaries were jointly recognized by the various tribes. The four major natural dividing lines in the area, the Aucilla, Suwannee, St. Johns, and Santa Fe rivers, all marked tribal boundaries.

6. An archeological tradition is a "way of life" (Goggin 1949:17), a cultural adjustment to an environment. Traditions are restricted geographically but extend through time from a few hundred years to a millenium or more. The beginning date of A.D. 800 for the tradition in Florida may be too early; a date of A.D. 1000 would not be surprising.

7. Prairie Cord Marked pottery was surface roughened by malleating the unfired clay pot with a wooden paddle wrapped with a twisted fiber cord. Alachua Cob Marked

United States, popularity of ceramic styles waxed and waned through time. Frequencies of specific types can be graphed and comparative frequencies noted. Thus, the point in time (A.D. 1250) when the frequency of cord-marked pottery equaled that of corncob-impressed pottery is used as the temporal division between the Hickory Pond and Alachua periods.

The change from the Alachua period to Potano I is marked by the appearance of Spanish artifacts at Alachua tradition sites. The A.D. 1600 date coincides approximately with the beginning of missionary activity among the Potano Indians. There seem, however, to have been few changes in Potano material culture (defined on the basis of archeologically derived data) until about 1630, the beginning of the Potano II period. From A.D. 800 to 1630, then, the Alachua tradition remained largely unchanged, except for increases and decreases of certain ceramic styles, a very minor trait. The techniques of construction and the types of ceramic, lithic, and bone artifacts, as well as the percentages of animal species used for food from Hickory Pond sites, are almost identical to those from Potano I sites, giving evidence of few changes in the Alachua way of life over this 830-year period (Milanich 1971a; 1972a). It is only after one generation of contact with the Spanish Franciscan missionaries that changes in Potano culture began to occur, at least those changes which can be recognized archeologically.

Earliest contact between the Potano and Europeans might have taken place in May 1528 when the Narváez expedition passed through extreme western Alachua County or eastern Gilchrist County. Cabeza de Vaca, however, reports that the expedition saw no Indians for almost a two-week period, until it reached the Suwannee River. The expedition probably traveled north through the swampy coastal flatlands west of Potano territory, an area between the coastal strand and the center of the state highland forests which was not well suited to Indian occupation. Certainly the later de Soto expedition spent several days in Potano territory during August 1539, passing through five villages: Ytaraholata, Potano, Utinamocharra, Malapaz, and Cholupaha (Smith 1968:39; Swanton 1939:144). Except for Malapaz, Spanish for "bad peace," a reference to an episode that occurred there between the Spanish and the Potano, all the towns are designated by their Timucuan names. Cholupaha must refer either to

---

pottery was roughened with a dried corncob. Occasionally some kernel impressions are evident.

the types or number of houses in the village, or perhaps to a certain house with ritual significance; Ytaraholata, Potano, and Utinamocharra all refer to chiefs, subchiefs, or political or religious officials. Thus, it might have been that specific tribal officials (such as war chiefs) traditionally came from certain villages and that these villages were referred to by the Indians by the name of the tribal position. Such religious-political organization would coincide quite well with what is known about other southeastern Indian tribes. It will remain unknown, however, whether or not these names, as recorded by the Spanish, accurately reflect Potano usage or if they are simply names picked up by the Spanish and applied to the villages.

As with the other western Timucuan tribes, the Potano were in contact with the French in 1562 and 1564–65. Laudonnière intrigued with the Utina in 1565 to attack the Potano, who were led by their tribal chief, also named Potano (Ningler et Confrontes 1927:163, 179–81). Again, as among the Utina and the Yustega, the Potano had one chief (probably the war chief) capable of summoning a large number of warriors together.

Between 1565 and 1600, there was sporadic contact between the Potano and Spanish Franciscan missionaries. More intense missionary activity began in 1600 when Father Baltazar López included the Potano region in his Cumberland Island, Georgia-to-Utina territory circuit (López 1933:28–32). López, in 1602, met with such great success among the Potano that a plea was made for the establishment of a full-time mission. In answer to this call, Fathers Martin Prieto and Alonzo Serrano were sent out from St. Augustine in 1606, either together or in close succession, to administer to the Potano (Oré 1936:112–14). Prieto established the San Francisco de Potano mission, presumably at or near the town of Potano. Archeological investigations (Symes and Stephens 1965) suggest that site A-272, Fox Pond, located northwest of Gainesville, was the location of this mission. Shortly after this time, the Santa Fe de Toloco (or Santo Tomas de Santa Fe) mission was established three leagues north of San Francisco, close to the St. Augustine–west Florida road, probably east of the present-day town of Alachua.

Both missions were flourishing when visited by Oré in 1616. In 1675, the two missions had a combined population of only 170 persons (Salazar 1675). This compares with the figure of 1,100 given by Father López in 1602 as the number of Potano receiving instruction in Christianity.

By 1689, the population of the two Potano missions had increased to 205 (Compostela 1689), reflecting the addition of non-Potano Indians to the mission population. Excavations at the Zetrouer archeological site, A-67, in Alachua County (Seaberg 1955), dated at ca. A.D. 1660–1700 (Milanich 1972a:36) and thought to have been a Spanish-Indian ranch, revealed 66 percent of the potsherds at the site to be alien to the Potano, reflecting a large non-Potano population. Two earlier Potano village sites, Richardson and Fox Pond, also in Alachua County and dated 1600–1630 and 1630–60, respectively, contained 8 and 30 percent of non-Potano aboriginal pottery.[8] These figures suggest an increase through time of non-Potano Indians into the Potano villages during the seventeenth century. At first, during the early seventeenth century, this movement was almost solely from the neighboring eastern Timucua, as evidenced by the Richardson site ceramic frequencies. At the site, 7 percent of the pottery was eastern Timucuan types (sample size 3,636 sherds). Later, by 1630, Apalachee and / or Utina and Yustega Indians had begun to enter the Potano region, living with the Potano at Spanish-Indian mission villages. Such a trend is evidenced by the Fox Pond site where ceramics from north and northwest Florida constituted 20 percent of the site total; eastern Timucuan pottery totaled 14 percent at the site, indicating increased movement from that area into north-central Florida (sample size from Fox Pond was 1,896 sherds). Such mid-seventeenth-century movements of Apalachee and / or other Indians into what was formerly western Timucuan territory also was suggested above for the Utina. During the period 1660–1700, there was an influx of Georgia coastal Indians into Potano territory, probably Guale Indians from the central and northern Georgia coast. This is shown by the high percentage of San Marcos–Guale associated pottery, 58 percent, at the Zetrouer site. Other ceramic frequencies at the site were Potano, 34 percent; eastern Timucuan, 7 percent; and Apalachee and / or Utina and Yustega, less than 1 percent (total sample size, 3,285). These somewhat surprising figures suggest that after 1660 there might have been reestablished and temporarily renamed Esperanza (Hope), with north-central Florida.

In interpreting these differences in ceramic percentages, it should be remembered that they represent relative frequencies and not raw numbers. The population of north-central Florida between 1660–1700 was much smaller than the population between 1600–1630.

8. The portion of the San Francisco mission village was evidently not the earliest village associated with the mission.

Thus the large percentage of Guale ceramics reflects only that population relative to the existing Potano population (if, indeed, ceramic frequencies do reflect human population frequencies). The real number of Guale might have been considerably less than the number of eastern Timucua in that territory in, say, 1620, when eastern Timucuan ceramics represented only 7 percent of the Richardson site total.

During the first decade of the eighteenth century, the population of the Potano territory was destroyed or forced to resettle closer to St. Augustine. Santa Fe was burned by the English and their Indian allies on May 20, 1702, and the population of the village was moved to San Francisco (Boyd, Smith, and Griffin 1951:37, 28). Sometime after July 1704, the San Francisco de Potano mission was moved toward St. Augustine. A 1717 census lists the village as being relocated near the presidio along with several other small villages, all seeking protection from the English (Escobar 1717). The Santa Fe village seems to have been reestablished and temporarily renamed Esperanza (Hope), with a population of fifty-one persons in 1711 (Córcoles y Martínez 1711). Soon after this, however, the village was moved to the outskirts of St. Augustine, probably occupied largely by non-Potano Indians. The name of the town continues to be found in Spanish documents until 1736 (Geiger 1940:138).

In addition to missions and mission stations (*visitas*),[9] a cattle ranch was established in Potano territory to furnish beef for St. Augustine.[10] Documents place the ranch four leagues from San Francisco de Potano (Boyd, Smith, and Griffin 1951:68), probably quite near the old Spanish road which passed through eastern Alachua County, near present-day Rochelle and Paynes Prairie. The Zetrouer site might have been associated with the ranch. The ranch was probably established about the same time as the Yustega and Utina ranches, before 1656. An important source of food for St. Augustine, the ranch was a target of attacks, first by the French in 1682 (the attack was on a hacienda called Rica, which might actually have been one of the Utina or Yustega ranches), then by the Yamassee Indians (incited by the

9. Visitas were villages which the Spanish priests visited on a regular basis to administer mass, hear confessions, etc.

10. The ranch was named *La Chua*, probably a combination of the Spanish article "the" and the Timucuan word for "sink" or "spring." Present-day Alachua County receives its name from the ranch. Most likely "the sink" referred to the sink found on the east part of the north edge of Paynes Prairie. Cattle may have been herded on the prairie.

English) in 1685, and finally by the Creeks (also possibly under English influence) in 1704 (Brooks n.d.:16; Bolton 1925:157; Boyd, Smith, and Griffin 1951:68). In the latter raid, one black worker at the ranch was killed and four were captured. These individuals were probably slaves held by the Indians or Spanish. The ranch was destroyed by April 30, 1706, and abandoned (Boyd 1953:475).

Archeological investigations at the Richardson site, dating from 1600 to 1630, suggest that culture change among the Potano occurred very slowly during the first quarter of the seventeenth century. It was only about 1630, after some twenty-five years of intense contact with Spanish missionaries, that changes, detectable through archeological field methods, took place. This is roughly the length of time for one generation to mature to adulthood.

The most notable change in Potano material culture was the adoption and continual increase in the use of European metal for tools and ornaments and a decline in the utilization of traditional raw resources, such as flint. Also, aboriginal pottery began to be made in shapes similar to the Spanish vessels. Plates, cylindrical vessels with loop handles, shallow bowls, and pitchers appeared.

Other changes are more complicated. Ceramic seriations from the Zetrouer and Fox Pond sites show the sites to have been occupied for only brief periods of time, perhaps as few as ten years. Surface collections from other historic Alachua tradition sites suggest a similar pattern. Also, there are no known sites which were occupied continuously from the sixteenth century into the post-1600 historic period. Traditional village locations seem to have been abandoned and new ones established (although names probably were retained, especially if villages were named for tribal chiefs). The new villages were not occupied long before being moved again. One possible explanation is that the Spanish missions drew the Potano away from older villages and consolidated them at the mission villages, as seems to have occurred among the Yustega and Utina. The introduction of new agricultural techniques, such as more intensive planting of corn and the use of new crops such as wheat, might have depleted the soils more rapidly, making changes in horticultural fields and villages more frequent.

As among the Utina and Yustega, changes in Potano subsistence and settlement patterns would have had widespread effects on many other aspects of Potano culture, especially those traits associated with a more nomadic way of life, including concepts of landownership and kinship, descent, and inheritance patterns.

SUMMARY

By the 1730s, the Yustega, Ocale, Utina, and Potano, grouped together as the western Timucua Indians, had been destroyed as cultures
and peoples. By 1704, the western Timucua had abandoned their
traditional lands in north-central Florida for villages nearer the protection of the presidio at St. Augustine. A few Timucua perhaps survived into the 1730s in the towns near St. Augustine, which were
populated largely by Georgia Guale Indians. By this time, however,
the cultures of the western Timucua were totally destroyed.

The extent of changes in western Timucuan cultures during the
seventeenth century may never be known. Spanish-introduced (or
Spanish-caused) changes can be said to have included the following:
among the Yustega and Utina and probably the Potano, the Spanish
priests were successful in their attempts to bring the Indians together
in villages and keep them there year-round. Hunting and collecting
trips to exploit the resources of specific habitats and sections of
habitats continued. But, by having influence over the village chiefs
and by bringing to the Indians new crops, livestock, and methods of
food storage and preparation over roughly a twenty-five-year period,
the priests were able to lead the Indians into a fully sedentary life-
style, one more dependent on agricultural production. This major
change is the basis for the relative success of the north-central missions. North-central and northern Florida were well suited to horticulture, as evidenced by the quantity and quality of agriculture in
those areas today. Without this precondition and the fact that farming
was practiced among the Indians before the arrival of the first Europeans, it is probable that the church's efforts at Christianizing the
Indians would have failed, as was the case in other areas of Florida.

After the collapse of the missions and the movement of the remnant Indian populations to the St. Augustine area, the sedentary pattern also broke down and a semi-nomadic pattern of life was established. This was true by 1728 at the villages of Nuestra Señora de
Guadalupe, San Antonio de Pocotalaca, San Francisco, San Buenaventura de Palica, Nuestra Señora del Rosario at Mose, Santa Catalina
de Guale, and San Antonio de la Costa, all located in the vicinity around
St. Augustine. The Indians of these villages were variously described at
the time as "gypsies, here today, there tomorrow" (Geiger 1940:134-
35). The change to a nomadic subsistence pattern can be attributed
both to poorer soils in the St. Augustine region and to a breakdown

of kinship ties and the political organization necessary for Indian horticulture.

The subsistence changes among the western Timucua would have led to settlement changes and changes in many other aspects of aboriginal culture. That settlement changes did occur is evidenced by archeological research among the Potano and by Spanish documents which indicate movement of villages on a much more frequent basis than was done prehistorically, and consolidation of Indian populations in fewer, but probably larger, villages. To date, the Potano have been the only western Timucuan tribe studied in depth.

Early documents concerning the Yustega, Utina, and Potano refer to one tribal chief to whom village chiefs were vassals. By the mid-seventeenth century, however, this system seems to have declined, and villages and village chiefs became more independent. This decentralization of tribal authority was related to the changes in settlement patterns and the influence of the Spanish priests in the selection of village chiefs.

Other Spanish-introduced changes in western Timucuan culture were tools, ceramics, and vessel forms at the expense of native industries; teaching the Spanish language to the Indians;[11] changes in inheritance patterns; and the introduction of European clothes, flour, and hardware, both as gifts (Canzo 1597) and as trade goods from Cuba (Marques 1582). The role of white traders in Florida has received little attention from historians or anthropologists, and whether or not such trade continued into the seventeenth century is unknown.

A second major agent of change was the movement into and within Florida of Creek, Guale, eastern Timucua, and other Indian tribes such as the Pohoys, whose linguistic affiliation and geographical origin are unknown. By 1660, these groups might have outnumbered the western Timucua. Their contributions to western Timucua culture change are not known, but might have been almost as important as were those of the Spanish missionaries.

Within a generation after 1660, the cultures of the western Timucuan tribes had been radically altered from the aboriginal cultures of the early historic period. Probably there was a joining of different Indian cultural traditions and a continual movement of peoples

---

11. In 1686, a royal edict was issued requiring all priests "using the most subtle methods they dispose" to teach all the Florida Indians the Spanish language (Carlos II 1686).

among Alabama, Florida, and Georgia. Out of this acculturation and diffusion process the Seminoles emerged, and they began occupying north Florida after the cessation of the English raids in the first quarter of the eighteenth century.

Interpreting post-1660 western Timucuan traits, those from both documents and field archeology, is made difficult by the presence of the non-Timucuan peoples in north-central and northern Florida. Thus, the presence of the southeast stickball game among the San Francisco de Potano villagers in 1678 (Vera 1678) might reflect its popularity among Creeks rather than its continuance among the Potano. The continual influx of Indians into Florida probably helped to prevent a more rapid destruction of the Indian population.

In this paper reference has been made to periods of time equal to one human generation during which culture changes were incorporated by the western Timucua. This suggests that traits were not immediately adopted by the Indian cultures during the acculturation process. Rather, there was generally a period of fifteen to thirty years during which certain traits were slowly incorporated into the aboriginal cultures. During this time a new generation of children grew to adulthood, gradually accepting and practicing the new traits.

The process of trait adoption, as the functional model of culture reveals, involves the changing of other culture traits to accommodate the new traits. Thus, the gradual acceptance of a more sedentary village pattern probably led to numerous other changes among the western Timucuan cultures. Those traits formerly circumscribed around a pattern of seasonally sedentary agricultural villages were altered. The extent of such secondary changes is at this time largely unknown.

Archeological field research, in any significant amount, has only been carried out among the Potano. It has, however, proved to be a useful methodology for gathering information on short-term culture change. Because historic sites are usually "thin" sites, accurate ceramic seriations are easy to obtain, and these give excellent temporal controls. Types and relative frequencies of Indian versus Spanish tools and ceramics at sites yield information on rates and degrees of acculturation and help to determine the type of site, i.e., mission village or cattle ranch. Information concerning changes in subsistence patterns and settlement patterning can also be produced from archeological excavation and simple site surveys and surface collections. The next decade should produce more experimentation with archeological field methods for historic Indian studies, which, in combination with documentary research, should provide meaningful anthropological interpretations of aboriginal acculturation and culture change.

REFERENCES

Abbreviations used: A.G.I., Archivo General de Indias; S.C.U.F., Stetson Collection, P. K. Yonge Library of Florida History, University of Florida, Gainesville.

Adam, Lucien, and Julian Vinson, eds.
1886.   Arte de la Lengua Timuquana Compuesto en 1614 por el P. Francisco Pareja. *Bibliotheque Linquistique Americaine*, tome 11. Paris.
Arredondo, Antonio de.
1736.   Manuscript, A.G.I., 87-1-1/60. [Testimony to the Spanish Crown, St. Augustine, November 27, 1736.] Photostat, S.C.U.F.
Barber, Bernard.
1941.   Acculturation and Messianic Movements. *American Sociological Review* 6:663–69.
Barcia Carballido y Zúñiga, Andrés González de.
1951.   *Chronological History of the Continent of Florida*. Translated by Anthony Kerrigan from the original Spanish edition of 1723. Gainesville: University of Florida Press.
Bolton, Herbert E.
1925.   *Arredondo's Historical Proof to Spain's Title to Georgia*. Berkeley: University of California Press.
Boyd, Mark F.
1953.   Further Consideration of the Apalachee Missions. *The Americas* 9:459–79.
Boyd, Mark F., Hale G. Smith, and John W. Griffin.
1951.   *Here They Once Stood: The Tragic End of the Apalachee Missions*. Gainesville: University of Florida Press.
Brooks, A. M., trans.
n.d.   Transcripts of Spanish Documents Relating to Florida. [Copied from original by Work Projects Administration, Statewide Writers Project, Miami, 1940.] On file, P. K. Yonge Library of Florida History, University of Florida, Gainesville.
Bullen, Ripley P.
1949.   The Woodward Site. *Florida Anthropologist* 2:49–64.
Bushnell, David I., Jr.
1908.   The Accounty of Lamhatty. *American Anthropologist* 10:568–74.
Canzo, Gonzalo Méndez de (Governor of Florida).
1597.   Manuscript, A.G.I., 54-5-16. [Letter to the Spanish Crown, St. Augustine, July 28, 1597.] Microfilm, S.C.U.F.
Carlos II (King of Spain).
1686.   Manuscript, A.G.I., 54-5-13/2. [Royal *cedula* to the Bishops of the Indies, Madrid, June 20, 1686.] Photostat, S.C.U.F.
Compostela, Diego Euclino de (Bishop of Cuba).
1689.   Manuscript, A.G.I., 54-3-2/9. [Letter to the Spanish Crown, Santiago, Cuba, September 28, 1689.] Photostat, S.C.U.F.
Córcoles y Martínez, Francisco de (Governor of Florida).
1711.   Manuscript, A.G.I., 59-1-30/20. [Letter to the Spanish Crown, St. Augustine, April 9, 1711.] Photostat, S.C.U.F.

Deagan, Kathleen A.
  1972. Fig Springs: The Mid–Seventeenth Century in North-Central Florida. *Historical Archaeology* 6:23–46.
Ehrmann, W. W.
  1940. The Timucan Indians of Sixteenth-Century Florida. *Florida Historical Quarterly* 18:168–91.
Escobar, Juan de Ayala (Governor of Florida).
  1717. Manuscript, A.G.I., 58-1-30/64. [Letter to the Spanish Crown, St. Augustine, April 18, 1717.] Photostat, S.C.U.F.
Fairbanks, Charles H.
  1957. Ethnohistorical Report of the Florida Indians. Testimony before the Indian Claims Commission, United States Department of Justice. Washington.
Fontaneda, Hernando d'Escalante.
  1945. *Memoir of Do. d'Escalante Fontaneda Respecting Florida, Written in Spain, about the Year 1575*. Translated with notes by Buckingham Smith, edited by David O. True. Coral Gables, Fla.: Glade House.
Franciscans of Florida.
  1735. Manuscript, A.G.I., 58-2-17/3. [Letter to the Spanish Crown, St. Augustine, March 8, 1735.] Photostat, S.C.U.F.
Gannon, Michael V.
  1965. *The Cross in the Sand*. Gainesville: University of Florida Press.
Gatschet, Albert S.
  1880. The Timucuan Language. *Proceedings of the American Philosophical Society* 18:465–502.
Geiger, Maynard J.
  1940. *Biographical Dictionary of the Franciscans in Spanish Florida and Cuba (1528–1841)*. Franciscan Studies 21. Paterson, N.J.: St. Anthony's Guild Press.
Goggin, John M.
  1949. Cultural Traditions in Florida Prehistory. In *The Florida Indian and his Neighbors*, edited by J. W. Griffin, pp. 13–44. Winter Park, Fla.: Inter-American Center, Rollins College.
  1952. *Space and Time Perspective in Northern St. Johns Archeology*. Yale University Publications in Anthropology no. 47.
  1953. An Introductory Outline of Timucuan Archaeology. *Southeastern Archaeological Conference, Newsletter* 3(3):4–17.
Goggin, John M., and William C. Sturtevant.
  1964. The Calusa: A Stratified, Nonagricultural Society (with Notes on Sibling Marriage). In *Explorations in Cultural Anthropology*, edited by Ward H. Goodenough, pp. 179–219. New York: McGraw Hill.
Granberry, Julian.
  1971. Final Collation of Texts, Vocabulary Lists, Grammar, of Timucua for Publication. *American Philosophical Society, Yearbook 1970*, pp. 606–7.
Haas, Mary R.
  1958. A New Linguistic Relationship in North America: Algonkian and the Gulf Languages. *Southwestern Journal of Anthropology* 14:231–64.
  1971. Southeastern Indian Linguistics. In *Red, White, and Black: Symposium on Indians in the Old South*, edited by Charles M. Hudson, pp. 44–54. Athens: University of Georgia Press.
Harris, Marvin.
  1971. *Culture, Man, and Nature*. New York: Thomas Y. Crowell.
Jones, B. Calvin.
  1972. Spanish Mission Sites Located and Test Excavated. *Archives and History News* 3(6). Florida Department of State, Division of Archives, History, and Records Management, Tallahassee.

Linton, Ralph.
1943. Nativistic Movements. *American Anthropologist* 45:230–40.

López, Atanasio.
1933. *Relación Histórica de la Florida Escrita en el Siglo XVII,* vol. 2. Madrid: Librería General de Victoriano Suárez.

Lorant, Stefan, ed.
1946. *The New World.* New York: Duell, Sloan, and Pearce.

Manuel (Chief of Asile).
1651. Manuscript, A.G.I., Escribanía de Cámara, legajo 155, folios 380–83. [Letter to the Governor of Florida, accompanied by a Spanish translation certified by Father Alonso Escudero, St. Augustine, December 9, 1651.] Photostat, National Anthropological Archives, Smithsonian Institution, manuscript no. 2446f.

Marqués, Pedro Menéndez (Governor of Florida).
1582. Manuscript, A.G.I., 54-5-16/27. [Letter to the Spanish Crown, St. Augustine, July 6, 1582.] Photostat, S.C.U.F.

Milanich, Jerald T.
1971a. *The Alachua Tradition of North-Central Florida.* Florida State Museum Contributions, Anthropology and History no. 17.
1971b. Surface Information from the Presumed Site of the San Pedro de Mocamo Mission. *Conference on Historic Site Archaeology Papers,* 5:114–21. Columbia, S.C.
1972a. *Excavations at the Richardson Site, Alachua County, Florida: An Early Seventeenth-Century Potano Indian Village.* Bureau of Historic Sites and Properties Bulletin 2, pp. 35–61. Tallahassee.
1972b. Tacatacuru and the San Pedro de Mocamo Mission, Cumberland Island, Georgia. *Florida Historical Quarterly* 50:83–91.
1973. The Southeastern Deptford Culture: A Preliminary Definition. *Bureau of Historic Sites and Properties Bulletin* 3, pp. 65–90. Tallahassee.
n.d. The Timucua. In *The Southeast,* edited by Raymond D. Fogelson, chap. 43. *Handbook of North American Indians,* edited by William C. Sturtevant, vol. 14. Washington: Smithsonian Institution. In press.

Milanich, Jerald T., and William C. Sturtevant.
1972. *Francisco Pareja's 1613 Confessionario: A Documentary Source for Timucuan Ethnography.* Florida Department of State, Division of Archives, History, and Records Management, Tallahassee.

Ningler et Confrontes, L., trans.
1927. *Voyages en Virginie et en Floride.* Paris: Chez Duchartre et Van Buggenhoudt.

Oré, Luís Gerónimo de.
1936. *The Martyrs of Florida (1513–1616).* Edited and translated by Maynard J. Geiger. Franciscan Studies no. 18. New York: J. F. Wagner.

Pareja, Francisco.
1627. *Cathecismo, y Examen para los que Comulgan.* Mexico: Imp. de Juan Ruyz. Microfilm, National Anthropological Archives, Smithsonian Institution.

Powell, J. W.
1891. Indian Linguistic Families of America North of Mexico. In *Bureau of American Ethnology, 7th Annual Report, 1885–1886,* pp. 1–142.

Salazar, Pablo de Hita (Governor of Florida).
1675. Manuscript, A.G.I., 58-1-26/38. [Letter to the Spanish Crown, St. Augustine, August 24, 1675.] Photostat, S.C.U.F.
1667– Manuscript, A.G.I., Escribanía de Cámara, legajo 156, folios 519-530v, i,
78 531-615v. [Letters and testimony to the Spanish Crown, St. Augustine and locations in provinces of Apalachee and Timucua, various dates 1677–88; filed under November 29, 1677.] Photostat, S.C.U.F.

88   *Jerald T. Milanich*

Seaberg, Lillian M.
 1955. The Zetrouer Site: Indian and Spanish in Central Florida. Master's thesis, University of Florida, Gainesville.
Serrano y Sanz, Manuel, ed.
 1912. *Documentos de la Florida y la Luisiana, Siglos XVI al XVIII.* Madrid: Librería General de Victoriano Suárez.
Smith, Buckingham, trans.
 1871. *Relation of Alvar Núñez Cabeza de Vaca.* Revision of original translated edition 1866. New York: J. Munsell.
 1968. *Narratives of de Soto in the Conquest of Florida.* Original translated edition 1866. Gainesville, Fla.: Palmetto Books.
Smith, Hale G.
 1948. Two Historical Archaeological Periods in Florida. *American Antiquity* 13:313–19.
Spellman, Charles W.
 1948. The Agriculture of the Early North Florida Indians. *Florida Anthropologist* 1:37–48.
Swadesh, Morris.
 1964. Linguistic Overview. In *Prehistoric Man in the New World,* edited by J. D. Jennings and E. Norbeck, pp. 527–56. Chicago: University of Chicago Press.
Swanton, John R.
 1922. *Early History of the Creek Indians and Their Neighbors.* Bureau of American Ethnology Bulletin 73.
 1929. The Tawasa Language. *American Anthropologist* 31:435–53.
 1946. *The Indians of the Southeastern United States.* Bureau of American Ethnology Bulletin 137.
 1952. *The Indian Tribes of North America.* Bureau of American Ethnology Bulletin 145.
Swanton, John R., ed.
 1939. *Final Report of the United States de Soto Expedition Commission.* 76th Cong., 1st sess., H.R. 71.
Symes, M. I., and M. E. Stephens.
 1965. A-272: The Fox Pond Site. *Florida Anthropologist* 18:65–72.
Vera, Martín Lorenzo de la.
 1678. Manuscript, A.G.I., Escribanía de Cámara, legajo 156, folios 519-530v, i, 531-61v. [Letter to the Spanish Crown, San Francisco de Potano, January 26, 1678; filed under November 29, 1677.] Photostat, S.C.U.F.
Wenhold, Lucy L.
 1936. *A Seventeenth-Century Letter of Gabriel Díaz Vara Calderón, Bishop of Cuba.* Smithsonian Miscellaneous Collections, vol. 95, no. 16.
Wilbert, Johannes.
 1972. *Survivors of Eldorado; Four Indian Cultures of South America.* New York: Praeger.
Willey, Gordon R.
 1949. *Archeology of the Florida Gulf Coast.* Smithsonian Miscellaneous Collection, vol. 113.
Zubillaga, Félix, ed.
 1946. Monumenta Antiquae Floridae (1566–1572). *Monumenta Historica Societatis Iesu,* 69; *Monumenta Missionum Societatis Iesu,* 3. Rome.

Cultures in Transition: Fusion and Assimilation among the Eastern Timucua

Kathleen A. Deagan

WHEN the eastern Timucua Indians first encountered the French in 1562, they were characterized by a way of life which appeared very much unchanged from that of at least a millenium earlier. This is reflected in the archeological record, which shows long continuity and homogeneity in the ceremonial and subsistence systems of the eastern Timucua tribes, as well as in their material technology. It took only one hundred years, however, for the effects of European contact to reduce and ultimately to eliminate the culture.

"Timucua" is a linguistic abstraction, referring to the language spoken by the historic Indians of north and central Florida and southeastern Georgia. These Timucua speakers by no means represented a cogent ethnic unit since the area referred to was crosscut by dialect, techno-environmental, ceremonial, political, and geographical differences. Several authors have attempted to divide the Timucua into groups based on geographical, technological, and dialect similarities resulting in a basic division into eastern and western Timucua, with smaller tribal units defined within each division (Milanich, this volume). The groups or tribes which are dealt with in this volume are in most cases those which were recognized by the French or Spanish in the sixteenth and seventeenth centuries and which have been subsequently defined by ethnohistorical and archeological research.

The eastern Timucua division is comprised of seven tribes or provinces in southeastern Georgia and northeastern Florida. The Cascange and Icafui tribes are sometimes listed separately (Swanton 1922:321; López 1602), but they will be treated here as a single unit on the basis of similarities in their environments, political affiliations, dialects, and archeological cultures. This group occupied the area to the northwest of Cumberland Island, Georgia, on the mainland, probably from the Satilla River northward to the mainland opposite Jekyll Island. This was the last Timucua province before Guale was reached (Swanton 1922:321). To the west of the Cascange was the Yufera tribe, mentioned in 1597 as being located west of the Cascange and east of the Yui (Serrano y Sanz 1912:145). The Yufera probably occupied the Georgia mainland opposite Cumberland Island. To the west of the Yufera were the Yui, or Ibi. They were bounded on the east and north by the north-south course of the Satilla River, which would have placed them close to the fourteen leagues inland from Cumberland Island as reported in the documents (Alas 1600). The south boundary of the Yui territory was approximately at the St. Marys River, and on the west they were bordered by the Okeefenokee swamplands. The Tacatacuru tribe was located on Cumberland Island itself. With the exception of the Tacatacuru (Milanich 1971a), these tribes of southeastern Georgia are the least known archeologically of the eastern Timucua groups.

Of the eastern Timucua tribes, the best known is the Saturiwa, who occupied the lower course of the St. Johns River and the coastal area from the mouth of the St. Marys River to below St. Augustine. To the south of the Saturiwa were the Agua Dulce, or Freshwater, Indians, who lived along the upper course of the St. Johns River and the coastal lagoons south of St. Augustine. In 1602, the Agua Dulce were reported to be twenty-four leagues from St. Augustine on the St. Johns River, extending along that river for eight leagues (Montes 1602). This is approximately the area between Palatka and Lake Harney on the St. Johns and from south of St. Augustine to Daytona Beach on the coast. The last eastern Timucua tribe, the Acuera, was probably located to the west of the Agua Dulce, between the east side of the Ocklawaha River and the St. Johns River. The Acuera are the only eastern Timucua group reported in the de Soto narratives, where it is said that they were a two-day journey east of the Ocale (Smith 1968:285). Two missions, each thirty-four leagues from St. Augustine, were listed in 1655 as Acuera missions (Geiger 1940:126). Using a conversion factor of two and one-half miles per league, the mouth of the Ocklawaha is very close to eighty-five miles (thirty-four leagues) from St. Augustine and seventy-five miles (a two-day journey) almost directly east of the Ocale location.

Among these seven tribes, at least five dialects, five political divisions, two archeological complexes, and three environmental zones were evident (see Table 1). Of the nine Timucua dialects distinguished in the writings of Fray Francisco Pareja (1602, 1627; Gatschet 1878), five of them, including Mocamo, Icafui, Yufera, Agua Dulce, and Acuera, were associated with eastern Timucua groups. The Mocamo dialect was spoken from Cumberland Island to St. Augustine (the Tacatacuru and Saturiwa), and was referred to as the main language of Timucua (Serrano y Sanz 1912:171; Oré 1936:71). While the Yufera had their own dialect, called Yufera by the Spanish, the interior tribes of mainland Georgia (Yui and Cascange) all spoke the same dialect, Icafui (Pareja 1602). The Agua Dulce and Acuera tribes each had a separate dialect known by the tribal name. The Tucururu dialect and tribe has been variously classified with the eastern Timucua (Swanton 1946:193; Granberry 1956:99), but the single mention of the Tucururu by Pareja (1627:37) and its isolated, little-known cultural position do not permit its inclusion with the eastern Timucua dialects at this time.

At the time of Pareja's observations on eastern Timucua language, the tribal dialects and tribal political affiliations were closely correlated (with the exceptions of Cascange and Yui). Timucua political organization was based on a loose association of towns for purposes of warfare and often tribute. Each town was headed by a *cacique,* but these were subject to a provincial head cacique. It was noted in 1601 that there were more than fifty caciques subject to the head caciques of Santa Elena, San Pedro, Timucua, and Potano (Canzo 1601). In 1602, the cacique of San Pedro (Cumberland Island) was the head of a political confederacy including the Tacatacuru, the Saturiwa, and the Cascange; the tribes of Yui, Yufera, and Agua Dulce were politically independent (Geiger 1937:147–50; López 1602). The Acuera, by 1600, also appear to have been independent from the other eastern Timucua groups, although at the time of initial contact they were affiliated politically with the western Timucua Utina (Hakluyt 1903b:21; Canzo 1598). Although the accounts of Laudonnière and Le Moyne describe political arrangements similar to these for the eastern Timucua in 1565, it is possible that the particular associations of the eastern Timucua by 1602 were at least partly the result of Spanish influence. The association of the Icafui-speaking Cascange with the Mocamo-speaking San Pedro (Tacatacuru) confederacy does suggest that the dialects of the St. Johns River tribes were not extremely divergent and that they were mutually intelligible.

The eastern Timucua tribes manifested at least two archeological

TABLE 1

LINGUISTIC, POLITICAL, ARCHEOLOGICAL, ENVIRONMENTAL AFFILIATIONS

Tribe	Dialect	Archeological complex	Political Affiliation		Environmental Zone
			At Contact	1602	
Yufera	Yufera	(?) Wilmington-Savannah/St. Johns	independent	independent	Mainland S.E. Georgia
Yui	Icafui	(?) Wilmington-Savannah/St. Johns	independent	independent	Mainland S.E. Georgia
Cascange	Icafui	(?) Wilmington-Savannah/St. Johns	(?) Guale	San Pedro	Mainland S.E. Georgia
Tacatacuru	Mocamo	Wilmington-Savannah derived	independent	San Pedro	Cumberland Island
Saturiwa	Mocamo	St. Johns	independent	San Pedro	St. Johns River
Agua Dulce	Agua Dulce	St. Johns	(?) Utina	independent	St. Johns River
Acuera	Acuera	St. Johns	(?) Utina	independent	Ocklawaha and St. Johns rivers

material culture complexes in protohistoric times which crosscut both linguistic and political affiliations. The tribes living along the St. Johns and Ocklawaha rivers (Saturiwa, Agua Dulce, Acuera) shared the St. Johns tradition in prehistoric times (Goggin 1952; 1953), while the Tacatacuru of Cumberland Island possessed an as yet unnamed complex, probably derived from the Wilmington-Savannah phases of the Georgia coast (Milanich 1971a). The eastern Timucua tribes of mainland Georgia have not been investigated sufficiently to identify the protohistoric culture complex, although they appear to have been related to the Wilmington-derived Savannah and Pine Harbor complexes of the central Georgia coast, as well as to the St. Johns tradition to the south (Moore 1897; Larson 1958). The area of Camden County, Georgia, southward to the mouth of the St. Johns River appears to have been a zone of transition between the Wilmington-Savannah derived material complex and the St. Johns tradition material and ceremonial complexes. Archeologically, the area is characterized in protohistoric times by the presence of some St. Johns ritual and ceramic features, as well as cord marking, sherd tempering, and other ceramic features which appear strongly related to the earlier Wilmington-Savannah phases to the north (Larson 1958; Milanich 1971a; Hemmings and Deagan 1973; Moore 1897).

The presence of Timucua speakers and Timucua political affiliations in southeastern Georgia poses a problem which is relevant to the cultural history of the eastern Timucua group. The Camden County area, occupied in historic times by the Cascange, Yufera, Yui, and Tacatacuru, appears to have conformed to the general cultural evolutionary sequence of the Georgia coast until the end of the Savannah phase, about A.D. 1100 (Larson 1958; Milanich 1971c). Undoubtedly, the area was also subject to influence from the adjoining St. Johns area throughout its history. At the end of the Savannah phase, however, the Camden County area failed to participate in the Irene–Pine Harbor phase of coastal Georgia and was instead subject to the St. Johns region as a major source of cultural influence, either through a movement of St. Johns people into the area or through increasing diffusion of the St. Johns culture (see discussions by Larson 1958; Milanich 1971a).

A hypothesis to account for this situation may be formulated, based on the development of the St. Johns tradition and its relationship to its marginal-area neighbors. From historic times, the application of the direct historical method reveals an absence of population movements into this area, and a strong technological continuity for more than two thousand years (Goggin 1952). By the end of the Savannah times, the bearers of the St. Johns culture had been developing and refining their adaptation to a riverine environment for more than a thousand years and, at this time, began to spread more rapidly and intensively than at any time previously. The areas of closest proximity to the St. Johns region were marginal or transitional culture areas and accepted elements of language and social organization resulting in the linguistic and political situation encountered by the first Europeans. These areas, however, were quite different environmentally from the St. Johns culture region, and techno-environmental factors may have prevented the acceptance of St. Johns material culture.

Population estimates for the eastern Timucua at the time of contact are tentative at best. Most estimates of Timucuan population have been based on data pertaining to the seventeenth century (Mooney 1928; Swanton 1946, map 33), when the eastern Timucua had already been subject to European influences for nearly fifty years. These estimates were also based in part on the number of Christian Indians, and no data have come to light which would permit a reliable conversion factor to be developed which could give us the total number of Indians from the number of Christian Indians.

One of the earliest comments on eastern Timucua population was made by Nicholas Bourguignon, a member of Laudonnière's expedition, who was captured by British pirates. In 1568, he related that between St. Helena and St. Augustine there was a powerful cacique who commanded ten thousand Indians (Hakluyt 1903b:113). Although this cannot be taken as a completely reliable figure, Bourguignon was probably referring to the coastal eastern Timucua confederacy noted by Laudonnière (Hakluyt 1903b:100–104) and Menéndez (1566). His figures suggest a sizeable pre-contact population. A conservative estimate of total Timucua population might be fifteen to twenty thousand Indians.

By 1600, with rare exception, only the Christian Indians were enumerated in the documents. Table 2 shows the population trend for Christian eastern Timucua Indians. It should be noted that the mission effort increased throughout the seventeenth century and reached its height at about 1675, after which time it declined (Gannon 1965). As more Indians were reached by the missions, presumably the number of Christians would increase. However, this was not the case for the eastern Timucua, since the population declined as the mission system expanded. Epidemics of pestilence struck the eastern Timucua in 1613–17, in 1649–50, and in 1672 (Swanton 1946:144). Probably there were undocumented epidemics and other incidents of disease prior to the seventeenth century which caused the steady population decline. By 1650, the eastern Timucua were severely decimated, and this was very likely a large factor in the Franciscan's turning to the western Timucua and the Apalachee areas as the major foci of mission activity in the seventeenth century. It was also after 1650 that the archeological and documentary record indicates an infusion and replacement of eastern Timucua culture with Guale cultural elements.

TABLE 2
POPULATION FIGURES FOR CHRISTIAN EASTERN TIMUCUA
1597–1711

Date	Number of Christians	Source
1597	1,400	Swanton 1946:194
1602	1,400	Pareja 1602; López 1602; Montes 1602
1606	1,023	Altamirano 1606
1655	787.5[a]	Geiger 1940:125
1675	210	Salazar 1675; Wenhold 1936
1689	540[b]	Compostela 1689
1711	119	Córcoles y Mártinez 1711
1717	loose count: 189 total Timucua	Escobar 1717

a. This estimate is based on the number of eastern Timucua Christian towns mentioned in the 1655 list, times the average number of families in an eastern Timucua village (given by Compostela 1689) multiplied by 4.5 as the average family size: $7 \times 25 \times 4.5 = 787.5$.
b. The number of families per village is given by Compostela (1689). This estimate is based on 4.5 persons per family.

The first European contact with the eastern Timucua came with the establishment of Fort Caroline by the French in 1564. The accounts of Ribault, Laudonnière, and Le Moyne provide a great deal of early ethnographic data for the eastern Timucua, although the accounts concentrate almost exclusively on the Saturiwa. This is also the case in the early Spanish records, beginning with the establishment of St. Augustine in 1565. The French and Spanish documents, in addition to focusing primarily on a single tribe, were written with sixteenth- and seventeenth-century European biases and often reflect a distorted image of Indian culture. Particularly in the areas of political activity, religion, and kinship, care must be taken to detect European interpretations.

It was not until the establishment of the Franciscan mission system
in 1583 that the eastern Timucua experienced intensive European
contact and that much of the ethnographic and religious data pertaining to the Indians were recorded. The writings of Freys Balthazar
López (1602) and especially Francisco Pareja (1602; 1613; 1627;
1886; Milanich and Sturtevant 1972) are very revealing of the eastern
Timucua culture at the turn of the seventeenth century. Again, however, most of the data pertain to the Saturiwa, who were subject to the
longest and most continuous European contact and who by 1600 had
been under European influence for a full generation. For this reason,
the ethnograpical and cultural history of the eastern Timucua must
be considered that of a culture in a state of transition.

The focal issue, therefore, in a consideration of eastern Timucua
culture, is the definition of the patterns and processes of European-
induced change and the nature of acculturation by the eastern
Timucua. Within this framework, a number of specific problems
needing clarification emerge: (1) the correlation of archeologically
known prehistoric eastern Timucua area cultures with those known
from historic times; (2) the definition of changes taking place in the
subsistence and settlement patterns of the eastern Timucua after contact; (3) the explanation of documentarily indicated changes in political organization, social structure, and ceremonialism after contact;
and, (4) the clarification of the passive acceptance of Guale cultural
elements in the seventeenth century by the eastern Timucua and the
rapid replacement of indigenous cultural elements with these more
northern ones.

An examination of the archeological and documentary data pertinent to these problems will help clarify them and permit the generation of hypotheses concerning the patterns and processes of acculturation among the eastern Timucua. Since the various eastern
Timucua tribes occupied varied environmental areas and the data
pertaining to each tribe differ in quantity, quality, and kind, each tribe
will be discussed separately, with an attempt at synthesis at the end of
the article.

SOUTHEASTERN GEORGIA EASTERN TIMUCUA TRIBES

With the exception of the Tacatacuru, all of the eastern Timucua
tribes of the southeast Georgia mainland occupied and exploited environmental zones of the coastal plain. They appear to have utilized
the freshwater marshes, rivers, and lakes, as well as the pine forests of

the area. Although no archeological information about the food procurement systems of these tribes has been recovered, a theory that
they exploited a number of habitats may be postulated. These would
include forest, riverine, and coastal resources, with fish, deer, shellfish, and, in historic times at least, maize horticulture providing the
subsistence base.

Cascange-Icafui

Located inland from Cumberland Island, the Cascange territory bordered on that of the Guale Indians. Earlier studies have suggested
that the Cascange and the Icafui were two distinct tribes, one Guale
and the other Timucua (Swanton 1922:321), since the Cascange were
believed to have participated in the Guale rebellion of 1597. Letters
written in 1602, however, refer to the Cascange as being part of, or
included with, the Icafui group (Pareja 1602; López 1602). It is possible that this was a historical development. But, since the Cascange-
Icafui were linguistically distinct from the Guale, and part of the
Tacatacuru confederacy in 1602 (Pareja 1602), they will be considered here as a single tribe.

No archeological excavation can be attributed with certainty to
have been in the Cascange territory. Lewis H. Larson's survey of the
Camden County area (Larson 1958) suggests late prehistoric affiliations with the St. Johns area. The Woodbine mound, near present-
day Woodbine, Georgia, may have been in the southern part of the
Cascange territory. Excavated by C. B. Moore (1897), the mound
contained tobacco pipes, a red sand mantle, and several conch shells,
which are characteristic of the northern St. Johns area (Goggin 1952),
as well as complicated stamped ceramics, which appear to be typical of
the late prehistoric Lamar-Irene pottery of the upper Georgia coast
(Caldwell 1952:319).

No missions are reported to have been established in the Cascange
territory, although the Cascange were periodically visited by the missionary at San Pedro on Cumberland Island (López 1602), and the
Indians in the Cascange province came each day to visit Christian
towns (Pareja 1602). In 1602, Cascange contained eight towns and
1,100 Indians who were tribute-paying subjects of the cacique at San
Pedro (Tacatacuru) (López 1602). Since it was also reported that this
was the only interior district subject to San Pedro (Pareja 1602), the
Guale rebellion may have provided a convenient opportunity for the
Indians of Cascange to rebel against the Tacatacuru. An alternate

possibility is that the Cascange became subjects of the Tacatacuru through Spanish intervention as a result of the rebellion. Nothing is recorded of the Spanish retaliation on the Cascange after the Guale rebellion, but by 1600, they are described as "villages of pleasing Indians" (Canzo 1600).

Cascange contact with the Spanish was minimal, comprised of intermittent visits from the missionary at San Pedro and occasional military parties passing through their territory. Governor Pedro de Ibarra went through the Cascange territory during his visit to the provinces of San Pedro and Guale in 1604 (Serrano y Sanz 1912: 164–93). He spoke of visiting two towns in the interior which were subject to San Pedro. These towns, Alatuc and Olatayco, were probably Cascange towns. He also lists as chiefs "of the pine forests of the interior lands who are subjects of Doña Maria" (the chieftainess of San Pedro) Exangue, Lamale, Heabono, Aytire, Tahupe, and Punuri (Serrano y Sanz 1912:186).

The tribe is not mentioned in documents after this time, and it is likely that the Cascange were replaced and encroached upon by Guale and Yamassee Indians, who in turn were being forced south by pressure from British colonists.

Yufera

The Yufera occupied the area inland from Cumberland Island south and west of the Cascange, bordering the Satilla, Cumberland, and St. Marys rivers. Again, very little archeological research has been done in this area. C. B. Moore (1897) noted two burial mounds on Cumberland Sound which were probably constructed by the prehistoric Yufera or their predecessors. These mounds (the Fairview mounds) do not indicate an elaborate ceremonial system. Like the mounds of the St. Johns area, they are located on water and contain chalky, check-stamped pottery (probably St. Johns tradition in origin) with the burials. Other than ceramics, however, few burial goods were recovered, and the mounds were low, single-component structures with no indication of reuse in historic times.

The Yufera had a long, but sporadic history of European contact. The earliest reference to the group is by the French who mentioned a tribe twelve leagues north of the mouth of the St. Johns River, which was governed by a beautiful and revered queen named Cubaconi (Hakluyt 1903b:75; Le Moyne 1875:12). Cubaconi was the widow of King Hiocaia, and her domain was called Hiocaia, or Hioucara, by the French.

French narratives refer to what is now known as the Satilla River as the Somme. The Indian name for this river was Iracana (Hakluyt 1903b:75). It was near this waterway, probably in Yufera territory, that the caciques of the area, including Athore (son of Saturiwa), Apalou, and Tacatacuru, often met (Hakluyt 1903b:75). Here they exchanged gifts with the queen of the land. The chiefs of the northeastern Timucua tribes (Saturiwa, Tacatacuru, Athore, Halmancanir, Harpara, Helmacape, Helicopile, and Molloa) met here in 1567 to pledge support for Dominique de Gourgues in his punitive expedition against Pedro Menéndez (Hakluyt 1903b:107).

References were made by the French to the beauty of the Yufera queen, who sent acorns, millet, and cassina to Laudonnière (Hakluyt 1903b:53). Laudonnière noted that in this land were "the fairest maids and women in all the country" (Hakluyt 1903b:73). The Yufera were also governed by a woman at the time of Ibarra's visit in 1604. He stated that the queen's heir was her nephew, which suggests a matrilineal organization.

No missions were established in the Yufera province, although it is likely that they, like the Cascange, were visited by the missionary from San Pedro. Reports by Governor Canzo in 1600 and 1601 describe the Yufera as "towns of Indian friends" (1600) and subject to San Pedro (1601). The latter statement was probably a misinterpretation of the situation, for it was specifically reported by Ibarra that the Yufera were an independent group, separate from but allied with the Tacatacuru (Serrano y Sanz 1912:185).

The Yufera seem to have maintained their independence from both the Spanish and other Indian confederacies in historic times. No mention is made of them after the first decade of the seventeenth century, and the increasing British slave raids, enemy Indian harassment, and encroaching Guale probably eliminated those Yufera remaining in their traditional territory, while the Christian Yufera were probably assimilated into the Tacatacuru mission group.

Yui (Ibi)

The Yui, or Ibi as the tribe was sometimes called, was the farthest inland of any of the southeastern Georgia, eastern Timucua tribes. Located fourteen leagues from Cumberland Island (Alas 1600), Yui seems to have been the only inland Georgia Timucua province subject to mission activity. Variously referred to as Ibi, Ibys, Yoa, Yui, and Yua, the Indians of this area were able to exploit the resources of the St. Marys River, the upper course of the Satilla River, the

Okeefenokee swamplands, and the interior pine forests. Unlike the Cascange and Yufera, the Yui did not have access to the coastal strip environmental zone.

The investigation of the Owen's Ferry mound by C. B. Moore (1897) is the only archeological research which can be tentatively attributed to the Yui area. The mound is located on the upper course of the Satilla River and did not differ significantly in structure or content from the Woodbine mound (in the Cascange area).

Little is recorded of the Yui's relations with either the Spanish or the other Timucuan tribes. They were not mentioned by the French, and they appear to have been independent from the Tacatacuru confederacy in historic times (Pareja 1602). An early Franciscan mission was established among the Yui in 1596, but activities were discontinued there after the Guale rebellion of 1597 (Geiger 1937:120). The Franciscans apparently abandoned the interior lands after this incident, and except for occasional visits to the interior, they concentrated their efforts on Cumberland Island. The Yui were probably not involved in the Guale rebellion since there is no mention of retaliation against them, and the chief of Yua was listed as one of the caciques whose allegiance was to the Spanish crown (Canzo 1598).

In 1602, the Yui had five towns and a population of 700 to 800 Indians. Although they had no missions, there were Christian Yui who visited the Christian towns near San Pedro (Pareja 1602). Pareja also noted that the Yui and the Cascange spoke the same language.

This tribe is not mentioned again in documents after 1607. The Yui were probably dispersed in the same manner as the Yufera and the Cascange. As the southward movement of the Guale increased the pressure on the southeastern Georgia tribes, those Indians who did not join the Christians at San Pedro were eliminated or assimilated.

Tacatacuru

Instead of being adapted to the pine forest and riverine habitats of mainland Georgia, the Tacatacuru exploited the salt marsh lagoons and live-oak hammocks of the coastal islands. Their food procurement system was most likely based on shellfish, fish, and the mammals of the live-oak hammocks in prehistoric times. By historic times maize horticulture was practiced.

Surface surveys at the presumed site of the Tacatacuru village and San Pedro de Mocamo mission provide some information about the historic Tacatacuru way of life (Milanich 1971a). Community patterning traits include the suggestion of a rectangular village plan and small, circular shell piles thought to reflect individual dwelling sites (Milanich 1971a:14). This pattern is a departure from the St. Johns River area Timucua middens, which are typically consolidated areas or mounds. The pottery made by the historic and protohistoric Tacatacuru also differs from that of the St. Johns River area. Instead of St. Johns chalky ware, the Tacatacuru made a sherd-tempered, often cob-marked ware reminiscent of the protohistoric ceramics found on the upper Georgia coast.

European contact with the Tacatacuru was long and intensive. René de Laudonnière and Dominique de Gourgues both refer to the cacique Tacatacuru (Hakluyt 1903b:75, 102), who in 1567 was one of those chiefs pledging support to de Gourgues.

After the Spanish seizure of Fort Caroline and the establishment of a colony at St. Augustine, Jesuit missionaries arrived in Florida, and the Tacatacuru were the object of one of the earliest, though unsuccessful, attempts at conversion. Father Pedro Martínez and a group of companions attempted to establish themselves at Cumberland Island on September 29, 1566, but they were repulsed by the Tacatacuru. Between 1566 and 1569, Martínez, three of his companions, and eleven Spanish soldiers were killed by the Tacatacuru (Lowery 1905:272-79).

That the Tacatacuru still felt allegiance to the French after this time is shown in their pledge of support to de Gourgues in 1567. Two years later, however, a Spanish garrison was established on Cumberland Island to subdue the Tacatacuru and to act as a link between the settlement at Santa Elena to the north and St. Augustine (Lowery 1905:289).

From 1587 until at least 1689, Cumberland Island was the site of one or more Franciscan missions. The first was established by Frey Balthazar López who arrived in 1587 (Geiger 1940:68). The mission was apparently located at the town of Puturiba, since Frey Fernandez de Chozas, who joined López in 1596 (Geiger 1940:87), was listed the next year as being at Puturiba (Geiger 1940:51). The San Pedro de Mocamo mission continued to be listed until 1659 (Díaz de la Calle 1659). By 1675, however, a mission called San Phelipe, or San Felipe, de Athulteca, was established on Cumberland Island (Swanton 1922; Salazar 1675). It was at this time also that Salazar (1675) noted that all of the Indians on the Isle of Mocamo (Cumberland) were infidels, suggesting a repopulation of the area. Probably between 1650 and 1675, the Timucua population of Cumberland Island was relocated as a result of the Guale-Yamassee pressure. Part of this population may have relocated in the western Timucua area. In 1657, the first mention of the mission San Pedro de Potohiriba appears, placing it in the western Timucua area (Rebolledo 1657). Potohiriba is quite possibly an alternate form of Puturiba (Swanton 1922:328). This would not have been the first time that the Tacatacuru had relocated a village. In February 1598, the Indians of San Pedro were at San Juan del Puerto after the Guale rebellion forces were repulsed by the Christian Tacatacuru, although they later returned to Cumberland Island (Geiger 1937:80).

It is probable that the new mission of San Felipe served the Yamassee rather than the Tacatacuru or other southeastern Georgia eastern Timucua remnants. In 1670, the garrison was abandoned (Lowery 1905:355), and its last mention in the mission documents was in 1689 (Compostela 1689).

In 1605, there were 300 Christians in the province of San Pedro, including the island of Napoyca (Amelia Island) and the towns of Santo Domingo, Santa Maria de Sena, San Antonio, and La Madalena (López 1602). This is substantiated by the statement of Bishop Altamirano who confirmed 308 Indians during his visit to San Pedro in 1606 (Altamirano 1606).

From the beginning of Spanish contact, the political system and structure of the Tacatacuru underwent changes. At the turn of the seventeenth century, the town of San Pedro was the head of a confederacy extending from Cumberland Island to St. Augustine (Geiger 1937:147–50; López 1602), including the Tacatacuru, Cascange, and Saturiwa. This may not have been the case at the time of initial contact, since de Gourgues noted in 1567 that Saturiwa's domain extended as far north as the River Seine (St. Marys) (Hakluyt 1903b: 101). Also, in 1566, Pedro Menéndez described a confederacy between the St. Johns River and St. Augustine (Menéndez 1566). At this time the Tacatacuru seem to have been allied with, rather than subordinate to or superordinate over, the Saturiwa.

The first European intervention in Tacatacuru affairs occurred with the order for the execution of Tacatacuru himself for the death of the soldiers and Jesuit priests (Lowery 1905:289) and the establishment of the Spanish garrison in 1569. By 1587, the Franciscan mission of San Pedro de Mocamo had been established. The cacique at this time was probably Don Juan, or Juanillo. Six years after the location of the mission, Don Juan was described as "sustaining the faith in the land" (Meestas 1593). Not only did he require his subjects to attend church in his town, but he also partially supported the missionaries through the tribute he exacted from his subjects.

The conversion of Don Juan decreased the burden of missionization for the friars, and it resulted in protection for them. During the Guale rebellion of 1597, the Tacatacuru were attacked by rebel Indians, who were repelled by the Christian Indians under Don Juan (Geiger 1940:79–81). It is not known whether the Cascange, who were possibly involved in the incident, became subject to San Pedro after they were subdued by the Spanish, or whether they joined the revolt to escape Tacatacuru subjugation.

Upon Don Juan's death in 1600, he was succeeded by Doña Ana, his sister's daughter, following the custom of the land (Swanton 1922:337). By 1604, she was replaced as *cacica* by Doña Maria Melendez (Serrano y Sanz 1912:171), a move which has overtones of Spanish influence. Doña Melendez was the cacica of Nombre de Dios, the province of which St. Augustine was a part in 1597 (Canzo 1598). Governor Canzo described her as "a good Christian" married to a soldier, and he praised her efforts at proselytizing the other Indians (Canzo 1598). During Pedro de Ibarra's visit to the province of San Pedro in 1604, Doña Maria was specifically named as the princess of San Pedro, and Ibarra's observations shed an interesting light on the Spanish role in Timucua political affairs. Ibarra, Frey Pedro Ruíz, and Doña Melendez met with the chiefs of the villages subject to San Pedro. At the meeting Ibarra asked Doña Maria if the chiefs had disobeyed her or had given cause for Spanish reprisal (Serrano y Sanz 1912:172). While she did not complain of any disobedience, the incident seems to imply strong Spanish support of Doña Maria's authority. It was also at this time that the San Pedro to St. Augustine confederacy was first mentioned. This suggests a pattern of using Christianized Indians in positions of power to promote pro-Spanish and pro-Catholic sentiments. This is not an unprecedented situation since the intervention in cacique succession by the Spanish was listed as one of the reasons for the Guale rebellion in 1597 (Canzo 1600). It is also known that Doña Maria's heir was her son, rather than her niece or nephew, as was the traditional custom. As early as 1593, the Spanish were aware of the Indian inheritance rules and were eager to change them. Responding to a report from Florida, the Spanish king commented on attempts to change infidel inheritance patterns: "concerning what you noted about the custom that upon an Indian nobleman's death his nephew, the son of his sister, inherits his dignity and his estate. The Christianized Indians complain and do not want to follow this law, but to inherit from their fathers. It would be well to support them in this" (Phillip II 1593).

Although the movement of the Tacatacuru from Cumberland Island between 1660 and 1675 is not documented, archeological evidence indicates that at least some of them relocated at San Juan del Puerto mission. In one portion of the San Juan del Puerto site, a series of individual shell piles and the presence of sherd-tempered and cord-marked ceramics strongly suggests community patterning features of the Tacatacuru sites encountered on Cumberland Island rather than those of the Saturiwa (McMurray 1973). The last mention of the Tacatacuru is in 1717, when the occupants of the village of San Buenaventura de Palica, a refugee Indian settlement near St. Augustine, were listed as being of the Mocamo tribe, probably Tacatacuru (Escobar 1717).

FLORIDA EASTERN TIMUCUA TRIBES

Saturiwa

The best known of the Eastern Timucua tribes, both archeologically and ethnographically, are the Saturiwa. They are the only group for which enough ethnographic data are available to reconstruct the aboriginal culture of about 1600. They occupied the lower course of the St. Johns and the coastal area opposite the river. This region included the St. Johns, extensive pine flatwoods, and coastal lagoons and estuaries. All of these habitats were exploited by the Saturiwa. Their subsistence system was based on shellfish, both fresh and salt water, as evidenced by extensive shell middens along the river and coast, and on fishing, hunting, and gathering. Deer, alligator, fowl, and turtle were important food items. In historic times the Saturiwa were horticulturalists, tilling for only half the year and hunting in the forest and gathering during the winter months (Hakluyt 1903a:456). They grew maize, beans, pumpkins, cucumbers, citrons, and gourds (Hakluyt 1903a:455; Ribault 1964:73).

The Saturiwa's first European contact was with the French under Jean Ribault in 1562. By 1564, René de Laudonnière had established Fort Caroline near the mouth of the St. Johns River in Saturiwa territory. Their relations with the French were generally amicable and were based on trade. Deer, fish, turkey, and corn were exchanged for hatchets, mirrors, knives, beads, combs, and cloth (Le Moyne 1875:10).

Although the Saturiwa helped build portions of Fort Caroline and provided food to the whites, they were frequently alienated by French demands for supplies "extorted by blows" (Le Moyne 1875:14). The French were also involved in the military affairs of the tribe, since the Saturiwa were anxious for assistance against the Utina confederacy, their most ancient enemies (Hakluyt 1903b:12). Laudonnière agreed in 1565 to send some of his soldiers against the Utina, although his goal was to form alliances with all of the Indian confederacies (Hakluyt 1903b:12). Laudonnière's men in 1565 also aided the Utina in their war against the Potano (Swanton 1946:173).

Although Saturiwa contact with the French was close and friendly, it was not until the advent of the Spanish Franciscan missions that major changes were brought about in Saturiwa culture. During the earliest phases of contact with the Spanish, the Saturiwa's sympathies were with the French, to the extent that they aided de Gourgues in his punitive expedition against the Spanish in 1567 (Hakluyt 1903b:102-4).

Jesuit efforts at missionization between 1566 and 1572 ended in failure, but in the period 1577-96, Franciscan missions had been established among the Saturiwa at St. Augustine (Nombre de Dios) and near the mouth of the St. Johns River (San Juan del Puerto). These remained the main church centers among the Saturiwa until the destruction of the mission system in 1702-4. From these bases the Franciscan priests reached most of the Indian towns in the Saturiwa area.

After the middle of the seventeenth century, expanding British colonization and slave raids, combined with attacks by enemy Indians, forced the Guale population of the Georgia coast to move south, both encroaching upon and replacing the eastern Timucua population, which by this time had seriously declined in number. This is reflected both in documents and from archeological evidence.

In 1658, the Guale town and mission of Santiago de Tolomato was relocated three leagues from St. Augustine (Phillip IV 1660), and in 1680 all of the Guale mission Indians were relocated at the missions of San Pedro, Santa Maria (Amelia Island), and San Juan del Puerto (the last in Saturiwa territory). This movement is demonstrated archeologically by the presence of Guale Indian San Marcos ceramics rather than St. Johns ceramics in seventeenth-century Saturiwa sites (Smith 1948).

In prehistoric and protohistoric times the Saturiwa area was characterized by the St. Johns archeological complex, including chalky pottery, burial mounds, and diffuse shell middens (Goggin 1952). This complex was continued into early historic times, as evidenced by burial mounds containing European trade material. The Dunn's Creek mound (Moore 1894:8), which is in the southern part of the Saturiwa territory, contained burials with St. Johns ceramics associated with historic material, including ornaments, metal implements, and a bell. Lower levels of the mound revealed trade material from aboriginal cultures of west Florida, but these were no longer present in the historic level. Another site in this area—North Mound, Murphy Island—contained historic burials intrusive into a mound constructed during earlier (ca. A.D. 1000) times (Moore 1896b:503–15). Ar-cheological evidence indicates that by the late sixteenth century, mound burial was being replaced by cemetery burial among the Saturiwa. The Fountain of Youth site in St. Augustine contained a group of Indian burials; individuals were extended flat on their backs, with their arms crossed over their chests. One group was oriented with their heads to the east and a second with heads to the west. Few grave goods were encountered, but the presence of glass beads and an iron spike imply that the cemetery dates from the late sixteenth cen-tury (Goggin 1952:54; Hahn n.d.).

Possible mission sites in the Saturiwa area contain small amounts of the indigenous St. Johns ceramics, but the predominant pottery type is San Marcos Stamped (Smith 1948). The site of San Juan del Puerto, excavated by William Jones of Jacksonville, reflected this situation and also yielded evidence of a palisaded village (McMurray 1973). Majolica, olive jar, and other nonceramic European artifacts were found at the site in addition to the aboriginal elements.

Wrights Landing (SJ-3), an archeological site known only from sur-face collections (Goggin 1953:6), similarly contains large amounts of San Marcos ceramics and minor quantities of St. Johns ceramics. Wrights Landing is believed to be the site of Nuestra Señora Guadalupe de Tolomato, a Guale town which was relocated near St. Augustine in 1658 (Phillip IV 1660). The Rollestown site, Pu-64b, (Goggin 1953:5) may have been the site of the mission of Salamatoto. This mission did not appear in documents until 1675 (Wenhold 1936:8), and it is likely that it was a mission for relocated Guale Indi-ans. It seems also to have been the site of an earlier Saturiwa village, as evidenced by a diffuse shell midden typical of the St. Johns Timucua region, as well as a ceramic sequence including late Archaic (Orange fiber-tempered) pottery, Deptford pottery, and St. Johns pottery (40 percent). Fifty-six percent of the ceramics, however, were San Marcos types, and occupation at the site seems to have been heavy only during the historic period (Goggin 1953:6; Smith 1956:46). The Spanish material included San Luis Blue-on-White majolica, a type most common in the last half of the seventeenth century (Goggin 1968:157).

Few nonmission sites of the historic period have been investigated in the Saturiwa area, and these generally show Guale rather than Saturiwa occupation. The Harrison site on Amelia Island, Na-41, has been identified as a Guale or Yamassee village dating from the seventeenth century (Hemmings and Deagan 1973). The site was a single component occupation, represented by San Marcos pottery, olive jar, and majolica in a thin shell midden. This was probably one of the infidel Yamassee villages reported by Salazar in 1675.

The site of San Francisco de Pupo, C1-10, on the west bank of the St. Johns River, is another nonmission aboriginal site, although it is best known for its historic Spanish occupation (Goggin 1951). It illustrates the replacement of Timucua culture elements by those of the Guale, even outside of the mission settlements. Ceramics again provide the evidence; a gradual, then rapid replacement of St. Johns ceramics by Guale (San Marcos) ceramics in the aboriginal levels of the site. By the levels representing historic occupation (post-1658) this process was complete.

From the writings of Frey Francisco Pareja, Jacques Le Moyne, Jean Ribault, and René de Laudonnière, the Saturiwa culture of the late sixteenth and early seventeenth centuries can be reconstructed. Detailed summaries of Saturiwa culture traits and ethnographic data can be found in Swanton (1922:345–87) and in Milanich and Sturtevant (1972:39–48). Much of these data are probably applicable to other eastern Timucua tribes. Saturiwa social organization was similar to that of many other southeastern tribes, featuring ranked, matrilineal clans with names such as Deer, Panther, Bear, Fish, Earth, Buzzard, and Quail (Gatschet 1878:492–93). Inheritance was through the mother's brother (Phillip II 1593), and clan membership determined the chiefs and other officials (Gatschet 1878:492). The White Deer Clan gave rise to the head chief, or *holata ico*.

The writings of Francisco Pareja indicate a caste-like social system similar to that postulated by William H. Sears for the circum-Gulf region (1954). Each village had its own chief, and these were under the jurisdiction of a head chief who exacted tribute from his subjects (Canzo 1601).

Priest-shamans were present among the Saturiwa; they were powerful religious-medical practitioners. The role of shamans in the culture is illustrated in Pareja's 1613 *Confessionario* (Milanich and

Sturtevant 1972:40–43), and constituted an area toward which much Franciscan-directed change was aimed.

The Saturiwa lived in palisaded villages with circular, thatched huts of palm "after the fashion of a pavilion." Villages also contained a central longhouse "with reed setees all about," which were set two feet off the ground and used both as seats and beds (Ribault 1964:84). This community pattern has not yet been archeologically confirmed in the Saturiwa area.

At the time of Laudonnière's account (1565), the Saturiwa towns formed a confederacy under Saturiwa, the chief of a town near the mouth of the St. Johns River. There were thirty chiefs under Saturiwa, including Sarranay, Allimacany, Marracou, Patica, Homoloa, Serauhi, Malica, Casti, Molloa, and ten of Saturiwa's brothers (Hakluyt 1903b: 21, 32, 88). Warfare was highly ritualized and was usually carried out against the two large western Timucua confederacies of Potano and Utina (Hakluyt 1903a:454), although this pattern of conflict had ceased by the time of Pareja's writing.

Spanish intervention in the political affairs of the Saturiwa, like the Tacatacuru, seems to have been affected by religious conversion and by interference in inheritance patterns. The extent to which the Saturiwa settlement patterns changed is unknown, but missions seem to have been located near, and adapted to, established Saturiwa villages. The seasonal migration practices of the Saturiwa were not eliminated, for as late as 1728, the friars near St. Augustine complained about the seasonal migrations of the Indians and presumably were still trying to prevent it (Valdez 1728). The Saturiwa population declined steadily throughout the historic era (Valdez 1728:7–8), and by the time of James Moore's raids in 1702–4, the Saturiwa remnants were mixed with Tacatacuru and Guale elements. Moore's raids from South Carolina dealt a death blow to the Indians remaining in the Saturiwa area, and the survivors were relocated near St. Augustine, where their last remnants were destroyed by pestilence and by slave raids.

Agua Dulce

The Agua Dulce, or Freshwater, Indians occupied the area south of St. Augustine along the coast and along the St. Johns River to approximately the vicinity of Lake Harney. Within this area—from Palatka to Lake Harney—the broad character of the St. Johns River changes to a series of interconnected lakes and marshes, comprising part of the

Florida lake region (see Goggin 1952:18–19). The Agua Dulce Indians were able to exploit riverine, coastal, marsh, lake, and pine forest habitats. The coastline in the Agua Dulce area is made up of lagoons, a feature that was not present in the Saturiwa coastal area.

Seasonal migrations from the coast to the river seem highly likely and are documented by Jonathan Dickinson's account of his shipwreck on the Florida coast in 1697. Dickinson traveled through the Agua Dulce area in the late fall and noted a diet consisting mainly of palm berries and occasional fish. The population apparently was sparse (Andrews and Andrews 1945). Along the river, freshwater molluscs were an important food resource in historic and prehistoric times. The large shell heaps of the St. Johns River are not often seen north of Palatka (Moore 1894; Goggin 1952:41), which is outside the Agua Dulce area.

Although the Agua Dulce Indians shared the St. Johns archeological complex with the Saturiwa, they were recognized by the Spanish as a separate province, with a separate language. The historic mound sites in the Agua Dulce area are larger and more elaborate than those in the Saturiwa area. It has been suggested, however, that about A.D. 1000 there was a population shift from the Agua Dulce and Acuera areas to the Saturiwa areas (Goggin 1952:48). This suggestion is based on the changes in relative frequencies of burial mounds in the three areas over time.

The Mount Royal mound, Pu-35 (Moore 1894:141), located on the St. Johns River in the northern part of the Agua Dulce area, was a large mound with associated earthworks, containing numerous Mississippian elements (Goggin 1952:54). There was also a midden area occupied by the Agua Dulce in historic times, which was characterized by extensive "shell fields." In the southern part of the Agua Dulce territory, near Lake Harney, is another site, the Thursby Mound, Vo-36 (Moore 1894:64–82), which was also used in historic times. It is notable because of a cache of effigy ceramic forms deposited close to the mound surface. The 292 pottery objects represent important food or ritual items for the Agua Dulce. They include effigies of fish, turtles, cats, bears, squirrels, turkeys, dogs, beavers, gourds, conch shells, squash, alligators, frogs, acorns, and several plants and animals which have not been identified. The mound also contained intrusive burials, accompanied by historic trade material. It is not certain whether the pottery cache, which is at approximately the same level as these burials, was deposited in historic times or at the end of the original mound construction period (ca. A.D. 1000).

Also in the Lake Harney vicinity are two smaller mounds which were used in historic times. Both Cook's Ferry Mound, Se-13 (Moore 1894:89–90), and Raulerson's Mound, Vo-136 (Moore 1892:918; 1894:91–94), are associated with village middens and contain burials accompanied by European trade goods dating from the early sixteenth century. While the stratigraphic situation is not clear, at both mounds the historic burials were intrusive to the main mound construction.

The Spruce Creek Mound, Vo-99 (Douglass 1885:78, 191), in the northern part of the Agua Dulce area, seems to have been constructed in the historic era. This is a large sand mound on the St. Johns River which contained five crania burials accompanied by European material, including a *Carlos y Joanna* coin dated 1516. The archeological evidence in the Agua Dulce area suggests that these people continued in historic times to practice burial mound religious ceremonialism with more intensity and duration than their neighbors to the north.

The Indians inhabiting this area were named "Agua Dulce" by the Spanish. French accounts noted several kings living along the St. Johns River south of the Saturiwa, including Mayaca, although it is not clear whether Mayaca was considered part of the Agua Dulce province by the Spanish. Since they shared material culture and, possibly, linguistic elements with the Agua Dulce, however, they will be considered part of the Agua Dulce Indians here.

From the French accounts it seems clear that the Agua Dulce were allied with the Utina confederation at the time of first contact. Laudonnière noted a king living two days south of Fort Caroline on the St. Johns River, who was called Molova and was a vassal of Utina (Hakluyt 1903b:21). (Molova is not to be confused with Molloa, or Homolloa, who lived three leagues from Fort Caroline and was an ally of Saturiwa [Hakluyt 1903b:23].) Molova was also listed in 1602 as an Agua Dulce town (Pareja 1602). On another voyage up the St. Johns River, Laudonnière noted a "mighty lake" in the river, which was Lake George. He then continued down the river, arriving at a place called Eneguape, or Enecaque, where the sister of Utina lived and where Laudonnière received corn (Hakluyt 1903b:54). The town or king of Encape was also listed as a vassal of Utina (Hakluyt 1903b:21).

By 1587, a Franciscan mission, the convent of St. Anthony (Geiger 1940:119), had been established in the Agua Dulce area. This was probably the San Antonio de Encape (Oré 1936) and Antonico (Montes 1602) mentioned in later documents. Towns in the Agua Dulce area listed in 1602 included Tocoy, San Julian, Filache, Antonico, Equale, Anacabila, Mayaca, San Sebastian, and Molova, which had a population of two hundred Christian Indians (Montes 1602; Geiger 1940:122). Although San Sebastian, Molova, Antonico, and San Julian had churches, the mission activity was not as successful as it had been in the Saturiwa area. A letter written in 1600 referred to San Sebastian as "a town of annoying Indians who shrug their shoulders at this place (the mission?) and that much given to them will not be heeded" (Alas 1600). This circumstance was partially blamed on the missionaries who were said to be awaiting new assignments and who also left the *doctrina* to visit friars who worked in other missions (Montes 1602).

The mission of San Antonio de Encape does not appear on the 1659 mission list (Díaz de Calle 1659), although it is listed in 1680 as a "new conversion" (Swanton 1922:322–23). This new conversion probably referred to the Guale-Yamassee Indians who by this time had pushed as far south as the Agua Dulce area. Meanwhile, another new conversion, San Salvador de Mayaca, had appeared. This may actually have referred to the Indians of the Mayaca village rather than to insurgent Indians, since no previous missions were mentioned for Mayaca. In 1697, the Mayaca Indians rebelled against the Spanish, presumably over "false fears of mistreatment" by Juan Alonso de Esquivel, who had a hacienda in this province (Sierralto 1698). Many of the rebel Indians were relocated in the vicinity of St. Augustine, although the crown ordered the rebel villages to be reestablished (Carlos II 1698). The rebellion, which spread also to the Jororo (Sierralto 1698), severely damaged the mission effort in the Mayaca–Agua Dulce province. The last mention of the Agua Dulce group was in 1735, when it was reported that the Mayaca were completely annihilated (Franciscans 1735).

Acuera

The Acuera tribe probably occupied the area between the Ocklawaha and St. Johns rivers. Little is known of them, either archeologically or from documentary sources. Their territory included the Ocklawaha River drainage and consisted mainly of pine/oak scrub forests, with numerous springs and lakes. The Acuera food procurement system was probably based on the exploitation of the river and its swamps and lakes. What was procurable from the scrub, in addition to fish, deer, and freshwater molluscs, was utilized for food. The extent to which horticulture was practiced is unknown.

The Acuera possessed the St. Johns material complex in prehistoric times, although burial ceremonialism seems to have been less strongly developed than in the Saturiwa or Agua Dulce areas. Burial mounds in the Acuera area are generally single-component, low sand structures with few burial goods (Moore 1896a; Abshire et al. 1935; Sears 1959; Deagan 1969). Middens in the area are either shell fields or heaps, representing what appears from the limited data to have been a sparse population, centered mainly around the river and lakes.

Archeological research in the Acuera area has revealed only one mound used in historic times. The Fort Mason Mound, La-43 (Moore 1896a:534), is in the western part of the Acuera territory, probably bordering on that of the Ocale. It was constructed during the historic period, and all of the burials are accompanied by European trade material.

The French referred to the "Aguera" as vassals of Utina (Hakluyt 1903b:21), although there is no indication of French-Acuera interaction. The earliest record of contact between the Acuera and the Spanish was in 1598, when the Spanish governor noted that the princess of Acuera was one of twenty-two caciques who came to St. Augustine to offer obedience (Canzo 1598). It was in the period between 1616 and 1655 that missions were established in the Acuera territory. The names of the missions of San Luis de Acuera and Santa Lucia de Acuera appear on the 1655 list (Geiger 1940:126). They are not, however, mentioned again in the documents, and they may have succumbed during the western Timucua rebellion of 1656. There is no further mention of the Acuera, and Spanish interaction with them may also have ended with the western Timucua rebellion.

Conclusion: Change among the Eastern Timucua

From the review of ethnohistorical and archeological data pertaining to the eastern Timucua, a model may be suggested to explain the processes of change for this group in historic times, and the problems stated in the introduction may be at least partially clarified. (1) Change in eastern Timucua social organization, political structure, and religious ceremonialism resulted from a program of directed change which was channeled through the missions. This type of change for the eastern Timucua may be categorized as assimilative (Spicer 1961:531), i.e., acceptance of the dominant culture's elements in the terms of the dominant cultural system to replace parallel elements in the subordinate culture. (2) Change in eastern Timucua material culture and demographic factors (such as population size and composition) developed through a process of nondirected change. The agents here were alien (Guale-Yamassee) Indians, who in turn had been subject to British-initiated change. The results of this process can be categorized for the eastern Timucua as "fusion" (Spicer 1961:533), i.e., the combination of elements from two or more cultures producing new forms. In the case of the eastern Timucua, elements of Guale, European, and Timucua cultures were involved.

The stress produced by the processes of change could not be supported by the eastern Timucua cultures, resulting in their disintegration within 150 years. It seems likely that these stresses also resulted in the breakdown of communication and contact between the eastern Timucua and the aboriginal inhabitants of the Florida Gulf coast area. This is indicated by the presence of west Florida trade material in prehistoric and protohistoric sites and their absence in historic levels or sites.

Subsistence and settlement patterns of the eastern Timucua appeared to have been little changed by European contact. Missions were originally located in the vicinity of existing Indian towns, and it was not until after the Guale rebellion that settlements were relocated by the missionaries. In nearly all cases, it was because of the intrusion of Indian populations from the north that the eastern Timucua were relocated, as illustrated by San Juan del Puerto. House types also did not seem to have been affected by European construction techniques; Calderón noted in 1675 that although the Indians knew carpentry and built wooden churches, their own houses were still of thatch (Wenhold 1936:12). He also noted that the aboriginal villages were built around a large council house, a pattern with continuity from prehistoric times and one that does not seem to have been usurped by the presence of a church.

The basic subsistence pattern of part-time horticulture was also not radically changed by mission contact. As late as 1728, the missionaries in St. Augustine complained that the Indians lived like gypsies and took to the forest as they pleased (Valdez 1728). The mission system encouraged horticulture, and probably winter hunting, since the friars subsisted on the produce and game which the Indians gave them as "alms" (Wenhold 1936:13). Although archeological evidence indicates that the Spanish introduced European farming implements, such as hoes, and horticultural techniques, they do not seem to have caused basic changes in the aboriginal subsistence patterns.

The most obvious areas of change in eastern Timucua culture were those of political organization and religious ceremonialism. Political organization was manipulated through the conversion of the caciques and when this was ineffective, pro-Catholic and pro-Spanish Indians were installed and supported as caciques by the Spanish. At least two instances of this practice occurred in the sixteenth and seventeenth centuries: the intervention of the Franciscans in Guale succession, which was a cause of the Guale rebellion, and the sudden appearance of Doña Maria Melendez as the head of a previously unmentioned Tacatacuru-Saturiwa confederacy in 1604.

With the arrival of Europeans, the early historic and protohistoric pattern of ritual warfare between Timucua tribal confederacies of Saturiwa, Potano, and Utina ceased, and in 1598 the caciques of nearly every eastern and western Timucua tribe came to St. Augustine in a body to pledge obedience to the Spanish (Canzo 1598).

Frey Pareja's *Confessionario* (Milanich and Sturtevant 1972) is particularly revealing of the extent to which the mission system attempted to change or eliminate most aspects of eastern Timucua ritual and ceremonialism. Archeologically, this is apparent in the abandonment of mound burial during the early historic period. This occurred rapidly in the Saturiwa area, which was subject to the longest and most intensive European contact, and is evidenced by the Fountain of Youth cemetery in St. Augustine, containing Indian burials in the Christian method dating from the sixteenth century.

In areas of less intensive contact, burial mounds were constructed and used in the historic period with greater frequency and duration. The Fort Mason mound in the Acuera area and the Spruce Creek mound in the Agua Dulce area were both constructed in the historic era. No such sites are present in the Tacatacuru or Saturiwa areas.

The mission system altered eastern Timucua social organization by encouraging inheritance from father to son, rather than from uncle to nephew (Phillip II 1593), attempting to prohibit polygyny, and the appointment of favored individuals to the chieftainship who may or may not have belonged to the White Deer Clan from which chiefs normally came. This may have contributed to the disruption of clan structure.

The changes in social, religious, and political structures were particularly manifest in the generation following the one which experienced initial European contact. Although Oré noted in 1616 that the younger Indians ridiculed their elders who still maintained the old beliefs and practices (Geiger 1937:13), the process of dual enculturation which this younger generation of Indians underwent undoubtedly produced a considerable degree of stress and cultural disorientation.

It was during this period, when the cultural system of the younger eastern Timucua generation was not an integrated and functional whole, that the Guale began to move into the eastern Timucua territory. The full acceptance of Guale cultural elements as replacements of eastern Timucua elements can be seen archeologically in the replacement of St. Johns ceramics by Guale ceramics during the seventeenth century, a process which was virtually complete by 1700. Population movements are archeologically indicated by such sites as San Juan del Puerto, which yields evidence of patterning traits typical of the Tacatacuru, and by Wrights Landing, which indicates a sudden, non-Timucua population increase in the seventeenth century.

With the raids of Colonel James Moore and his Carolinians in 1702 and 1704, the Florida mission system was destroyed and the Indians of Florida were relocated near St. Augustine. Geronimo Valdez, Bishop of Cuba, noted in 1729 that four out of five mission Indians were killed as a result of Moore's raids. The Timucua were especially hard hit, since out of obedience to the church they remained and fought the invaders. Even after their relocation in St. Augustine it was noted that "they are the most hated of all the other tribes, and war is waged on them so much that they are being destroyed" (Valdez 1729). By 1725, Indian slave raids had reduced the Timucua to fifteen men and eight women, and these Indians for their own security moved to within a cannon's shot of the fort. They were struck by a pestilence, however, and only the cacique survived (Valdez 1729). The cacique and forty newly converted Indians of unknown tribal affiliation then moved to Mosa (near St. Augustine) with the Apalachee. There is no further mention of the Timucua Indians.

REFERENCES

Abbreviations: S.C.U.F., Stetson Collection, P. K. Yonge Library of Florida History, University of Florida, Gainesville; A.G.I., Archivo General de Indias, Seville, Spain; N.A.A., National Anthropological Archives, Smithsonian Institution, Washington, D.C.

Abshire, A. E.; Alden Potter; Allen Taylor; Clyde Neil; Walter Anderson; and John Rutledge.
  1935.   Early Man in the Ocala National Forest: Some Further Papers on Aboriginal Man in the Vicinity of the Ocala National Forest. Mimeographed. Civilian Conservation Corps Co. 1420, Ocala, Florida.
Alas, Alonso de las.
  1600.   Manuscript, A.G.I. 54-5-14 (Santo Domingo). [Letter to the Spanish Crown,

January 12, 1600.] Microfilm copy, Lowery Collection, University of Florida, Gainesville.

Altamirano, Juan de las Cabezas de.
  1606.   Manuscript, A.G.I. 54-5-20. [Letter to the Spanish Crown, June 27, 1606.] Photostat, S.C.U.F.

Andrews, Evangeline, and Charles Andrews, eds.
  1945.   *Jonathan Dickinson's Journal; or God's Protecting Providence*. New Haven: Yale University Press.

Caldwell, Joseph R.
  1952.   The Archeology of Eastern Georgia and South Carolina. In *Archeology of the Eastern United States*, edited by James B. Griffin, pp. 312–21. Chicago: University of Chicago Press.

Canzo, Gonzalo Méndez de (Governor of Florida).
  1598.   Manuscript, A.G.I. 54-5-9. [Letter to the Spanish Crown, February 24, 1598.] Microfilm copy, Lowery Collection, University of Florida.
  1600.   Manuscript, A.G.I. 54-5-9. [Letter to the Spanish Crown, January 12, 1600.] Microfilm copy, Lowery Collection, University of Florida.
  1601.   Manuscript, A.G.I. 54-5-9/4. [Letter to the Spanish Crown, April 24, 1601.] Microfilm copy, Lowery Collection, University of Florida.

Carlos II (King of Spain).
  1698.   Manuscript, A.G.I. 58-1-22/458. [Letter to the Governor of Florida, May 10, 1698.] Photostat, S.C.U.F.

Compostela, Diego Euclino de (Bishop of Cuba).
  1689.   Manuscript, A.G.I., 54-3-2/9. [Letter to the Spanish Crown, September 28, 1689.] Photostat, S.C.U.F.

Córcoles y Mártinez, Francisco de (Governor of Florida).
  1711.   Manuscript, A.G.I. 58-1-30/20. [Letter to the Spanish Crown, April 9, 1711.] Photostat, S.C.U.F.

Deagan, Kathleen A.
  1969.   A Small Sand Burial Mound in the Ocala National Forest. Mimeographed. Florida State Museum, Gainesville.

Díaz de la Calle, Juan.
  1659.   Manuscript (Noticias Sacras y Reales de los Ymperios de las Yndias de la Nueva Espana 1659), 2 vols. Biblioteca Nacional, Madrid, 3023–24. Microfilm copy, Lowery Collection, University of Florida.

Douglass, Andrew E.
  1885.   Some Characteristics of the Indian Earth and Shell Mounds of the Atlantic Coast of Florida. *American Antiquarian* 7:78–82, 140–47.

Escobar, Juan de Ayala (Governor of Florida).
  1717.   Manuscript, A.G.I. 58-1-30/64-65. [Letter to the Spanish Crown, April 18, 1717.] Photostat, S.C.U.F.

Franciscans of Florida.
  1735.   Manuscript, A.G.I. 58-2-17/3. [Letter to the Spanish Crown, March 8, 1735.] Photostat, S.C.U.F.

Gannon, Michael V.
  1965.   *The Cross in the Sand*. Gainesville: University of Florida Press.

Gatschet, Albert S.
  1878.   The Timucua Language. *Proceedings of the American Philosophical Society* 17:490–504.

Geiger, Maynard J.
  1937.   *The Franciscan Conquest of Florida, 1573–1618*. Washington: The Catholic University of America Press.
  1940.   *Biographical Dictionary of the Franciscans in Spanish Florida and Cuba (1528–1841)*. Franciscan Studies 21. Paterson, N.J.: St. Anthony's Guild Press.

Goggin, John M.
   1951.   Fort Pupo: A Spanish Frontier Outpost. *Florida Historical Quarterly* 30:139–92.
   1952.   *Space and Time Perspective in Northern St. Johns Archeology.* Yale University Publications in Anthropology no. 47.
   1953.   An Introductory Outline of Timucua Archaeology. *Southeastern Archaeological Conference, Newsletter* 3(3):4–17.
   1968.   *Spanish Majolica in the New World.* Yale University Publications in Anthropology no. 72.
Granberry, Julian.
   1956.   Timucua I: Prosodics and Phonemics of the Mocama Dialect. *International Journal of American Linguistics* 22(2):95–105.
Hakluyt, Richard.
   1903a.   *The Principal Navigations, Voyages, Traffiques and Discoveries of the English Nation,* vol. 8 (1600). Reprinted by James MacLehose, Glasgow.
   1903b.   *The Principal Navigations, Voyages, Traffiques and Discoveries of the English Nation,* vol. 9 (1600). Reprinted by James MacLehose, Glasgow.
Hahn, Paul.
   n.d.   Burial Excavation at the Fountain of Youth Cemetary. Manuscript, Department of Anthropology, University of Florida.
Hemmings, E. Thomas, and Kathleen Deagan.
   1973.   *Excavations on Amelia Island in Northeast Florida.* Florida State Museum Contributions, Anthropology and History no. 18.
Larson, Lewis H.
   1958.   Cultural Relationships between the Northern St. Johns Area and the Georgia Coast. *Florida Anthropologist* 11:11–12.
Le Moyne, Jacques.
   1875.   *Narrative of Le Moyne, an Artist Who Accompanied the French Expedition to Florida Under Laudonnière, 1564.* Translated from the Latin of De Bry. Boston: Osgood Co.
López, Balthazar.
   1602.   Manuscript, A.G.I. 54-5-20. [Letter to the Spanish Crown, September 16, 1602.] Photostat, S.C.U.F.
Lowery, Woodbury.
   1905.   *Spanish Settlements within the Present Limits of the United States: Florida, 1562–74.* New York: G. P. Putnam's Sons.
McMurray, Judith A.
   1973.   The Definition of the Ceramic Complex at San Juan del Puerto. Master's thesis, University of Florida, Gainesville.
Meestas, Hernando de.
   1593.   Manuscript, A.G.I. 14-7-37. [Carta de Hernando de Meestas, October 1593.] Microfilm copy, Lowery Collection, University of Florida, Gainesville.
Menéndez, Pedro de.
   1566.   Manuscript, A.G.I. 54-1-31/167. [Letter to the Spanish Crown, October 20, 1566.]
Milanich, Jerald T.
   1971a.   Surface Information from the Presumed Site of the San Pedro de Mocamo Mission. *Conference on Historic Sites Archaeology Papers,* 5:114–21.
   1971b.   *The Alachua Tradition of North-Central Florida.* Florida State Museum Contributions, Anthropology and History no. 17.
   1971c.   The Deptford Phase: An Archeological Reconstruction. Ph.D. diss., University of Florida, Gainesville.
Milanich, Jerald T., and William Sturtevant.
   1972.   *Francisco Pareja's 1613 Confessionario: A Documentary Source for Timucuan*

Ethnography. Florida Department of State, Division of Archives, History, and Records Management, Tallahassee.

Montes, Juan de.
1602. Manuscript, A.G.I. 54-5-17. [Letter to the Spanish Crown, September 16, 1602.] Photostat, S.C.U.F.

Mooney, James.
1928. *Aboriginal Population of North America North of Mexico.* Smithsonian Miscellaneous Collections, vol. 80, no. 7.

Moore, Clarence B.
1892. Certain Shell Heaps of the St. Johns River, Florida Hitherto Unexplored. *American Naturalist* 26:912–22.
1894. Certain Sand Mounds of the St. Johns River, Florida. *Journal of the Academy of Natural Sciences of Philadelphia* 10:5–105, 129–246.
1896a. Certain Sand Mounds of the Ocklawaha River, Florida. *Journal of the Academy of Natural Sciences of Philadelphia* 10:518–43.
1896b. Two Sand Mounds of Murphy Island, Florida. *Journal of the Academy of Natural Sciences of Philadelphia* 10:503–17.
1897. Certain Aboriginal Mounds of the Georgia Coast. *Journal of the Academy of Natural Sciences of Philadelphia* 11:4–138.

Oré, Luís G.
1936. *The Martyrs of Florida (1513–1616).* Edited by M. J. Geiger. Franciscan Studies 18. New York: J. F. Wagner.

Pareja, Francisco.
1602. Manuscript. A.G.I. 54-5-20/5. [Letter to the Spanish Crown, September 14, 1602]. Photostat, S.C.U.F.
1613. *Confessionario, en Lengua Castellana y Timuquana.* Viuda de Diego Lopez Davalos, Mexico. Photostat, N.A.A.
1627. *Cathecismo y Examen para los Comulgan.* Mexico: Imp. de Juan Ruyz, Microfilm, N.A.A.
1886. Arte de Lengua Timuquana Compuesto en 1614. Edited by L. Adam and J. Vinson. *Bibliotheque Linguistique Americaine,* tome 11. Paris.

Phillip II.
1593. Manuscript. A.G.I. 86-5-19. [Letter to the Governor of Florida, October 2, 1593]. Photostat, S.C.U.F.

Phillip IV.
1660. Manuscript A.G.I. 54-5-10/87 [Royal cédula to the Governor of Florida, February 26, 1660]. Photostat, S.C.U.F.

Rebolledo, Don Diego de.
1657. Manuscript [Letter to the Spanish Crown, January 16, 1657] Escribano de Consejo, Leg. 155, no. 18. Photostat, S.C.U.F.

Ribault, Jean.
1964. *The Whole and True Discouerye of Terra Florida.* Facsimile reprint of the London edition of 1563. Gainesville: University of Florida Press.

Salazar, Pablo de Hita (Governor of Florida).
1675. Manuscript, A.G.I., 58-1-26/38. [Letter to the Spanish Crown, August 24, 1675] Photostat, S.C.U.F.

Sears, William H.
1954. The Socio-Political Organization of the Pre-Columbian Cultures of the Gulf Coastal Plain. *American Anthropologist* 56:339–45.
1959. *Two Weeden Island Period Burial Mounds, Florida.* Florida State Museum Contributions, Social Sciences no. 5.

Serrano y Sanz, Manuel, ed.
1912. *Documentos de la Florida y la Luisiana, Siglos XVI al XVIII.* Madrid: Librería General de Victoriano Suárez.

Sierralto, Don Martin de (Conseja de Franciscans).
  1698. Manuscript, A.G.I. 58-1-22/463. [Letter to Franciscans, June 5, 1698.] Photostat, S.C.U.F.
Smith, Buckingham.
  1968. *Narratives of de Soto in the Conquest of Florida.* Gainesville, Fla.: Palmetto Books.
Smith, Hale G.
  1948. Two Historical Archaeological Periods in Florida. *American Antiquity* 13:313–19.
  1956. *The European and the Indian.* Florida Anthropological Society Publication no. 4.
Spicer, Edward H.
  1961. Types of Contact and Processes of Change. In *Perspectives in American Indian Culture Change,* edited by E. H. Spicer, pp. 517–43. Chicago: University of Chicago Press.
Swanton, John R.
  1922. *Early History of the Creek Indians and Their Neighbors.* Bureau of American Ethnology Bulletin no. 73.
  1946. *The Indians of the Southeastern United States.* Bureau of American Ethnology Bulletin no. 137.
Valdez, Bishop Geronimo.
  1728. Manuscript. A.G.I. 58-2-16/22 [Doctrineros Census, September 1, 1728.] Photostat, S.C.U.F.
  1729. Manuscript. A.G.I. 58-2-16/25 [Letter from the Bishop of Cuba to the Spanish Crown, January 14, 1729.] Photostat, S.C.U.F.
Wenhold, Lucy.
  1936. *A Seventeenth-Century Letter of Gabriel Díaz Vara Calderón, Bishop of Cuba.* Smithsonian Miscellaneous Collections, vol. 95, no. 16.

Historic Guale Indians of the Georgia Coast and the Impact of the Spanish Mission Effort

Lewis H. Larson, Jr.

FROM the time of their first intrusions into the Georgia coastal area, the Spanish were met by a homogeneous group of aboriginal people who spoke a language belonging to the Muskhogean group. These people, whom they called the Guale, occupied that area of the Georgia coast lying between St. Andrews and St. Catherines sounds. To the south in Florida were the neighboring Timucua. To the west was the area the Spanish referred to as the Province of Tama. Northward, in the area between St. Catherines Sound and the Savannah River, there seems to have been no aboriginal occupation, although the Cusabo were situated on the coast north of the mouth of the Savannah (Swanton 1922:81).

The Guale appear relatively briefly on the southeastern scene, yet the part that they played in the Spanish attempts at colonization of *La Florida* is important. They were called the Ouade by the French Huguenots who came to the St. Johns River area in 1562 (Swanton 1946:603). By 1692, they had completely retreated to the south of the St. Marys River in the face of continued English and Indian assaults on the Spanish missions. Some aligned with the English and were absorbed by the Yamassee. The others stayed in Florida where they gradually mixed with other groups who lived around St. Augustine for protection. The last information that we have of their existence as a group is in 1735 when one Fray Tomas de Aguilar was reappointed professor of the Indian language of Guale (Geiger 1940:23). In the year 1728, they were under the charge of this same priest of the mission of Santa Catalina de Guale, at that time located at Nombre de Dios near St. Augustine (Geiger 1940:23).

If the actual extent of Spanish influence cannot be accurately measured archeologically, certain inferences can be drawn. The original Spanish sources, which doubtless contain much in the way of ethnographic description of the Guale, were with few exceptions unavailable to me. The existing secondary source material is at best tantalizingly meager. One is forced to the opinion that the Spanish could not have occupied the Georgia coast for over one hundred years without noting its aboriginal occupants. This opinion is further strengthened when one considers that the Spaniards who lived on the coast were literate priests, who, for the most part, were limited in their human contact to the aborigines. There are a number of tempting hints in the literature which lead one to the conclusion that the Archives of the Indies in Spain contain much data that could fill the gaps in our knowledge of the coastal area of Georgia of that period and of its native inhabitants. It awaits a concentrated effort by historians.

For purposes of discussing Spanish cultural impact on the Indians of the coast, the Guale occupation can be divided into two categories: Pine Harbor complex, which refers to that cultural assemblage identified archeologically as Guale and is just immediately post-contact, and the Sutherland Bluff complex, which is post-1600 in time and Guale in culture.

The identification of the Pine Harbor complex as the archeological remains of the sixteenth-century Guale is dependent upon these factors: Pine Harbor complex is confined archeologically to the same area that the historic Guale occupied, and there is no known archeological assemblage which would fall temporally between Pine Harbor complex and Sutherland Bluff complex; and the pottery of the Sutherland Bluff complex is related to similar archeological assemblages in other areas of Georgia and the Southeast which have been stratigraphically demonstrated to be post-1600 in age. The identification of the Sutherland Bluff complex as the Guale of the Spanish Mission period is demonstrated by its correspondence to the area occupied by the Guale of the Spanish documents and also by the unquestionable association of Sutherland Bluff and Spanish cultural materials in an archeological context.

PINE HARBOR COMPLEX

For the most part, Pine Harbor villages were located along the mainland and on islands in offshore marshes on tidal rivers and creeks. Several of these villages were quite extensive, including the Pine

Harbor type site near Pine Harbor in McIntosh County, Georgia. This site extends for over a mile on high ground along the marshes bordering the Sapelo River and one of its small tributaries. Today, Pine Harbor villages appear as a series of low shell middens scattered haphazardly over the site. These middens average two to three feet in height and about fifty feet in diameter. No definite arrangement has been noted, although none of the sites has ever been mapped. A burial mound is usually found in association with the larger villages.

The proximity of the village sites to salt water and the large accumulation of shell in the middens offer ample evidence of the pre-Spanish Guale dependence upon a marine economy. The contents of Pine Harbor middens reveal a utilization of not only the local oysters, which form the bulk of the midden material, but also several other types of bivalves, many species of whelk, crabs, and a wide variety of fish. Fishing was supplemented by hunting; the bones of numerous deer, small game, and birds regularly appear in the middens. Agriculture was practiced, but its importance seems to have been slight. We have some information on agricultural practices from the Spanish accounts of the Guale of the late sixteenth century which gives clues about their pre-contact ancestors. Father Avila was forced to act as a human scarecrow to keep birds from maize fields during his period of captivity in 1598 following the Guale revolt of 1597. It was during this same period of captivity that he was beaten by Indians when he happened to pass them as they dug with rods (Oré 1936:92). It is not clear that they were working in a cornfield, but their implements seemed to be digging sticks.

The Guale cultivated pumpkins, beans, and corn (Geiger 1936:105). Corn was ground into flour in wooden mortars and made into bread. San Miguel found the Guale grinding their corn "in deep and narrow wooden mortars: the mano is a kind of rammer more than two yards in length and the rammer widens above and is slender in the mortar" (Garcia 1902:2).

The first missionaries in the Guale area complained bitterly about the fact that the Indians neglected agriculture in favor of hunting and fishing, which meant that permanent settlements were not the rule, for long seasonal junkets in pursuit of game mitigated against a settled populace. This mode of living on the part of the Indians proved distracting to the Spanish fathers; it was difficult to pursue a congregation which scattered so widely so frequently. Such was the experience of Father Rogel, a Jesuit and one of the first missionaries in La Florida. In 1570, in Orista immediately north of Guale, "Father Rogel tried to see if he could prevail upon the Indians to remain quietly in one location, where continued preaching might have some effect. He offered them a quantity of maize for their plantings and exhorted them to take care of the fields and not to go wandering. They accepted the maize and promised to establish a village, and they asked him for hoes to cultivate the ground. Father Rogel had only three so he sent to Esteban de las Alas for more. The latter sent him five, which the father gave to the Indians. They began to carry out Father Rogel's wish, building more than twenty dwellings at the site selected for the village, while two of the Indians sowed their fields with the maize given them by Father Rogel. In a short time, however, all the villagers (except those who had planted seeds) fled from the place from no other motive other than their natural weakness and inconstancy. Although Father Rogel followed them for twenty leagues, and tried to hold them with adornments, presents, and gifts (which are the things which most influence the disposition of these Indians), he could not get them to come with him.

"The Indians were so reluctant to receive the Catholic religion that no admonitions would curb their barbarity—a barbarity based on liberty unrestrained by the yoke of reason, and made worse because they had not been taught to live in the villages. They were scattered about the country for nine of the twelve months of the year, so that to influence them at all, one missionary was needed for each Indian" (Barcia 1951:151–52).

The Guale social organization generally followed that of their Creek cousins. The central figure of each town was referred to as the *mico*, who functioned as chief. It was through the mico that the Spanish conducted all of their dealings with a village and its inhabitants. While this may have been simply a matter of Spanish expediency, it does recall the Creek pattern whereby the mico received representatives of other towns (in this case the Spanish) and carried on diplomatic negotiations. There was also a head mico under whose leadership all of the towns in Guale were united. Swanton quotes a letter of Méndez de Canzo, governor of Florida, to the king, in which the function of the head mico is explained: "the title of head mico [*mico mayor*] means a kind of king of the land, recognized and respected as such by all the caciques in their towns, and whenever he visits one of them, they all turn out to receive him and feast him, and every year they pay him a certain tribute of pearls and other articles made of shells according to the land" (Swanton 1922:84).

A definite order of succession may have governed the choice of head mico, for Don Juanillo, who was to lead the revolt of 1597, is spoken of as the one "whose turn it was to be head mico of that province [Guale]." On the other hand, Barcia speaks of Don Juanillo only as the "eldest son and heir of the cacique of the island of Guale" (Barcia 1951:181). In addition to the head mico and the town mico, there was recognition of three or four chiefs who acted as leaders in specific districts of the province. These districts comprised a northern, a central, and a southern group of towns. The micos were probably assisted by a council made up of the leaders of the town. Perhaps a series of sub-chiefs existed as in the Creek pattern.

On many occasions the micos, when meeting with the Spanish, were accompanied by individuals whom the Spanish referred to as *mandadors*, lieutenants of the mico (Geiger 1936:78). During the visit of Governor Ibarra to the Guale area in 1604, to reestablish the missions destroyed in the 1597 revolt, the Spaniards were met by the micos of a number of towns in the area, including the mandadors of Asao and Yfulo, "en la junta el dicho mico Don Domingo . . . (el) pilotillo mandador de Asao y el mandador de Yfulo" (Serrano y Sanz 1912:179). On this same occasion, Ibarra was greeted by another official of Asao, referred to as the *aliaguita de Asao*. There is a question of his position, but there can be no doubt that he was a functionary in the social structure of Asao (Serrano y Sanz 1912:179).

There is evidence to support the contention that both the mandadors and the aliaguitas represented actual Guale political officials. In the Spanish document recounting Governor Ibarra's visit to Guale in 1604, it is related that he stopped on St. Catherines Island to address a gathering of important chiefs at the town of Guale. Here on November 22, he met with Don Bartolome, mico of Guale, the mico of Yoa, the *caciques* of Aluete, Otax, Uculegue, Culupala, Otapolas, Unallapa, Ahopo, the brother of the cacique of Otax, the aliaguitas of Guale, the head mandadors of Guale, and other principal Indians (Serrano y Sanz 1912:187). It is revealing to find that the aliaguitas and mandadors are included in a list of micos and caciques. The phrase "and other principal Indians" emphasizes the position of these individuals. The Spanish, without a doubt, regarded both the aliaguita and the mandador as Indian officials of some sort and were reflecting an aboriginal viewpoint in this attitude. It would be interesting to know why the Spanish distinguished certain personages by the term mico and others by the term cacique. All of the individuals were apparently heads of towns. In addition, the micos of Yoa and Guale were seemingly the overlords of a number of towns, yet the cacique of

Aluete complained to Ibarra that three of his vassals, the caciques of
Talapo, Ufalague, and Orista, had fled from his jurisdiction (Serrano
y Sanz 1912:188–98). Elsewhere the cacique of Aluete is spoken of as
a head (elder?) cacique (*cacique mayor*), while the caciques of Talapo,
Ufalaque, and Orista are referred to as minor (younger?) caciques
(*caciques menores*) (Serrano y Sanz 1912:191).

Positive information on clans is almost totally lacking. The only
thing which might indicate their presence is a statement by Oré: "they
[the Indians] consider themselves related provided they have the
same names or lineage" (Oré 1936:107).

An aspect of the social organization with which the Spanish were
concerned was the existence of polygamy. The degree to which it was
practiced is uncertain, but it was one of the Indian customs which the
priests regarded with unfriendly eyes, and their interference with the
practice contributed to the 1597 revolt. One would judge from the
stress which the fathers placed on it, and its continuous mention in the
Spanish documents, that it was a widespread and popular institution.
The abolishment of polygamy is cited by Don Juanillo, leader of the
Guale revolt, as an Indian grievance and justification for the insurrec-
tion. According to his addresses to the Guale: "They take away our
women, leaving us only the one and perpetual, forbidding us to exchange her" (Barcia 1951:182).

Oré provided information on other aspects of the social structure,
including an example of the problems that the friars faced in their
efforts to erase polygamy. "We have an example of this [polygamy] in
reference to the principal cacique of the province of Guale. During
the time of his apostasy he took to his house as a concubine and
mistress one of his sisters-in-law, the sister of his own wife, with whom
he lived all that time. By her he had three children, and by his own
wife four children. Knowing that he would be commanded to leave
his sister-in-law he spoke first and said to the father: 'I see the evil I
have done in committing this incest with the sister of my wife. I have
three children by her, but if I eject them from my house, they will
have to suffer and perish. Although she is in my house, I do not have
to have relations with her; if the Indians murmur at this, recall what I
said.' The fathers said nothing in order not to break immediately with
the cacique for it seemed proper to them to act in this manner until a
more opportune season presented itself, lest everything be lost. Afterwards, they treated with this cacique in resolving his difficulty.
They told him to eject his sister-in-law from his house and send her to
her father's house because her presence in his house was scandalizing

the Indians and was setting them a bad example. The fathers said the reformation of morals should start with him. All they accomplished with him was that he put her in a separate house, which was an ancient custom of the chiefs who placed in a separate house each one of the women or lovers they had. Even then the Indians complained, 'Until now the cacique had in one house two women and children; now he has two houses and in each house he has a woman as if he were a pagan.' The Indians urged him [the cacique] to marry her. Neither did he nor she wish [to marry], nor did anyone dare to marry her, for it was a custom that no one should marry or speak to the wives or the lovers of the caciques. God was pleased to call to Himself the wife of the cacique, while the sister-in-law gathered the children of her sister together with hers in her house" (Oré 1936:101–2).

If there is any indication of the regularity of the practice among the Guale of one man marrying several sisters, it is supposed that a sororate rule prevailed. Unfortunately, this is the only reference available that speaks at all of the marriage pattern in polygamous unions. The custom of a house for each wife suggests ownership of the house by the wife and matrilocal residence, although, here again, more definite evidence is required. The indication of some of the taboos which probably surrounded the micos is also of interest.

If the supposition is accepted that the Guale were culturally as well as linguistically akin to the Creeks, one finds much in the Creek social structure which might provide a sounder basis for the interpretation of certain Guale social practices. Both Creek and Guale shared the common trait of designating the town leader by the term mico. His function with respect to his town seems to have been the same with both groups. Speck says that the Tuskegee mico, "as the civil head of the town, was to receive all embassies from other tribes, to direct the decisions of the town council according to his judgement; and, finally, to stand as the representative of the town in foreign negotiations" (Speck 1907:113). The Spanish accounts present an almost identical description of the function of the Guale micos. From the various de Soto narratives, it is apparent that the Creeks lived under a system of head micos who controlled several towns in a particular area, e.g., the mico, or cacique, of Coosa (Garcilaso 1951:341–47). A similar situation is reflected among the Guale with the mico mayor.

The Creek political structure included, in addition to the mico, a number of individuals who held titles and assisted him in various ways. Two who were important were the *heniha*, whose functions were concerned with peace, and the *tastanagi*, who acted in matters having to do with war and internal policing. In some Creek towns a number of persons functioned collectively in each of these offices (Swanton 1928:276-334). Among the Guale there is a comparable situation; the mandador and the aliaguita were sub-chiefs similar, if not identical, in function to the heniha and tastanagi.

Perhaps where polygamous marriages took place among the Guale, a sororate rule was followed. In speaking of the Creeks, Swanton states, "where polygamy existed the wives were generally sisters and usually inhabited the same house, though there were cases in which a man had wives living in two or more distinct houses" (Swanton 1928:79). In addition the Creeks observed matrilocal residence, and the women owned the houses, also a practice of the Guale, according to Father Oré's account.

The aboriginal religious patterns of the Guale are scarcely hinted at in the Spanish documents. As a result, the archeological evidence offers the best information. During Pine Harbor times, burial mounds were constructed which have produced material of a religious nature. The bulk of this material, in the form of grave furniture, belonged to the Southern Cult. It includes engraved shell gorgets with the coiled rattlesnake and cross, stone and copper ceremonial celts, clay pipes with cult symbols, incised pottery vessels with cult motifs, and conch shell bowls. Clay figurines representing "eagle warriors" have been found at the Pine Harbor site (Larson 1955:75-81). The Southern Cult among the Guale was undoubtedly a peripheral manifestation of the broader southeastern pattern. Among them certain elements of this pattern are missing, while local developments within the overall framework seem to have taken place. The platform mound is absent, and many of the items of cult paraphernalia are missing, yet the clay figurines and clay pipes appear to be unique to the Guale area.

If one can equate certain, or even all, facets of the Southern Cult with the busk (Waring 1968), there is a partial explanation for the way in which the cult manifests itself on the coast. Agriculture did not play an important role in the pre-Spanish Guale economy; therefore, it could only have assumed a proportionate role in the religious activity. If the cult was primarily a maize fertility ceremony, then one would not expect the Guale to have taken over this ritual in its entirety or to have left those portions which they did take over unmodified. It is suggested that simply because the entire culture was basically oriented toward agriculture, the cult ceremonialism indirectly embraced many phases of southeastern culture which did not bear directly on farming. The Guale, when confronted with the cult, adopted those nonagricultural aspects of it and modified them to fit their own cultural situation.

The burial mounds represent a departure from a generalized late southeastern pattern of cemetery burial. The mounds are more or less accumulations of mortuary deposits in a restricted area. There are some instances where the mounds seem to have grown up over central burial pits or tombs, but many of the mounds have yielded burials from the mound fill only. The burials were varied in form: flexed and extended primary burials, cremations, and urn and bundle burials were used. Several bodies were usually buried together, yet a single body might be placed by itself. Grave goods were rare. While some mounds seem to have been constructed around and over an old shell midden, others show a deliberate attempt at construction and often attained a height of ten or more feet. Most appear, however, as irregular rises in the surrounding area, only two or three feet high. There would seem to be no single burial pattern aside from the general trait of mound interment.

There is a possibility that a mortuary temple may have existed among the Guale. The practice of urn burial and bundle burial points toward this usage. There was a mortuary temple at the coastal Irene site immediately north of the Guale area (Caldwell and McCann 1941:25–28). John White pictures such temples from the Virginia area, and they occur widely throughout the Southeast (Lorant 1946).

During the Guale revolt, Father Avila was taken captive and carried a short distance inland from the coast to the Guale town of Tulafina. There he suffered tortures and indignities at the hands of his captors. He rebelled when after that "they tried to make me serve in cleaning the house of the demon, for such we call it. They, however, call it a tomb. There they place food and drink for the dead which the dead are supposed to find at the morning meal. The Indians believe that the dead eat this food. However, they are already persuaded that the dead do not eat it, because the wizards eat it themselves, as they know by experience for we have made this known to them" (Oré 1936:91).

Avila's "house of the demon" with its attendant hungry "wizards" sounds suspiciously like a mortuary temple complete with priests. The wizards were apparently similar to those functionaries that the priest had railed against at the missions, and who had caused Father Avila to be precipitated into his unhappy state of captivity.

San Miguel recorded in some detail a ball game which gives some idea of the aboriginal ceremonialism. It is an eyewitness account recorded in 1595 near the Guale town of Asao: "We found the head cacique and his principals who were many, at the door of a [large] house on a large and clean plaza. . . . They tried to entertain us with a certain game. In order to begin it, they all went together with their cacique to a part of the plaza, each one with a rod or piece of sharp pointed antler of the shape and size of a dart. One of them [a cacique] did not assemble. [This] cacique had a stone in his hand the size and shape of a bread cake or a half real, and commencing the game, he who had it threw it, rolling it with all his strength, and everyone at one time and without order pursued the stone with their rods. At times they were inconsiderate of one another. I did not understand the game well, but it seemed to me that he who ran the fastest and arrived first with his rod and the stone, and without stopping a bit the speed of rolling to where they had left [scored]. In the same manner they took it and rolled it [again]. In this exercise they enjoyed a great length of time, and were so engaged in the effort, that perspiration ran all over their bodies.

"At the conclusion of the ceremony we all entered together into the hut. The Spaniards, caciques and important Indians sat down, each on a bed which was supported by poles from the floor. There was in the hut, near the door on the right side, an idol of human figure badly carved. It had the eyes and tail of a wolf, and the rest of the body was painted with red ochre. At the feet of the idol was a large earthen jar with a wide mouth, filled with a liquid that is called cassina. Round about the jar and the idol were a large number of jars of two types, also filled with cassina. Each Indian takes one in [his] hand and with reverence they go giving it to those who have just played, who are seated, each on a bed. Each one takes and drinks his, which makes their bellies like drums. When they have drunk it their bellies swelled and they were inflated, they were thus quite a long time. We hoped to see that this fiesta was finished, when we saw them opening their mouths with much calmness each one made a large stream of water through his mouth as clear as what he had drunk. Others on their knees on the floor, with affectionate hands were scattering the water which they made in all directions. All those who did that were important. This finished the solemn rite" (Garcia 1902:195–96).

The house at which the Spanish met the caciques and the hut where the cassina ceremony took place was undoubtedly the same building. It occupied a site on the plaza, a fact, which when coupled with information which San Miguel gives us regarding its interior arrangement and the use to which the building was put, suggests that it was a council house. The account of the game seems to refer to one similar

to chunkee, for it follows the general description given by Adair for
that game among the Creeks (Adair 1775:401–2). Among the Guale
each side was led by a cacique, which would indicate that a side represented a particular town. A third cacique acted as referee. In the
ceremony following the game, the players were served cassina by
Indians who did not participate in the game but who were important
functionaries. Here again there are parallels to similar rituals observed among other southeastern groups (Swanton 1928:538–44).

What is known of Guale material culture does not present a complete picture. Apparently they used a wide range of bone tools including awls, needles, ornamental pins, and projectile points. There were
hundreds of sherd hones on Pine Harbor sites. They were probably
used in sharpening bone tools. In addition to bone, shell, particularly
the conch shell, was used to make a number of tool types. Columella
chisels and conch shell hoes and hammers are found frequently on
Pine Harbor sites. Shell and pearls were used to make beads. Pottery
discs are found scattered around most of the refuse areas. Stone is not
found naturally in the area, and, as a result, stone was utilized only
rarely. No stone projectile points have been found which seem to
belong to the Pine Harbor complex.

Stone celts are discussed with some regularity on Pine Harbor sites.
The Spanish refer frequently to the *macana*, or stone axe, used by the
Guale during the early part of the mission period. It was with the
macana that the Guale killed a number of Spanish priests, so that the
implement seems to have been a weapon as well as a tool (Geiger
1936:89).

The pre-Spanish Guale made a wide variety of ceramic forms. Most
of these vessel shapes duplicate pre-contact contemporary forms in
other areas of Georgia and the Southeast. Large jars were the most
popular shape, others include casuela bowls, open bowls, and bowls
with rim effigies. Decoration was almost exclusively stamped (both
filfot cross and a large check). Two types of incising were used, Irene
Incised and McIntosh Incised, which was a fine incising used for cult
symbolism on pottery.

The Guale were fond of personal ornamentation, a fact borne out
by both documentary material and archeological information. Moore
found large quantities of shell beads with burials on the north end of
Creighton Island (Moore 1897:35). He also reports shell beads with
burials of the Pine Harbor complex elsewhere in the area. In 1595,
San Miguel saw Guale wearing beads on their wrists and upper arms
(Garcia 1902:194). The Guale used body paint as ornamentation.

Father Oré speaks of their warriors as "pagan Indians painted and smeared with red paste, and feathers on their heads. This among them is a sign of cruelty and slaughter" (Oré 1936:73). San Miguel also reported that they painted their faces, breasts, upper arms, and thighs (Garcia 1902:194). This use of body ornamentation came eventually to divide the Christian Indians from the pagans during the mission period. Father Oré relates that the Christian Indians often set upon the pagans who were referred to as the *hanopiras* because of the practice of body painting: "We religious find it necessary to become the defenders and protectors of the Hanopiras among the Christian Indians. This term signifies a painted man because the pagans in greater part go about smeared and painted with a bright reddish color, and when this is lacking they paint themselves with soot and charcoal" (Oré 1936:43–44).

The Guale used two house types: a small, roughly rectangular dwelling constructed of posts and a large communal building which probably served as a council house and temple. The dwelling house pattern was found under the edge of a shell midden at the Pine Harbor site. It is the only certain house pattern for this period in the Guale area, so there is some question of how typical it is. The priest San Miguel, who visited the Guale in 1595, said, "All of the houses are small, because, as they have little reason to keep in them, they make them only for shelter" (Garcia 1902:195).

The second type of Guale structure was an entirely different type of building, and its use does not seem to have been utilitarian. It was a huge circular structure of posts with a conical roof. At the time of San Miguel's visit, such a structure was occupied by the Spaniards of his party. The building is described as large and "circular in shape, made of entire pines from which the limbs and bark had been removed, set up with their lower ends in the earth and the tops all brought together above like a pavillion or like the ribs of a parasol. Three hundred men might be able to live in one: it had within around the entire circumference a continuous bed or bedstead, each well fitted for the repose and sleep of many men, and because there was no bed-clothing other than some straw, the door of the cabin was so small that it was necessary for us to bend in order to enter; and due to the cold although it was spring when we arrived; and so that one may not feel the cold at night and may sweat without clothing it is sufficient to cover the doorway at night with a door made of palmetto" (Garcia 1902:195).

It was this same type of house in which the shipwrecked Dickinson and his group were housed on their return northward from St. Augustine in 1696. His description of an Indian building at St. Marys on the Georgia coast closely parallels that of San Miguel: "We were conducted to the war-house, as the custom is, for every town hath a war-house. Or as we understood these houses were for their times of mirth and dancing, and to lodge and entertain strangers. This house is about 81 foot diameter built round, with 32 squares, in each square a cabin about 8 feet long of a good height being painted and well matted. The center of this building is a quadrangle of 20 foot being open at top of the house, against which the house is built thus. In this quadrangle is the place they dance having a great fire in the middle. One of the squares of this building is the gateway or passage in" (Dickinson 1946:67). Dickinson's description is more revealing as to the use of the building and leaves little doubt that it was definitely a council house.

Father Oré mentions the use of a *garita*, or granary. While not speaking specifically of the Guale, he would seem to include them in the use of such a structure. "These [garitas] are found all over Florida [La Florida], and in them the Indians place the maize they keep for their sustenance; it is a type of barn supported by four posts, high and bulky, raised from the earth" (Oré 1936:24).

SUTHERLAND BLUFF COMPLEX

The Guale, under Spanish influence and dominion, underwent many fundamental changes, yet they managed to retain certain important aspects of their culture which were purely aboriginal. The most important changes were in their economic orientation and their religious organization.

The Sutherland Bluff villages, like those of their pre-Spanish Guale ancestors, were located along the tidal creeks and rivers. These sites present a different picture from the Pine Harbor sites. The numerous shell middens of the earlier sites are absent during the Spanish period—not that shell was no longer present in the middens, rather the low moundlike heaps were not now built. The Sutherland Bluff shell seems to have scattered over the entire site in rather an even layer. Perhaps, as evidence from the Harris Neck site seems to indicate, the shell was deposited along the edge of the site bordering the marsh or river. One also has the feeling that, quantitatively, the amount of shell on the sites is much smaller than that on Pine Harbor sites. This was the result of the Spanish policy of forcing the natives into a sedentary agricultural economy.

The Spanish found such an attitude toward the Indians was necessary for many reasons. First, natives were settled in a particular spot, preferably around the actual mission site or in its immediate locality. This fact promoted Christianizing and permitted the Spanish to watch their wards at a time when both the French and the English were competing with the Spanish for Indian trade and for allies in an attempt to control the Atlantic coast.

The Spanish also knew that an Indian agricultural economy was necessary to support the missions and the secular installations at St. Augustine. Thus, Guale was soon covered with large fields and orchards which supplied the Indian as well as the Spanish needs. The result was that the Indians became settled farmers, turning from their former dependence upon the surrounding tidal waters. This explains the thin middens of shell which are a familiar archeological feature of the Sutherland Bluff sites. New crops and domesticated animals were introduced, including onions, peppers, garlic, limes, peaches, figs, oranges, swine, and chickens. Hunting and fishing were still carried on, as the excavated middens indicate, but their importance was sharply diminished.

The extent to which the Guale social organization underwent change is not known. That it did go through change is almost certain, however. The Spanish action which precipitated the Guale revolt of 1597 was the continued meddling with the mico succession, polygamy, and other aspects of the social structure on the part of the priests. The friars were trying to Christianize the Indians, and, in order to do so, found it necessary to destroy certain Guale institutions in the process. Undoubtedly, they were at least partially successful. In any event, the Spanish must have found some of the aboriginal social institutions practical from the standpoint of their dealings with the Indians, for there are references to micos up until the abandonment of the Georgia coast by the Spanish.

The Spanish, in fact, made a real effort to preserve the political organization of the Guale. In an account dealing with a visit to Guale in 1604 by Governor Ibarra of Florida, the cacique of Aluete asked him to order three former vassal chiefs to return to his jurisdiction after they had fled to the mico of Asao. Ibarra promised to do this and "said to him that on the return trip to Asao he would call them together and talk to them and admonish them that they obey him [the cacique of Aluete], as they had done in the past; that this was the wish of his majesty and his [Ibarra's] own, that the minor caciques did not disobey their principal chiefs, but that they obey and respect them and that his grace would remedy it and order them to do this" (Serrano y Sanz 1912:189).

In the area of religion, the Spanish were most proficient and probably made the greatest changes in the Guale culture. By Sutherland Bluff times, the burial mounds had disappeared and along with them all traces of the Southern Cult. While no burials have been found on the Georgia coast which are directly attributable to the Sutherland Bluff period, a number of Spanish mission period burials have been excavated in Florida which gives some idea of the burial practices, notably at the Fountain of Youth site in St. Augustine. These burials follow the Christian mode of cemetery interment—extended, on the back with the hands on the chest. One can assume that such practices prevailed on the Georgia coast.

The Catholic church apparently was successful in its efforts to win over the Indians. There is, of course, the question of degree to which the Guale embraced Christianity, but probably a situation similar to that which developed among the Mexican Indians occurred. Paraphernalia and associated symbolism of the Southern Cult vanish. The beliefs and practices seem to have followed suit or at least to have been modified and incorporated into the dominating Catholic pattern.

Records left by the Spanish clergy and civil authorities leave little doubt that wholesale conversions were made among the Guale and that the Indians had embraced most of the outward manifestations of Christianity. Calderón notes 13,152 Christianized Indians living in the provinces of Guale, Apalachee, Timucua, and Apalachicola in the year 1675 (Wenhold 1936:12). Describing these same Christianized Indians, he notes, "As to their religion, they are not idolators, and they embrace with devotion the mysteries of our holy faith. They attend mass with regularity at 11 o'clock on the holy days they observe; namely, Sunday, and the festivals of Christmas, the Circumcision, Epiphany, The Purification of Our Lady, and the days of Saint Peter, Saint Paul, and All Saints Day, and before entering the Church each one brings to the house of the priest as a contribution a log of wood. They do not talk in the church, and women are separated from the men; the former on the side of the Epistle, and the latter on the side of the Evangel. They are very devoted to the Virgin, and on Saturdays they attend when her mass is sung. On Sundays they attend the Rosario and the Salve in the afternoon. They celebrate with rejoicing and devotion the Birth of Our Lord, all attending the midnight mass with offerings of loaves, eggs and other food. They subject themselves to extraordinary penances during Holy Week, and during the 24 hours of Holy Thursday and Friday, while our Lord is in the Urn of the Monument, they attend standing, praying the rosary in complete silence, 24 men and 24 women and the same number of children of both sexes, with hourly changes. The children, both male and female, go to the church [and] on work days, to a religious school where they are taught by a teacher whom they call the Athequi of the church; [a person] whom the priests have for this service; as they have also a person deputized to report to them concerning all parishioners who live in evil" (Wenhold 1936:14).

At least one Indian religious practice seems to have made the transition from an aboriginal ceremonial base to a Spanish Catholic matrix. The reason for transfer of the ceremonial is found in the fact that both religious structures contained essentially the same practice. Father Oré records that the Guale "show reverence for the dead, for not only on the General Commemoration of the Dead [November 2] do they bring them an offering, such as pumpkins or beans or a basket of maize or a hamper of toasted flour, but also during the year they have mass said for them with some offering of the afore-mentioned articles which they offer as alms. On Monday, at the procession for Departed Souls, they come to be present at it and to hear mass" (Oré 1936:105). The pagan Guale brought offerings of food for the dead in the mortuary temple so that it was easy for them to adopt the Catholic celebration of the Commemoration of All Souls.

The material culture of the Guale probably did not undergo the sweeping changes which might be expected. The Spanish did not come as traders, and when compared to the English or the French, their distribution of gifts in an effort to win Indian friends was meager. On occasion mention is made of the distribution of gifts of axes, scissors, hoes, and cloth to various micos who came to St. Augustine to acknowledge the Spanish king. In the main, however, no attempt was made to extend to the Indians the material benefits of Spanish technology. The friars taught the Indians improved agricultural and construction techniques. Yet priests with the Eucharist were poor substitutes for the English offering guns and Venetian beads.

It was the matter of guns that actually may have caused the ultimate failure of the Spanish in Georgia. On only one occasion do the Spanish documents show that the Guale received guns from their warders. This was the occasion of an English-inspired and -led attack by the Yuchi on the mission of Santa Catalina de Guale. Some sixteen of the mission Indians were given firearms to aid a small Spanish

Lewis H. Larson, Jr.

garrison of five men in their defense of the island. This attack took place over one hundred years after the Spanish began their dealings with the Indians. The net result of the mission Indians' inability to meet the increasing English forays was panic. Finally the Georgia missions were abandoned, with the removal of the Indians to the shadow of the Castillo de San Marcos in St. Augustine some ten years later. Even this, however, failed to solve the problems for the Spanish, for many of the Guale rapidly began to drift back to the English in the Carolinas. One of the last Guale missions to be recorded in the Spanish documents, just before Florida became an English colony in 1763, was Tolomato, the very people whose ancestors had led the Guale revolt of 1597.

The Spanish influences on Guale material culture are most vividly manifested in the Indian pottery. The Spanish priests brought with them to the missions a limited quantity of glazed European ware—the majolica. This ware seems to have caught the eye of the local potters, for a variety of pot shapes in imitation of Spanish forms appear during Sutherland Bluff times. In particular, plates and pitchers with graceful handles became popular. Painted designs were used on these new shapes, yet all these European ceramic ideas were applied to a native base and framework. Nowhere is there evidence that the potter's wheel was introduced or that refined firing techniques were applied. The native clays and manufacturing methods followed pre-Columbian patterns in spite of the fact that the decorative use of paint followed a European mode.

Besides the Spanish-influenced wares, several types of aboriginal ceramic styles were popular (in fact, the most popular pottery type was pure Indian) and continued to develop from Pine Harbor forms. These native Guale styles became widespread and eventually were to be found in a variety of modified forms in much of Spanish Florida during the latter half of the seventeenth century.

There were changes to some extent in the Guale architecture. We know from Jonathan Dickinson's account that the Guale council house remained relatively unchanged during the Spanish period, although it undoubtedly lost all its ceremonial function. The dwelling house changed from the Pine Harbor period. Wall trenches replace post holes, and the houses become slightly larger with interior rooms and a sheltered entrance (Caldwell, n.d.). The Indians had, after all, carried out the construction of a number of churches and secular buildings under Spanish direction and using Spanish designs adapted to local raw materials, environment, and technical skill.

The Spanish introduction of material goods had little impact on the Guale. According to Dickinson, their women found European cloth such a rarity after 150 years of Spanish contact that they still wore skirts of Spanish moss (Dickinson 1946:88). Calderón, Bishop of Cuba in 1675, after an episcopal visit to Florida, left an excellent description of Indian agricultural practices. Describing in general terms the Guale, Timucua, Apalachee, and Apalachicola, he noted features which all held in common. In January, the fields were cleared by burning in order to prepare them for planting. During this burning, a hunt was staged to take advantage of the animals driven out of the area by the fire. In April, the actual planting was carried out with the men preparing the soil; "the man goes along opening the trench," while the women did the sowing. The fields which belonged to the caciques were cultivated and sown by his townspeople in common (Wenhold 1936:13).

For approximately a century and a half, the Guale were in contact with Spain and her representatives. Spain at this time was one of the great world powers, and she laid claim to much of the New World. The Guale, along with other Indians of La Florida, were but one of the hundreds of groups of native peoples with which the Spanish had to deal. Yet Spain's policy towards the Guale was radically different from that followed in the centers of high aboriginal culture in Middle America and Peru. Unfortunately, the Guale were viewed as being on the periphery of the Spanish empire. They had no gold and they were pagans, but they were living on the Bahama Straits. Therefore, they were worthy of attention, and it became painfully apparent by 1763 that they had deserved more.

At the time of the first Spanish contact and for a time thereafter, the Guale were a coastal people whose economy was centered on the tidal waters where they derived a subsistence from fishing. Agriculture and hunting were of relatively minor importance. The dead were placed in burial mounds which, together with mortuary temples, took a place in the overall religious complex. This religious complex, in turn, was part of the pan-southeastern pattern of the Southern Cult.

The people lived a semi-sedentary life, given to seasonal movements between their fields and their fishing and hunting grounds. Their houses were not large and, in the rather mild climate of the coastal area, served only as shelters. Large communal buildings functioned as temples and council houses. Their social organization seems to have paralleled that of their linguistic relatives, the Creeks. Their tools, weapons, and ornaments in general probably could have been duplicated among many of the other groups living in the immediate southeastern area.

The arrival of the Spanish naturally wrought many changes, although the form these changes took is surprising. The white man's efforts were directed primarily toward the nonmaterial aspects of the native culture, and the changes which took place elsewhere were only incidental and, for the most part, accidental. The priests sought to improve the Indians' souls, not their hunting skill. Thus, it is not surprising to find the Indians using much the same technology, tools, and raw materials when the Spanish left Georgia as they were when de Ayllón attempted his ill-starred colony in the sixteenth century. The basic modifications of the aboriginal culture were in those institutions centering about the nonmaterial elements of society. The mission program was effective in channeling the formal religious patterns from aboriginal to those embracing the Christian church of sixteenth-century Spain. Much that was aboriginal was merely reoriented in the process. Attempts were made to modify certain facets of the social structure, but they were only partially successful in this. Such changes were necessary before the missionary efforts were effective, and most of the Indians became at least nominal Christians. Changes were also deemed a requisite to the ultimate dominion of the Church over the natives in the matter of economic and settlement patterns. Here, too, the old forms seem to have yielded.

Yet, in spite of changes and attempted changes in purely nonmaterial matters, the Spanish made only halfhearted efforts or, in most cases, no effort at all to influence the technology, tools, dress, etc., of the Indians. No trade was carried on, no guns allowed, and there were only pitiful gestures on the part of the Spanish to teach the Indians skills. Spanish contact was reflected dimly in pot manufacture and in the substitution of the iron hoe for its conch shell counterpart, but only a handful of beads and no gun flints, rifles, mirrors, brass or silver ornaments, or white clay pipes ever found their way into Indian hands. These were the things that gave England superiority. With the exception of Spanish ceramics, there is an almost total absence of trade material from Guale sites in Georgia. Thus, the Guale continued almost unchanged in material culture throughout the Spanish contact period. This would seem to be contrary to "the general anthropological induction that the non-material culture of a people is much the more resistant to change ... (and) that those aspects of material culture which have persisted at about the aboriginal level tend strongly to be associated with ritual activity (Kluckhohn 1942:197).

Much more must be known about the Guale before accurate and final conclusions regarding them and their relationships with the Spanish can be drawn. It is almost certain that further archeological work and documents as yet undiscovered in the Archives of the Indies can provide some of the answers.

REFERENCES

Adair, James.
1775. *The History of the American Indians.* London: E. and C. Dilly.
Barcia Carballido y Zúñiga, Andrés González de.
1951. *Chronological History of the Continent of Florida.* Translated by Anthony Kerrigan from the original Spanish edition of 1723. Gainesville: University of Florida Press.
Caldwell, Joseph R., and Catherine McCann.
1941. *Irene Mound Site, Chatham County, Georgia.* Athens: University of Georgia Press.
Caldwell, Sheila.
n.d. Excavations at Ft. King George. Manuscript, Georgia Historical Commission, Atlanta.
Dickinson, Jonathan.
1946. *Jonathan Dickinson's Journal.* Edited by Evangeline W. and Charles McLean Andrews. New Haven: Yale University Press.
Garcia, Genaro.
1902. *Dos Antiguas Relaciones de la Florida.* Tip. y lit. de J. Aguilar vera y Comp. (S. en C.), Mexico.
Garcilaso de la Vega.
1951. *The Florida of the Inca.* Translated and edited by John Varner and Jeanette Varner. Austin: University of Texas Press.
Geiger, Maynard.
1936. *The Early Franciscans in Florida and Their Relation to Spain's Colonial Effort.* Washington: George Washington University Press.
1940. *Biographical Dictionary of the Franciscans in Spanish Florida and Cuba (1528–1841).* Franciscan Studies 21. Paterson, N.J.: St. Anthony's Guild Press.
Kluckhohn, Clyde.
1942. The Navahos in the Machine Age. *Technology Review* 44:178–80, 194–97.
Larson, Lewis H., Jr.
1955. Unusual Figurine from the Georgia Coast. *Florida Anthropologist* 8:75–81.
Lorant, Stefan, ed.
1946. *The New World: The First Pictures of America.* New York: Duell, Sloan, and Pearce.
Moore, Clarence B.
1897. Certain Aboriginal Mounds of the Georgia Coast. *Journal of the Academy of Natural Sciences of Philadelphia,* 11:4–138.
Oré, Luís Gerónimo de.
1936. *The Martyrs of Florida (1513–1616).* Edited by Maynard Geiger. Franciscan Studies 18. New York: J. F. Wagner.
Serrano y Sanz, Manuel, ed.
1912. *Documentos de la Florida y Luisiana, Siglos XVI al XVIII.* Madrid: Librería General de Victoriano Suárez.
Speck, Frank G.
1907. The Creek Indians of Taskigi Town. *American Anthropological Association, Memoirs,* no. 2, pt. 11, pp. 99–164.

Swanton, John R.
1922. *Early History of the Creek Indians and Their Neighbors.* Bureau of American Ethnology Bulletin 73.
1928. *Social Organization and Social Usages of the Indians of the Creek Confederacy.* Bureau of American Ethnology, 42d Annual Report, pp. 23–472.
1946. *The Indians of the Southeastern United States.* Bureau of American Ethnology Bulletin 137.
Waring, Antonio J., Jr.
1968. The Southern Cult and Muskhogean Ceremonial. In *The Waring Papers,* edited by Stephen Williams, pp. 30–69. Athens: University of Georgia Press.
Wenhold, Lucy L., trans.
1936. *A Seventeenth-Century Letter of Gabriel Días Vara Calderón, Bishop of Cuba.* Smithsonian Miscellaneous Collections, vol. 95, no. 16.

The Last of the South Florida Aborigines

William C. Sturtevant

THE cultures of the aborigines of South Florida are known to us from archeology and from documents that derive from the earliest Spanish contacts during the sixteenth century. There were no permanent garrisons or missions in the area, and the Spanish made no efforts to secure or patrol that part of Florida. As a result, almost nothing is known of two centuries of culture change and of the processes of biological and social extinction under the blows of Creek and English raids from the north at the end of the seventeenth and the beginning of the eighteenth centuries. According to an epitaph written in 1775 by Bernard Romans, utilizing local sources of information, Key West and Vaca Key "were the last refuges of the *Caloosa* nation; but even here the water did not protect them against the inroads from the Creeks, and in 1763 the remnant of this people, consisting of about eighty families, left this last possession of their native land, and went to the Havannah" when Spain handed the Floridas over to the British (Romans 1775:291).

New data on the final period of South Florida aboriginal history should be welcome. Documents relating to a Jesuit mission in 1743 in the area which is present-day Miami are in a single *legajo* of the Archivo General de Indias, Seville (formerly catalogued as 58-2-10 [13, 15]—thus they are labeled on the Stetson Collection photostats in the P. K. Yonge Library of Florida History, University of Florida, Gainesville—but now called Santo Domingo 860). Woodbury Lowery mentioned these documents in 1912 (p. 288), citing Torres Lanzas (1900:109–10), and there are typed abstracts in the files of the Florida

Ethnohistoric Survey and the Catholic Historical Survey of Florida in the P. K. Yonge Library of Florida History. The Jesuit historian Francisco Javier Alegre knew of the mission as early as 1764–66 when he was writing his *History of the Province of New Spain of the Company of Jesus,* first published in 1841–42 and republished in 1956–60. Alegre, who did not cite his source, knew some details that are not revealed in the Seville documents. (His brief account was used in Goggin and Sturtevant's 1964 ethnographic sketch of the Calusa.)

The purpose of this essay is to exploit the historical and ethnographic details given in the legajo in Seville. It contains several related documents dated 1743 and 1744, including some transcripts of earlier documents; the important item is the *informe* (printed here as an appendix). This article is based on these documents, except where other sources are cited.[1]

HISTORICAL BACKGROUND

In early February 1743, Juan Francisco de Güemes y Horcasitas, governor and captain-general of Cuba, received a petition purporting to be from three Calusa leaders who were in Havana on one of their frequent visits: *Cacique* Don Pablo Chichi, *Capitan Grande* Don Domingo, and *Sargento Mayor* Sandino (or Fandino). This document, written in good Spanish, provided no ethnographic information—not even any local color—but demonstrated accurate knowledge of the bureaucratic practices of the colonial government and the church. Evidently it was written by someone other than the three Indians. It is a request that missionaries be sent to the Florida Keys (*Cayos*) to provide religious instruction. It was noted that similar requests had been made earlier. In addition to the religious arguments, it was claimed that the Indians of the keys had welcomed fishermen and other Spaniards who visited them. There were willing missionaries already available in Havana, and the royal treasury always had supported missions "ever since the Indies were conquered." To provide a clinching precedent, a copy was enclosed of a royal order of October 10, 1728, in which Phillip V remonstrated with the Bishop of Durango for delay in providing the missionaries requested by the Upper Pimas and ordered that Jesuits be sent at the expense of the viceroy of New Spain.

1. Angelina López Fuentes of Seville prepared a typewritten transcript of the documents. Her transcript of the informe has been checked and revised by comparing it with a microfilm of the original.

Immediately on receipt of the petition, the governor consulted with the bishop of Cuba, Jamaica, and Florida, the rector of the Jesuit college in Havana, the royal commissary (who was also in charge of ship construction), and the counsellor of the Audiencia of Santo Domingo. This group cited royal orders of December 13, 1730, February 22, 1734, and August 21, 1735, which directed that Florida Indians should be settled in Cuba and there indoctrinated; the group pointed out that sending missionaries to the keys would be a different and more costly proposition. They authorized expenditure of funds from the royal treasury to support an expedition consisting of two Jesuits from the college, along with one servant and, as pilot, Captain Lucas Gomes who was "universally loved and respected by the Indians" and "like a father, because of the good services he has always provided them." The Jesuits were to report on the number and attitude of the Indians and the nature of the place and to make recommendations to the Crown for further action. The college was short of personnel, and it was not until June 2, 1743, that the rector was able to appoint Fathers Joseph Xavier de Alaña and Joseph María Mónaco as the priests chosen for the expedition.[2]

In a report to the court, Governor Güemes y Horcasitas set forth the arguments for sending missionaries to the keys rather than trying to settle Florida Indians in Cuba. The latter had been the policy, he said, since 1704 when the cacique of Key West (*Cayo de Guesos*) and other Indians had arrived in Cuba, where all or most of them had died. In 1710, he recalled, 280 Florida Indians had arrived in Cuba with the hereditary cacique of the Calusa (*de Carlos*), the Calusa capitan grande, the caciques of Jove, Maimi, Tancha, Muspa, and Rio Seco, and the principal chief (*cacique principal*) who was baptized Felipe. Felipe, three other caciques, and nearly two hundred Indians soon died of sickness. The survivors were scattered until they returned to the keys in 1716 or 1718. In 1732, some others fled from the keys, sending their children ahead, and went to Jagua Bay (Bahía

---

2. Burrus (1967:43–45; Alegre 1960:399) identifies these two men as Giuseppe Saverio Alagna, who was born in 1707 in Palermo, became a Jesuit in 1722, went to Mexico in 1730, and worked for twenty-six years in the college at Havana, where he died in 1767; and José María Mónaco, who was born in 1704 in Naples, became a Jesuit in 1720, was a missionary in Nayarit in 1737, went to the residency in León in 1741 and worked in the one in Havana from 1743 until the Jesuit expulsion in 1767, and died in 1774. Alegre was acquainted with Alaña in Havana from 1755 to 1762—he learned Italian from him (Burrus 1967:43)—and may well have known Mónaco there at the same time. That, presumably, explains the details he was able to include in his *History*. (The expedition is described in Alegre 1960:397–401.)

de Cienfuegos), Cuba. This policy obviously had not been a success. Not only could the Indians be more readily converted in the keys, the governor argued, but there was a potential "harvest of souls in the copious number of children who die" there. Furthermore there were other important reasons in favor of this plan. Even as pagans the Keys Indians succored shipwrecked Spaniards and chastized their English enemies. The governor cited examples of the English ship *Tiger* which was lost in the Tortugas, and the Indians' killing twelve men from an English launch and sloop they had surprised. They had also used arms provided by Spaniards to defend Spanish sailors against the English in 1738 and 1742, and they were friendly to the many Spanish fishermen visiting their territory. Furthermore, the governor believed that the Keys Indians, together with their friends and allies, the adjacent Maimies, would, if Christianized and pacified, form a bulwark against the barbarous Indians to the north.

Fathers Alaña and Mónaco left Havana on June 24. On the following day, as reported by Alegre, they cast anchor at Key West, where they were forced to remain because of contrary winds and because they sighted an English brigantine. Father Alaña, trained in mathematics, took advantage of the delay to make detailed observations of the keys, which he recorded on maps. While there, a Spaniard fishing at Cayo Frances informed them that the Indians had gone to Santaluz to celebrate a peace they had recently concluded with the Indians living there. The Santaluces, according to the informant, were planning to sacrifice a little girl in honor of the occasion. Distressed, the Jesuits sent a Spaniard in a small canoe with a letter imploring the Santaluz chief to desist, and he acceded to this plea.

The Spanish fathers finally reached their destination at the mouth of the Miami River on July 13. The priests erected a hut (*choza*), where they celebrated mass on St. Ignatius Day, according to Alegre. Father Alaña reported that he and his colleague proposed to name the settlement "el Pueblo de Santa Maria de Loreto" (after the famous pilgrimage center in Italy). Alegre describes the wooden fort that was built there with the help of the sailors and Indians. In the shape of an equilateral triangle measuring twenty-four yards (*varas*) on a side, it had stone mortars in the corner bastions which dominated the settlement, the river, and the path from the interior, with a surrounding embankment, ditch, and stockade. The Spanish flag was raised on August 8, 1743.

By September 9, Father Alaña had returned to Havana in the galley *Santa Ysabel*, whose commander had agreed to leave behind twelve soldiers and a corporal to protect Father Mónaco. The latter would remain until the decision of the Crown was known. Forwarding Father Alaña's report to Madrid, the governor announced that he had reprimanded the commander for this action and had ordered the return of Mónaco and the soldiers. Alegre adds that the fort was razed to deny it to the English and their allies, the Uchizas (i.e., the Creeks). The governor felt that the methods proposed by the Jesuits for establishing a mission would be very costly and would not be likely to succeed, due to the mobility of the Indians and the necessity to fortify and garrison the place against the English.

Fathers Alaña and Mónaco had not been well received by the Keys Indians, who denied having asked for them in Havana. The natives threatened to kill Captain Gomes, whom they blamed for the coming of the priests. They distrusted the black servant Manuel Hernandez since, with his accurate knowledge of the country, he could reveal to the Spaniards their hiding places. They would permit the establishment of a mission (according to Alegre because, otherwise, the Spaniards might leave without distributing the clothing, food, axes, knives, and other things sent by the governor). However, conditions were placed on this agreement. The cacique denied the king's dominion over his territory and required tribute for allowing a church to be built or Spaniards to settle on his land. The Indians demanded food, rum, and clothing from the Spaniards, without laboring in return. They rejected burlap as being suitable only to clothe blacks. They refused to abandon their "superstitions," and they refused to allow their children to be punished by missionary teachers. The plan proposed by the Jesuits required, as protection against the Uchises, the building of a redoubt or stockade, to be garrisoned for several years with twenty-five soldiers. These troops would help destroy the native idols, serve as sentinels to keep the Indians from running away at night, protect the missionaries, punish the Indians for drunkenness, control the rum trade, keep peace among the local Indian groups, and protect them against the Uchises raiders from the north. A settlement of Spanish families would be established to grow food for both Spaniards and Indians, to teach agriculture to the Indians, and to provide a Spanish presence in a dangerous area which gave signs of productivity in agriculture and naval stores and which in ten or twelve years might supplant the settlement at St. Augustine that was so difficult to support. Finally, two ships would be required, one for trips to Havana and the other to permit the missionaries to minister to outlying and temporary Indian settlements.

When this report was read by the Council of the Indies, it was not difficult for the councillors to decide, on February 14, 1744, that the proposed mission was both costly and impractical: "Thus, given the circumstances, one can judge that this reduction is not now according to God's will, and there are many other regions in which these religious can exercise their apostolic ministry and with more hope of fruitful results than could be promised in this conquest, so it does not have to be attempted now." The recall of the mission was approved. The governor and bishop were directed to pay particular attention to the good treatment of Keys Indians who might come to Cuba subsequently, in order to convert them and to "keep them friendly and in some manner subordinate to us without inclination towards our enemies."

Five years later, in July 1748, an English sloop returning to New England with a cargo of logwood from the Bay of Honduras ran aground five leagues off Cape Florida. About sixty Indians came out in some twenty canoes, shot to death eleven men aboard, and took as prisoner Briton Hammon, a black man from Marshfield, Massachusetts, whose captivity narrative (Hammon 1760) supplies all that is known of the incident. The Indians, threatening in "broken English" to kill him also, took him to their "hutts" where they watched him closely but did not mistreat him. He was fed "boil'd Corn, which was what they often eat themselves." After five weeks Hammon was rescued by a Spanish schooner passing on its way from St. Augustine to Havana. His captors followed and arrived in Havana four days after he did, demanding that the governor return their prisoner. The governor, however, ransomed Hammon for ten dollars. As Professor John M. Goggin of the University of Florida pointed out in his oral testimony before the United States Indian Claims Commission in 1961, these events imply that Spain lacked sovereignty over the South Florida Indians at this date.

ETHNOGRAPHY

Briton Hammon, in his account, gives a few minor fragments of cultural data: the aborigines of the Miami area in 1748 lived in huts, ate boiled corn, had canoes in which they could sail to Havana, and knew a few words of English. Considerably more ethnographic data, as of 1743, is in the informe written by Father Alaña, supplemented by some details he provided to Alegre. According to this information, at the mouth of the Miami River (as it was later named) lived about 180 people, half of them children, in a settlement "without huts." These "Indians of the Keys" were the survivors of three distinct tribes or "nations": Cayos, Carlos, and Boca Raton. (To judge by the names, the first were the Keys Indians proper, the second the Calusa who originally had inhabited Mound Key in Estero Bay, and the last were from the present-day Miami Beach area.) Alegre notes that continual war with the Uchises (allies of the English) and drunkenness had reduced the whole "nation" of the keys' "islanders" to only a few families. The site at the Miami River was not occupied throughout the year, according to Alaña. The Indians did not farm but subsisted on fish ("even the women and children live more in the sea than on land") and on a few wild fruits. The latter varied seasonally, and the people followed them by leaving their Miami River location at the end of September and moving to Pejchel Key and the northwest coast (perhaps Estero Bay?), whence they were transported by fishermen from Havana. After that season, they moved to Vaca Key.

The priests were told that three other "nations" lived [respectively?] one, two, and four days' journey into the mainland: the Maymies, the Santaluses, and the Maiacas. There were very few of these natives remaining; the total population for all three was estimated at only one hundred or a few more. Alegre used the spellings Maimíes, Santaluces, and Mayacas and reported that the caciques of four or five settlements of these and a few other nations visited the missionaries soon after they arrived at Miami.

According to Alaña, most of the adult men he met could understand and speak Spanish moderately well; they had learned the language through trading contacts with sailors from Havana. The Indians liked rum, which they acquired from the shipwrecks near the keys and the coast and from Cuban fishermen who paid them with spirits for help in fishing. They had even exchanged most of the guns they had been given for rum. Immoderate drunkenness created problems, Alaña reported.

According to Alegre each settlement (*ranchería*) of the Keys Indians had a separate chief, or *casique,* with an assistant for each whom the Indians referred to as *capitan grande,* and a priest they called *obispo* (i.e., bishop). Alaña reported that the cacique and his children were worshipped by smoking or fumigating supervised by the obispo. At their deaths and at the deaths of other leaders, children were sacrificed to serve them in the afterlife. (Alegre reported that one or two children were killed to accompany a cacique.) This custom is not inconsistent with the very high value that was placed on children. The

Spaniards were surprised that children were not required to show respect to their elders and were even allowed to slap them with impunity, while parents would cut and burn themselves to demonstrate distress at an accident befalling a child.

At the installation of a new obispo, the candidate ran around continually for three days, only drinking (not eating at all? or, drinking rum?), so that he fainted many times. They believed that in this way he died and was revived as a sanctified being. Alegre reported that the obispo could call the wind by whistling and divert storms with various cries. There was another religious functionary who divined events regarding future and distant matters, and who, while he was decorated with paint and feathers, cured the sick by running about and gesturing over them.

Although Alaña claimed that the Indians believed the soul did not survive the body—"thus swallowing the absurdity of being no better than beasts"—he also reported a mortuary cult. The dead were greatly feared, and there was a taboo on their names. Food, tobacco, and herbs were offered to them daily, and graves were covered with mats and sprinkled. Guardians were stationed in the cemeteries, which were located apart from the settlement due to a fear of the dead, but were nevertheless visited on "pilgrimages." In the graveyard there was a temple which contained two "idols." The main one, called *Sipi,*[3] was a small board on which appeared a fish and other figures shaped like tongues. Alegre is a bit more specific on this matter: the figure was a very gross and badly formed depiction of a barracuda (*picuda*) crossed by a harpoon and surrounded with various small tongue-like figures. Evidently associated with this image was a long pole, with silver taken by the Indians (from wrecks, apparently) buried at its foot. This pole was decorated with flowers and feathers for celebrations. Also in the temple were "very ugly masks" for the fiestas of the main image. The men painted themselves daily "in honor of the principal idol." Otherwise, both men and women were "naked except for the most necessary minimum." The other temple image was "the god of the graveyard," which was a "horribly good representation" of a bird's head, carved in pine. According to Alegre, the graves were decorated

3. This single item increases the known lexicon of south Florida languages by 10 percent. But unfortunately it seems no more useful for comparative purposes than the ten words with meanings given by Fontaneda (1945) that were struggled with unsuccessfully by Buckingham Smith, Albert S. Gatschet, and John R. Swanton. The languages of aboriginal south Florida remain of unknown affiliation.

"with turtles, barracudas, and other animals, tobacco and similar things, in order to keep [the dead] content."

After discussing religion with the Indians, Father Alaña was impressed with the strength of their belief in "superstitions" and with their ridicule of the "contrary truths" which he tried to explain to them. They denied God the Creator, claiming that everything makes itself, denied that God could prevent men from acting as they wished, and "they multiplied the Divinity oddly."

MAP

There are two known versions of Father Alaña's map. The one reproduced here is in the Archivo General de Indias, filed under *Mapas y Planos México* 147; earlier it was kept with documents now in *Santo Domingo* 860. It measures 40.5 x 28.75 centimeters. It has been reproduced nearly full size by Burrus (1967, vol. 2, no. 18), quite legibly but without a transcription of the names that appear on it. The bits missing in the central tear in our recent photograph, in Burrus' reproduction and in the Stetson Collection photostat, are preserved in a full-sized tracing received by the Map Division of the Library of Congress in 1911, which is now kept in the Geography and Map Division, Library of Congress (Vault, Florida, Florida Keys, 1743).

Another version of the same map, measuring 39 × 36 centimeters, is attributed to Alaña and is in the Servicio Geográfico del Ejército, Madrid (LM 8ª, Iª, a, Núm. 128). This one has been well reproduced, accompanied by a transcription of the place names that appear on it, as No. 52 in Servicio Geográfico e Histórico del Ejército (1953).

The redrawn version printed here has been prepared from a modern photograph of the A.G.I. map, with the missing pieces restored from the Library of Congress tracing. The place names have been transcribed from the photograph and the tracing, assisted by transcriptions from the original made by Angelina López Fuentes, and by comparison with the published transcriptions from the Madrid version. In the following list the numbers, keyed to the redrawn map, indicate the positions of the legends. Following the number, the first version is a direct transcript of the legend; then, in parentheses, the version on the Madrid map; next, within quotation marks, an expanded and / or modernized spelling of the legend on the Seville map; finally, in brackets, a translation, modern identification, or remark.

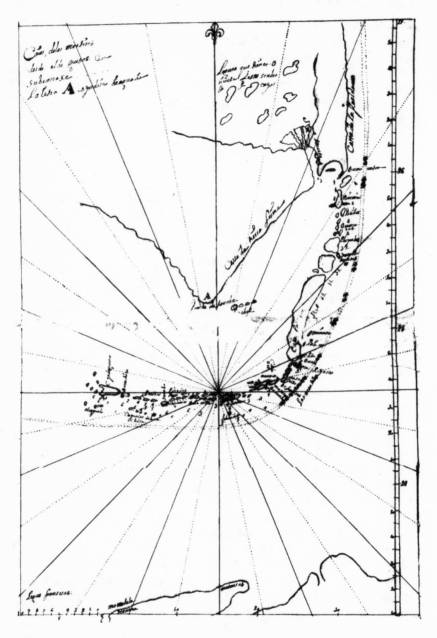

Fig. 1. Map of Florida Keys by Joseph Xavier de Alaña S.J., 1743.
Courtesy Archivo General de Indias, Seville.

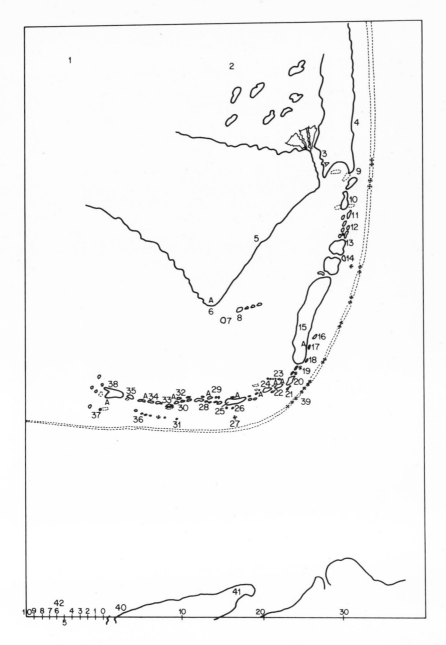

Fig. 2. Father Alaña's map redrawn.

1. Caios, de los martires / desde el de guesos. Con / su braseaxe
_ _ _ _ _ / La letra A es yndises de aguada (Cayos de Los / Martyres)
"Cayos de los Martíres desde el de Huesos con su braceaje. La letra A
es índice de aguada." ["Keys of the Martyrs from that of Bones (i.e.,
Key West), with their depths of water. Watering-stations are indicated
by the letter A." The numerals indicating depths are omitted on re-
drawing.]

2. Laguna que tiene / orisonte y esta senbra / da de cayos (Laguna
q^e haze / Horizonte y esta / sembrada de cayuelos) "Laguna que tiene
horizonte y está sembrada de cayos" ["lake which has a horizon and is
strewn with keys." According to Goggin (1950:19n11), this "is the first
map to indicate the presence and nature of the Everglades."]

3. S M^a de loreto (S. M.ª de Loreto), "Santa María de Loreto"
[legend pertains to a spot on the north shore of the modern Miami
River, probably the site of old Fort Dallas, where the location of the
mission is indicated by a small rectangle and triangle on the Seville
map and by three rectangles on the Madrid map.]

4. Costa de la Florida (Costa de la Florida) ["Florida coast"]

5. Costa de Tierra Firme (Costa de la Tierra firme) ["coast of the
mainland"]

6. Punta de tanche (Punta de Tanche) ["Tanche point," i.e., Cape
Sable]

7. Axi (C. de Axi) "Cayo de Ají" ["pepper key"(?)]

8. C. Pexchel (C. Pexchel) "Cayo Pejchel"

9. Boca raton (Boca raton) [evidently modern Miami Beach]

10. Biscaino (C. Biscaino) "Cayo Vizcaíno" [Key Biscayne]

11. Paridas (Paridas)

12. Mascaras (Mascaras) ["masks"]

13. Playuelas (Playuelas) ["small beaches"]

14. res^{ga} de las tetas (restinga de las Tetas) ["tits shoal"]

15. Cayo Largo (Cayo Largo) ["long key," i.e., Key Largo]

16. escriuano (C. Escrivano) "Cayo Escribano" ["secretary key"]

17. Palomo (C. Palomo) "Cayo Palomo" ["cock pigeon key"]

18. C. de tabanos (C. de Tavanos) "Cayo de Tábanos" ["horsefly
key"; Madrid map has an anchor here.]

19. Boca de Yerro (Bocas de Guerrero) "Boca de Hierro" or "Bocas
de Guerrero" ["iron" or "soldier entrance"]

20. mate / Veixo (Mate.^{e} Viexo) "Matacumbe Viejo" ["old
Matacumbe," i.e., Upper Matecumbe Key]

21. C. Franses (C. Franzes) "Cayo Francés" ["French key"]

22. matacumbe nuebo (Mat.ᵉ Nuevo) "Matacumbe Nuevo" ["new Matacumbe," i.e. Lower Matecumbe Key; the Madrid map adds a cross here, perhaps to indicate a visit by Father Alaña.]

23. Cᵒ de leñas (C. de leña) "Cayo de Leña" ["firewood key"]

24. Biboras (Vivoras) "Cayo de Víboras" ["snake key"; Madrid map adds a cross here.]

25. Bacas (C. de Vacas) "Cayo de Vacas" ["cow key," i.e., Vaca Key; Madrid map adds a cross here.]

26. Sonbrero (Sombrero) ["hat"; modern Sombrero Key]

27. Labandera (Lavandera) ["washerwoman"; a name with no island shown, for, as a legend on a 1768 map—number 54 in Servicios 1953—explains, this "tip of the keys" was simply a rock that was always visible.]

28. Baia onda (Bayo honda) "Bahía Honda" ["deep harbor," i.e., modern Bahia Honda key]

29. (Pinales) ["pines"; the legend does not appear on the Seville map.]

30. Caguamas (Caguamas)

31. (Cayuelo de Caguamas) ["little Caguamas key"; the legend does not appear on the Seville map.]

32. Pinales (Pinales) ["pines"; the Madrid map has two keys named thus, one of which may be modern Big Pine Key or both may be the earlier Pine Islands.]

33. Sambo (Sambo) "Cayo Sambo"

34. Pineiros (Piñeiros) [This is shown as Piñero Grande on Liguera Antayo (1742), and so may represent modern Big Pine Key.]

35. Boca chica (Boca chica) ["little entrance"; modern Boca Chica key]

36. Cayuelos de boca chica (Cayuelos de Boca chica) ["little keys of Boca Chica"]

37. el cayuelo (el Cayuelo) ["the little key"]

38. Cayo de guesos (C. de guessos) "Cayo de Huesos" ["bone key," i.e., Key West; Madrid map adds a cross, probably to show Father Alaña's visit that began June 25, 1743.]

39. Los martires (Los Martyres) "Los Martíres" ["the martyrs," i.e., the Florida Keys]

40. Morro de la Hauana [Havana, Cuba]

41. matansas [Matanzas, Cuba]

42. Leguas fransesas (Leguas franzesas) ["French leagues"]

APPENDIX

The informe of Father Alaña in *Santo Domingo* legajo 860 is a clerk's copy, which appears on leaves 10–16 of a transcript that has a title page reading "Año de 1743. Thestimonio de los autos sobre hauer impetrado los Yndios naturales principales De los Cayos de la Florida el s[an]to Baptismo, y que para su logro y lo demas que exponen, Pasen a ellos Ministros correspondientes; Y lo que en el asumpto se ha providenciado. Gou[ier]no de la Hau[an]a." The informe reads as follows:

Ynforme que Presentan a el Exc[elentisi]mo señor d[o]n Juan Fran-[cisc]o Guemes de Horcasitas theniente General de los Reales ex[ercit]os Gov[ernado]r y Cap[ita]n Gen[era]l de la Ciudad de la Hauana, e ysla de Cuba los Padres Joseph Maria Monaco, y Joseph Xavier Alaña de la Compañia de Jesuz sobre el estado en que han hallado a los Yndios de la Florida, austral y sus Cayos con lo que jusgan nesesario para su constante Reduccion = Exc[elentisi]mo señor: Salidos de la Hauana en Veinte, y quatro de Junio de este presente año de mill setecientos quarenta y tres No pudimos hasta el dia trese de Julio Dar fondo en la Voca del Rio / [10r] que Queda como Dos leguas al S[ur] O[este] de boca ratones en donde se camino supimos que se hallauan los Yndios de los Cayos, ya por el poco favor de los Vientos, ya por el extravio que nos causo vn Vergantin, que nos Dio Casa, y supimos tarde hera Español.

Hallamos a la boca de d[ic]ho Rio vn Pueblo esto es sin chosas en q[ue] Vivian de monton hasta Ciento, y ochenta personas, en hombres mugeres, y niños los que hazen como la mitad de esse numero Los varones de hedad perfecta por la mayor parte entienden y hablan mediamente el Castellano, por el Comercio frecuente con los Barqueros de la Hauana, y todos son Reliquias de tres naciones, Cayos Carlos, y Boca Raton. Fuera de estos averiguamos que de otras tres naciones Maymies, Santaluses, y Maiacas que moran, a vna, Dos, y quatro Jornadas en la tierra firme, se podran agregar otras Cien Almas o pocas mas. Los Yndios de los Cayos segun comunmente les llaman o del Pueblo de santa Maria de Loreto segun deseamos se llamen en adelante, tienen prinsipalm[en]te tres mansiones, en que Reparten el año: La de d[ic]ho Rio en que perseveran hasta fines de Septiembre La de Cayo Pexchel, y costa del N[or]O[este] a donde los lleuan los pescadores de la Hauana, y por vltimo la de Cayo de Vacas: La Rason potisima de esta ynconstancia es su indolencia supina: pues sin querer cultibar la tierra se contentan con el Pescado, y poca fruta silvestre que los paraxes d[ic]hos de por si subministran sucecsivamente.

El resevimiento que nos hisieron fue bien seco, y hauiendonos quitado con intolerables porfias el basti/[10v]mento para ellos destinado, declararon abiertam[en]te el disgusto de n[uest]ra ida hasta negar Repetidas vezes con evidente falsedad el que hauian pedido en la Hav[an]a Padres q[ue] los hisiesen Christianos: Desian no obstante que querian serlo de temor q[ue] V[uestra] E[xcelencia] los castigase. Mas esto de ser christianos no tiene en voca de ellos otra significacion sino resevir la Agua Sacramentar con estas condicciones: Que sin trauajar ellos los ha de sustentar el Rey n[uest]ro señor, los ha de vestir, y no de cañamasos, que lo abominan como propio de Negros siendo assi que andan desnudos hombres y mugeres esepto lo mas presiso; Les ha de subministrar aguardiente alegando exemplos de la Florida: se han de quedar en su punto las superticiones, de que estan llenos; y por vltimo no se ha de vssar castigo en la enseñada de los niños, y fue esta la primera Condicion que en nombre de todos nos propuso el Casique. Ni es de admirar pues la passion que para los Hijos tienen llega al extremo de sufrirles bofetadas, y de quemarse, o cortarse electivam[en]te por muestra de dolor de hauer susedido otro tanto por contingencia a el hijo sin que de el desfruten jamas Señal alguna de reuerencia.

El proponer atrebidamente estas condicciones hase de estar persuadidos que en admitir de qualquier modo N[uest]ra Religion Nos hasen favor tanto que llegaron a desirnos, que de hauerse de fabricar /[11r] Yglesia en su Pueblo abremos de pagar a los Yndios el Hornar, y de haverse pasar Españoles a poblar abran de pagar a el Casique tributo de las tierras que suyas son, y no del Rey de España: Palabras nasidas de perversos Colaterales; porque en el Casique hemos reconosido buenas ynclinaciones.

Los herrores, Ydolatrias, y Supertisiones de esta gente son de lo mas brutal: mas lo que admira es el apegatenasisimo con que todo lo mantienen, y la irrision que hasen de las verdades contrarias, y sus rasones. Vimos dos idolos: el prinsipal es vna pequeña tabla con la Ymagen de vn Peje, y otras figuras como de Lenguas: esta por hauerla Pisado vn dia vno de los de nosotros, a fin de quitarles experimentalmente el temor de los Desastres que pensavan se seguirian a su menor desprecio la han escondido, y sin violencia tenemos poca esperanza de Arrancarsela el otro Ydolo que es el Dios de el Sementerio teatro de sus mas frequentes superticiones era vna cabeza de pajaro esculpida en Pino, la que en lo orrible representaua bien su original, y la que hecha pedasos quemamos juntamente con la choza que tenian por Yglesia quando nos parecio se haria sin Aluoroto de los Yndios por tener sobre si vna Galera armada q[ue] estubo de paso viniendo de la Florida: Assi sucedio; mas no sin muchas señas de dolor, y aun gemidos, y lagrimas de las Mugeres.

Tenian en d[ic]ha Yglecia feisimas Mascaras destinadas para las fiestas de el Ydolo prinsipal alli colocado / [11v] q[ue] llaman *Sipi* con vn palo largo q[ue] en ciertos dias enfloran, empluman, y Celebran, a cuyo pie hauia enterrada alguna plata q[ue] los mismos Yndios Sacaron. Tienen vn Yndio q[ue] llaman Obispo Consagrado con tres dias de Carreras en q[ue] solo bebe hasta desfalleser muchas vezes; y piensan q[ue] el tal muere, y resusita Santificado. Ay otro Yndio q[ue] afirman Ser Bruxo, y como Dios terminos p[ara] ellos sinonimos: A este consultan lo futuro, lo distante, lo venidero: A este tienen por Medico del Lugar, y son sus remedios grandes Ahullidos, y ademanes, q[ue] sobre el Enfermo hase Emplumandose, y pintandose horriblemente: Es a la verdad hombre q[ue] tiene en su Aspecto No se que señas de Instrumento diabolico. Veneran al Casique, y a sus hijos con sahumerios en q[ue] interbiene el obispo, y a sus Muertes, y de otros prinsipales Matan Niños para q[ue] los bayan a servir Crueldad q[ue] practican aun en las pases, la q[ue] estorbamos hauiendo Savido en Cayo franses q[ue] hauian de celebrarlas con d[ic]hos Yndios Embiando por delante en vn Cayuco a un Español con Carta para el casique.

Tienen grande pavor a los Muertos, y su Efecto parece el no Sufrir que se les nombren, y ofreserles Cotidianamente Comestibles, tavaco, Yerbas, Cubriendo con esteras y regando las Sepulturas, y aun Manteniendo guardias en el Sementerio q[ue] frequen / [12r]tan con romerias, y tienen algo distante de el Pueblo de temor no les hagan mal los defuntos: sin que fuese posible Conseguir Nos entregasen el Cadaver de vna Niña que por riesgo de Muerte baptisamos sino q[ue] la enterraron con los demas Yndios Gentiles, y con sus Seremonias, Y para enterrar otro niño baptisado con los Vistos Christianos fue nesesaria alguna violencia, en medio de esto tenazmente afirman que no sobre viven las Almas humanas a los Cuerpos tragando el absurdo de no ser ellos mejores que las bestias, Viendose de las rasones mas fuertes, y bolviendo las espaldas quando se les recombiene con sus mismas herradas practicas, q[ue] acabamos de referir.

Todos los dias se pintan los hombres costumbre que hemos aberiguado ser practicada ahorra del Ydolo prinsipal que veneran a el paso que menos precian el Dios de los Christianos contra quien han proferido blafemias [sic] q[ue] nos han abrasado ya, negandole la Creacion de las Cossas, y afirmado q[ue] de si mismas se hazen, ya negandole el poder ympedir a los hombres la Execucion de lo q[ue] quieren, ya multiplicando Extrañamente la Divinidad.

En fin Exc[elentisi]mo señor dejando por abrebiar otras frequentes superticiones a los hallamos igualmente apegados, como lo son todos los Yndios Americanos en vista de la dobles Espesial, Osadia, y obstina / [12v]cion que estos añaden tenemos por nesesario se apoye la conquista de sus Almas en el medio mismo, que lo ha sido para el resto de las Americas: Esto es que si quiera por algunos años le acompañe a los Misioneros la Escolta de veinte, y cinco soldados de costumbres selectas; con cuyo resguardo se podra vssar el rigor nesesario para desarraigar hasta las reliquias de la Superticion, como es asolumptamente [sic] nesesario a fin de que no la aprendan los Niños, sin peligro de extremos gorrosos a los Misioneros, pero muy notorios a los mismos Yndios o de vna fuga repentina como otra vez practicaron, y esta nos insinuaron ser de su yntencion: la que no se podra ympedir sin Centinelas de noche, y la que es facill[is]imo execute vna gente Vaga, y que mas vive en la mar que en la tierra hasta los Niños, y las mugeres.

En el d[ic]ho paraxe a la Voca del Rio se podra formar vn reducto, o estacada con poquisimo costo por hallarse a la mano lo nesesario; sin que pueda ser batida desde la mar por estar la Ensenada quando mas enbraza de fondo, y la Voca del Rio en quatro palmos aunq[ue] este baxa alla dentro, has dies, y dose palmos: N[uest]ros Yndios tienen pocas Armas de fuego que las q[ue] V[uestra] E[xcelencia] les dio. Las han trocado casi todas por Aguard[iente] / [13r] fuera de que han dado muestras de temor al soldado español. Los Vchises, o Yndios brabos de la Florida hallaron resistencia, si acasso con extrahordinario exfuerzo por ser d[ic]ho Sitio lo mas distante en la tierra firme de sus Provincias yntentaren Dar sobre el Pueblo.

Otra rason nos mueve Exc[elentisi]mo señor a tener por nesesario el auxilio militar; y es la inerrible pacion que tiene esta gente para el Aguardiente. Ha sido quexa quotidiana el no hauerles traido nos han alegado mill rasones que el Diablo les sugiere, nos han llegado a redarguir con el Vino de la santa Misa, y en fin nos han d[ic]ho claro, que sin Aguardiente, ni piden, ni quieren ser Christianos. Por otro lado embriagandose (y susede siempre, que tienen con que, que esperar de ellos moderacion en este es ymprudencia) pierden la poca rason que tienen, y se revisten de vna brutalidad estrabagante; No hay hijo para Padre, ni muger para marido echando mano de todas Armas por relacion de quien los ha Visto en sus tierras, en donde parecen de otra espesia, que los que bienen a la Havana, y aun por lo que colegimos por n[uest]ros Ojos vn dia en que embriagandose el Casique Cap[ita]n grande, y otros dos, o tres se siguieron estos efectos. Hablo vno vno de Nosotros, y a n[uest]ros Oidos calumnias atroses: hizieron las Mugeres de los borrachos/[13v] a el monte en que se mantubieron la noche de miedo no las matasen o golpeasen como suelen los maridos: Corrio el Cap[ita]n grande con vna hachuela tras n[uest]ro Negro sin auerle dado este la menor ocacion: profirio el Casique ynjurias contra Lucas Gomes hasta amenazarle con la escopeta. Y por vltimo como en el vino segun se dise esta la verdad descubrieron sus pecho los borrachos, y aun los que no lo estanban, disiendo que tenian intento de matar a d[ic]ho Lucas, y a Manuel Hern[ande]z. Contra estos en otras muchas ocaciones manifestaron odio formal: Miran a Lucas Gomes como causa prinsipal de n[uest]ra ida, y que siendo Pardo los quiere (disen) mandar: indicios claros de que todo el afecto, y subordinaz[io]n que le mostrauan en la Hauana hera superfisial, y ordenado a el baxo intento de cogerle quanto podian. Miran a Manuel como practico de todas sus tierras, y que los a de hallar adonde quiera que huigan: siendo assi que es este hombre, y por d[ic]ha prenda, y por las demas que hemos en el experimentado muy nesesario p[ar]a la conquista: thestimonio que deuemos a la Verdad, y nos arranca la gratitud a el amor, y esmero con que nos han asistido, y ouedesido en cossas importantes a el bien de la Mision, que por no ser este su lugar omitimos.

Voluiendo pues al Aguardiente algo se Estorbara entimando graves penas contra los barqueros en la Havana, y en la Florida; mas fuera de la que los Yndios adquieren, por la perdida annual de embarcaciones en los Cayos, y Costas de la Florida; dificil sera contener / [14r] la codicia de vn pobre pescador que save d[ic]ho liquor el medio principal para que el Yndio le ayude en su pesca, y la de otro qualquiera que sabe dara el Yndio el valor de Cien pesos por vn frasco de Aguardiente En cuya comparacion, nada aprecia, como nos consta por muchos cassos particulares, siendo pues nesesario que no obstantes los exfuersos de los Superiores, y Misioneros haya de hauer borrachos en el Pueblo, es consiguiente la nesesidad del castigo para ympedir los mas perniciosos efectos, y a el vicio su prodominio: lo que ynfiere la nesesidad de auxilio militar, sin el q[ua]l no es aquello practicable sin peores incombenientes pues esto de castigar es cossa nunca practicada entre los Yndios, ni aun por el Casique.

Por vltimo es conducente este auxilio a la concervacion de los Yndios a cada paso pelean estas nacionsillas, y se disminuyen como aseg-
ura la mem[ori]a de el mucho mayor numero, que havia Veinte años
ha, de suerte que si se dejan en sus barbaros estilos a pocos a[ño]s se
habran acauado ya por las Guerrillas, ya por el Aguardiente que
veven hasta reventar, ya por los Niños que matan, ya por los que se
lleuan las Viruelas, a falta de remedio, y ya finalmente por los perecen a
manos de los Vchises en el qual casso caresemos de las vtilidades que a
n[uest]ra Nacion traen estos pocos Yndios, assi por la advercion que
mantienen a los Yngleses como por la devocion a n[uest]ros aunque
solo fundada en el interes.

Otro medio hallamos igualmente nesesario a / [14v] la reduccion de
esta gente, y es que se transporten a poblar la tierra algunas familias
españolas, y aun por vn año vayan vna doz[en]a de forsados a des-
molerla: pues las riueras hasta que de alli a vna milla entran los
Pinales todas son de Arboleda espesa y muchas maderas resias; y por
consiguiente de esto y de lo arriua d[ic]ho hasta que la tierra sub-
ministre alimentos, es presiso mantener no solo a los españoles mas
aun a los Yndios, por lo menos todo el tiempo de el año que por
faltarles en d[ic]ho Pueblo van Vagando por los Cayos los forsados se
piden por que entre los Yndios seran Veinte los que estan hechos a el
trabajo ligero de la pesca; Los demas, ya por prinsipales, ya por Soldados han estado hasta ahora esemptos de el trabajo. No hay duda,
que a estos, y a Aquellos hemos de enseñar a el Cultivo; pero ni la
piedad permite que oprimamos a tales Yndios desde luego; pues esto
por lo menos fuera retraerlos dela religion Christiana: Y si nos Con-
tentamos con el poco a poco que de ellos con vn Moderado rigor se
puede Alcanzar se prolongara notablemente el tiempo en que sera
nesesario sustentarlos de los r[eale]s erarios. Las familias españolas se
piden porque los Yndios son del todo cassi ignorantes de la agricul-
tura que aprenderan agregandose a los n[uest]ros fuera de que la
poblacion de Españoles en d[ic]ho paraxe se reconose vtil porque esta
en medio de los Cayos, y de la costa de la florida: Sitios los mas
apeligrados, y en donde perecen a cada paso / [15r] embarcaciones
n[uest]ras y de otras naciones: La tierra esta llena de Pinales, y teas
vtiles para Brea y Alquitran, y quizas con el tiempo se descubriran
palos de provecho para Nauios: todo lo qual se podra facilmente
conducir por el Rio que atrabiesa los Pinales. hay tambien tierra segun
voz comun admirable para siembras, y Crias de Serdos, y ganado
mayor. Parece en fin capaz de vn Pueblo tal, que con dies, o Dose años
de cultivo arrastre las familias que con tantos sustos, y gastos se man-

tienen en san Augustin de la Florida dejando alli solo el Castillo con su Presidio.

Mas por ahora sera tambien nesesario que su Mag[esta]d mantenga a la micion dos barcos: el vno para los viages a la Hauana, el otro para que el Padre pueda acudir a las administraciones a que fuere llamado: ♦ pues aunque, se proyecta formar el Pueblo en la tierra firme regularm[ent]e haura Yndios dispersos en los Cayos, ya por la pesca, ya por otras ocurrencias.

En Vista de lo referido Exc[elentisi]mo señor tan diverso de lo que en la Hauana, se hauia ideado por informes avidos desde lexos, en vista de lo peligroso q[ue] hera a la micion el que Quedase Padre sin escolta o nos bolviesemos los Dos (que el vno hera nesesario biniese a informar) y en fin por la atencion que / [15v] nos asistio a que fuese accion de V[uestra] E[xcelencia] a continuar, o suspender lo Comensado; Nos determinamos a pedir auxilio a la Galera, y tropa que biniendo de la Florida hubo de esperar algunos Dias en Cayo Viscayno barios atrasos. Con este auxilio cooperando por temor, y buen Arte sin violencia los mismos Yndios en algo Quedo formada en tres dias vna Estacada a la voca del Rio sobre el Pueblo con algunos Pedreros, y dose hombres de guarnicion: Numero que parecio sufisiente mientras se avisaba a V[uestra] E[xcelencia] atento a que se trajeron al mesmo tiempo con maña los mas de los Yndios revoltosos. Logrose tambien en los mismos dias quemarles sin Aluoroto la Yglecia, y aquel Ydolo que pudimos auer a las manos.

Este es Exc[elentisi]mo señor el estado en que Queda la micion que nos Da buena esperanza se lleue a perfeccion con los medios propuestos, o los que V[uestra] E[xcelencia] hallare mas proporcionados De los Yndios eseptos los que como mala leuadura corrompen a los demas a quienes tocan prinsipalmente los Cargos expresados: Los demas muestran alguna docilidad: Los Niños se nos agregauan a porfia para aprender la doctrina en lengua Castellana, aunque varias veses por instigacion de los grandes se nos retiraron. Rason sera reprimir a los que impiden la promulgacion del Evangelio a los que / [16r] con manifiestos Engaños hazen irricion de la nacion Española, y de su Santisima Religion manteniendo casi a n[uest]ra vista la adoracion sacrilega de vnos brutos. No es ya tiempo de sufrir que vnos desnudos despues de hauer ocupado a V[uestra] E[xcelencia] y demas Ministros de S[u] M[agestad] despues de hauer causado graues gastos a los Reales Erarios, con vn no Queremos lo frusten todo. Con los medios propuestos si fueren de la Aprouacion de V[uestra] E[xcelencia] a imitacion de todas casi las Misiones de la America se extirpara la

Ydolatria, y se fundara la Verdadera Religion a Despecho de los Obstinados que por Castigos entenderan lo que por rasones no quieren = Joseph Xauier Alaña de la Compañia de Jesuz.

Es conforme a los Autos preincertos que Originales Quedan en mi poder a que me remito; y el Mapa Exivido por el R[euerendo] P[adre] Joseph Xavier de Alaña de la Compañia de Jesuz va puesto al final de este Ynstrum[en]to y en virtud de lo prevenido en la providencia de nueve del que corre Doy el pres[en]te en la Hauana a veinte y ocho de Septiembre de mill setecientos quarenta y tres años.

Hago mi signo [mark] en thestim[onio] de verdad.

[Signature and rubric:] Miguel de Ayala
es[criba]no m[ayo]r de
Go[bier]no y G[ue]rra;

Damos fee que d[on] Miguel de Ayala de quien este Thestimonio / [16v] esta signado, y firmado Es escriuano mayor de Gov[ier]no y G[ue]rra de esta Plasa e ysla de Cuba por S[u] M[agestad] fiel, Legal, y de Confianza, y como tal vssa, y exerse, y se le Da entera fee, y Credito. Havana, y septiembre Veinte, y ocho de mil setecientos quarenta, y tres años.

[Signatures and rubrics:]

Pedro Ant[onio] de Florencia
es[criba]no R[ea]l.

Manuel Ramirez
es[criba]no R[ea]l.

Cristoual Vianes de Salas
esc[riba]no Pu[bli]co.

REFERENCES

Alegre, Francisco Javier.
 1960. *Historia de la Provincia de la Compañía de Jesús de Nueva España*. Tomo IV: Libros 9-10 (años 1676-1766). [Nueva edición por Ernest J. Burrus S.J. y Felix Zubillaga S.J.] Bibliotheca Instituti Historici S.J. Vol. 17, Rome.
Burrus, Ernest.
 1967. *La obra cartográfica de la Provincia Mexicana de la Compañía de Jesús (1567-1967)*. 2 vols. Colección Chimalistac . . . Serie José Porrua Turanzas, Vols. 1, 2. Madrid: Ediciones José Porrua Turanzas.
Fontaneda, Hernando d'Escalante.
 1945. *Memoir of Do. d'Escalante Fontaneda Respecting Florida, Written in Spain, about the year 1575*. Translated by Buckingham Smith, edited by David O. True. Coral Gables, Fla.: Glade House.
Goggin, John M.
 1950. The Indians and History of the Matecumbe Region. *Tequesta* 10:13-24. (Reprinted on pp. 39-48 of Goggin's *Indian and Spanish: Selected Writings*. Coral Gables: University of Miami Press, 1964.)
Goggin, John M., and William C. Sturtevant.
 1964. The Calusa: A Stratified, Nonagricultural Society (with Notes on Sibling

Marriage). In *Explorations in Cultural Anthropology: Essays in Honor of George Peter Murdock*, edited by Ward H. Goodenough, pp. 179–219. New York: McGraw Hill.

Hammon, Briton.
1760. *A Narrative of the Uncommon Sufferings, and Surprizing Deliverance of Briton Hammon, A Negro Man, Servant to General Winslow, of Marshfield in New-England; who returned to Boston, after having been absent almost Thirteen Years.* Boston: Green & Russell.

Liguera Antayo, Juan de.
1742. Plano de los Cayos de la Flor[i]da. Manuscript map in Biblioteca Nacional, Madrid; photocopy in Geography and Map Division, Library of Congress (Florida, Florida Keys [Reg] 1742), and in Clements Library, Ann Arbor (Karpinski Collection, No. 115).

Lowery, Woodbury.
1912. *A Descriptive List of Maps of the Spanish Possessions within the Present Limits of the United States, 1502–1820.* Edited with notes by Philip Lee Phillips. Washington: Government Printing Office.

Romans, Bernard.
1775. *A Concise Natural History of East and West Florida.* New York: Printed for the Author. (Reprinted in facsimile, with an introduction by Rembert W. Patrick, University of Florida Press, Gainesville, 1962.)

Servicio Geográfico e Histórico del Ejército.
1953. *Cartografía de Ultramar. Carpeta II: Estados Unidos y Canadá, Toponomía de los mapas que la integran, Relaciones de Ultramar.* Madrid: Imprenta del Servicio Geográfico del Ejército.

Torres Lanzas, Pedro.
1900. *Relación descriptiva de los mapas, planos, &c., de México y Floridas existente en el Archivo General de Indias.* Tomo 1. Sevilla: Imp. de El Mercantil.

The Ethno-Archeology of
the Florida Seminole

Charles H. Fairbanks

THE archeology of the Florida Seminole can be placed in meaningful relationship with the ethnographic documentation of these Indians in several ways. The historic origins of the Seminole in the Creek nation to the north can be examined with attention to specific similarities and differences between these two genetically related peoples. The subject can be approached also by attempting to define Seminole adaptations through space and time. One could examine and describe recent Seminole cultural patterns and attempt to "upstream" from the modern base to earlier sorts of cultural expression. The most fruitful discussion, however, would be an investigation of what has been learned about Seminole archeology within the framework of Seminole ethnohistory from the time of their separation from their ancestral homes in Central Georgia and Alabama until the present. This conjunctive approach should give the most information and explanation of the characteristic Seminole living styles. In this study, Seminole history is divided into five periods: colonization, 1716–63; separation, 1763–90; resistance and removal, 1790–1840; withdrawal, 1840–80; and modern crystalization, 1880–present. What is known of their archeology within each of these phases is discussed. For an understanding of the cultural processes at work one must depend on both written documents and archeological evidence.

A peculiarity of Seminole culture is that its antecedents lie outside the area where the population was historically located. While migrations are known to anthropologists, examples are rather hard to find in archeological contexts. In 1710, Thomas Nairne, the most knowledgable South Carolinian on Indian affairs, noted, "There remains not now, so much as one village with ten houses in it, in all Florida, that is subject to the Spaniards; nor have they any horses or cattle left, but such as they can protect by the guns of their Castle of St. Augustine, that alone being now in their hands, and which is continually infested by the perpertual Incursions of the Indians, subject to this Province" (Nairne 1710:34).

Thus was proclaimed the destruction of the Timucua and the missions dependent on them by raids of Carolina slavers. Nairne was exaggerating, but only slightly. These raids were to continue for some years; Georgia was not the only British colony to serve as a base for operations against Spanish Florida. During the Yamassee War of 1715, attacks were checked briefly until the English recovered from that holocaust. Colonel James Moore's raid of 1704 had occurred at a time when Carolina was turning her attention westward as well as southward. The really major penetration of the interior parts of the southeast began in earnest (Crane 1956).

The period following the 1710 statement by Nairne until the end of the Yamassee War six years later saw Spain trying ineffectually to rebuild her Florida colony. With the destruction of the cattle ranches in Alachua and Apalachee, St. Augustine suffered real privation (Barcia 1951:356). The Yamassee War had resulted in an abiding Creek-Cherokee enmity, in the awakening of British colonial authorities to the danger of French encirclement, in a constitutional revolution in South Carolina, in far-reaching migrations among many southeastern Indian tribes, and in a reorientation of frontier diplomacy, especially by the Creeks. Emperor Brim of the Creeks had conceived the strategy of alternating gestures of friendship toward the British, French, and Spaniards, combined with sequential attacks against each of the colonial powers until, he hoped, all were eliminated and Indians once again controlled the southern heartland. This was to continue as the central theme of Creek national policy until the elimination of France, England, and Spain at the end of the American Revolution left the Creeks surrounded by a single power, the United States. What is of interest is the aftermath of that war since it motivated the movement of some Creeks into Florida.

Both Emperor Brim of the Creeks and his son were married to Apalachee women. The son was known as Chipacafi to the Spaniards, and as Secoffee, or Seepecoffee, to the English (Barcia 1951:362). Whether these wives were Florida refugees from Moore's raid of 1704 is not known, although many Apalachee fled to the Creeks for protection. Neither is it possible to evaluate how much this involvement of influential Creeks with Apalachee may have been responsible for the subsequent movement of other Creeks into Florida. It is certain that Brim's heirs maintained a strong interest in the area.

The Spanish government in Florida seems to have acted with rare decision upon the news that Yamassee and Creeks were at war with the Carolinians. When the newly appointed Spanish governor Don Pedro de Oliver y Fullana arrived in St. Augustine, he found the Lower Creek emissary Chisla Scaliche, a brother of Brim, waiting. As a result of their conversations, Governor Oliver sent Lieutenant Peña on a diplomatic mission to the Creek towns along the Lower Chattahoochee. He was instructed to encourage them to settle in the unoccupied areas of Florida where recently there were Timucua and Apalachee settlements (Boyd 1949). Lieutenant Peña reported that the chiefs of these lower towns had agreed to remove to the Apalachee area (Boyd 1949:24). There was also renewed Creek activity at Pensacola, and much of it seemed friendly (Barcia 1951:358).

As a result of Peña's second expedition in 1717 he secured promises that a number of Creeks would settle in Apalachee and in the vicinity of the newly rebuilt Fort San Marcos de Apalachee. The towns involved were Tasquique, Apalachicola, Oconee, Euchitto (Hitchiti or Chiaha), Yuchi, and Sawokli. Peña also reported that he had encountered small bands of Apalachee, probably those who had fled to Mobile, scattered in their old territory (Boyd 1952). Peña's third expedition to recruit settlers in 1718 penetrated as far as the Upper Creek country of interior Alabama.

These Spanish activities, along with a generally high state of tension between the British and Creeks, resulted in the migration of many Apalachee refugees and an indeterminate number of Creeks into Florida. Migration was probably further stimulated by Cherokee raids as far south as the Creek town of Kasita, near present-day Columbus, Georgia. While there were certainly some Apalachee, Yamassee, Yuchi, and perhaps even Calusa in Florida after 1716, most of the Indians were Creeks from the towns along the lower Chattahoochee. That the Seminole until after 1815 spoke mainly the Hitchiti dialects found along the lower Chattahoochee strengthens this assumption. These efforts by the Spaniards called attention to the opportunities for settlement in Florida and for the removal of the Indians from the British sphere of influence to the north (Fairbanks 1957).

COLONIZATION PHASE

The period from 1716 until 1763, the colonization era, saw the movement of Creeks—individuals, families, and perhaps parts of whole towns—into Florida from the area of the lower Chattahoochee River and from the fall line area of the Oconee and Ocmulgee rivers in central Georgia. Data on the presence of Creek towns along the middle course of the Flint River are fragmentary, but the area probably also contributed some migrants. Two major factors were involved: the invitation of the Spaniards to settle an unoccupied territory, and the pressure, or anticipated pressure, from Carolina as retaliation for the Creek involvement and leadership in the recent Yamassee War. While these migrants may have been joined by some refugees of aboriginal Florida tribes such as the Timucua and Apalachee, they were predominantly Creek.

The known archeological remains of this phase of colonization show no relationship in material culture to previous Florida Indians. While in many cases earlier town sites may have been reoccupied, most of the locations apparently were new. Ceramics in the southeast are one of the most conservative elements of material culture, and the emerging Seminole possessed pottery closely related to that of Creek towns in central Georgia. The type Chattahoochee Brushed, or Walnut Roughened, was not known to the Apalachee or Timucua sites of the mission period. Both the mission sites and early Seminole sites do show some similiarity of a few types. Aucilla Incised found on mission sites has a resemblance, and generic relationship to the type Ocmulgee Fields Incised. These similarities are derived from a common ancestry in Late Mississippian incised rather than from each other. The incised type seems not to have been at all common among the Seminole (Goggin 1958). Available information indicates that the archeology of the migrants represents Creek rather than Apalachee or Timucua patterns.

Missions were not reestablished among the new Creek towns in northern Florida. It is not clear whether this was due to the inclinations of the Spaniards or to the resistance by the Indians. Likely the dismemberment of the Spanish mission apparatus in Florida left little capability for a new program. There seems to have been some attempt by the Spaniards to give the Indians the sorts of things they wanted— trade goods. A royal *cédula* in 1745 (Phillip V 1745) directed the establishment of a trading store in Apalachee, evidently in conjunction with Fort San Marcos de Apalachee. Spain at that time had difficulty in supplying the necessary trade goods, and the colonial authorities found it difficult to maintain the store. They did, however, persevere in spite of rather continuous trouble and fierce competition from English traders to the north (Wenhold 1956; Alden 1944:9–12).

The Spaniards were not able to reestablish the cattle ranches in the Alachua and Apalachee regions that had contributed to the subsistence of St. Augustine, Pensacola, and St. Marks. Instead they began to depend more on the hunting and farming skills of the growing mestizo population in and around St. Augustine. Recent excavations in that city indicate that the bulk of household ceramics were of Indian style and manufacture (Deagan 1974). It can be assumed that the food cooked in them was also procured from the Indians. The Seminole never seem to have lived in St. Augustine in large numbers. Few extant accounts mention Creek or Seminole Indians, and Seminole brushed pottery has not appeared in any quantity in St. Augustine. Evidently mestizos, mainly from the Guale group, and escaped blacks from Carolina were the major suppliers of food, both wild and domestic. The Seminole remained aloof, in large part because they had left their Georgia homes to escape contact with the English and did not propose to substitute Spanish contact.

Little is known archeologically about the Seminole in this period. Documents locating towns or settlement areas are scarce and unsatisfactory (Cline 1973). No site clearly representing the Colonization Phase has yet been excavated. It is possible, nevertheless, to indicate at least three areas where the Seminoles were settled during the middle years of the eighteenth century. The oldest settlement was probably in the vicinity of present-day Tallahassee (the name dating back to this period). Secoffee, a son of Brim, was the likely founder, and Tonaby was chief there at the end of the Spanish dominion (Porter 1949). To the east were a series of settlements around Lake Miccosukee. This name has come to be identified with the Hitchiti-speaking element of the Seminole Nation from this early time onward. Perhaps the largest settlements were in present-day Alachua County near Lake Cuscowilla. The main town here was the headquarters of Cowkeeper, one of the major figures in early Seminole history. The Cowkeeper band supposedly was the Oconee band who removed there at the end of the Yamassee War. There may have been a fourth area along the Apalachicola River from the junction of the Chattahoochee and Flint rivers down to or near the coast. As this area was remote from both St. Marks and Pensacola, details of the towns are fragmentary. The Tallahassee, Miccosukee, and perhaps Apalachicola bands traded with the store at St. Marks and caused constant trouble. Rum, cane syrup, tobacco, and pipes were the most popular items sold at the store, and the deer skins offered by the Indians often exceeded the supply of trade goods. The Indians often contacted traders within the British dominion. The Alachua band traded eastward to St. Augustine or northward into Georgia.

It is likely that the Tallahassee-Miccosukee and Alachua areas settled were a rather conscious occupation of the old Apalachee and Potano homelands by the Seminoles. The fact that these two areas had been occupied previously meant that they suited Indian community needs. In both areas there were at least small patches of loamy or sandy clay soils suitable for agriculture. Numerous lakes provided aquatic resources and hardwood hammocks where deer were more abundant than in the south Georgia and north Florida pine barrens. Perhaps the major attractions were the old Apalachee and Timucua agriculture fields together with the herds of feral cattle present in these regions. It was at this time that the Seminole began utilizing these cattle. The lack of excavation at any site of the colonization phase settlements makes it difficult to describe with any accuracy the subsistence base of the population, although some inferences can be drawn from the sparse archeological and historical data. As yet no major divergence from the Creek cultural pattern had occurred; pottery, at least, strongly resembles that of the Georgia piedmont. The difficulty of locating Seminole sites strongly suggests a more diffuse settlement pattern than had been characteristic of either the central Georgia ancestral region or the antecedent Fort Walton and Mission periods in northern Florida. Of course, the Seminole occupation was relatively short as archeological phases are reckoned, and this also contributes to the paucity of remains.

The Seminole "kept" cows in much the fashion of the southern British frontiersmen, that is the free ranging cattle were periodically rounded up. The cattle were used for food, and it seems highly probable that their hides were traded along with deer skins. Except for the aspect of hunting feral cattle for meat and hides, this growing involvement with horned cattle was foreign to southeastern Indian cultural patterns. They must have been developed in the northern Florida areas rather than brought from the central Georgia piedmont, since before removal the Creeks had not yet had enough contact with the Carolinians or Georgians to have developed such skills. It is unlikely that the Seminoles were actively breeding cattle, rather they depended on the natural increase of the herds. The Alachua area seemed ideal for cattle. Herds maintained their strength and increased after the destruction of the missions and ranches in the first decade of the eighteenth century. As expected these activities increased the masculine roles at the expense of the feminine activities; hunting is usually a distinctively male pursuit. Women, however, remained strong because of their involvement in agriculture so that female activities and artifacts were less affected by European cultural impact. In this period the isolation of the Seminole from British and Spanish settlements meant that only selected aspects of the two European cultures were accepted into Seminole culture. The major sources of change would have been internal—the adaptation to a new environment.

A major factor in this new adaptation was the complex relationship to environmental conditions of soil, rainfall, and temperature, specifically different from those in central Georgia. While the red clay hills of the Tallahassee area probably were not too different, there was a longer growing season, somewhat more moderate summer-winter temperature variations, and probably more varied natural resources. The Indians also had to adapt to a much different European domination, that of the Spaniards, whose attitudes were changing because of a variety of factors. Destruction of the missions and ranches had demonstrated the need for another Indian policy. The need for labor and food in St. Augustine was acute. New crops such as watermelons, sweet potatoes, and domestic animals—cattle, pigs, and chickens— had to be integrated into the Indian food-procurement patterns.

Following the settlement of Georgia in 1733, the rivalry between Britons and Spaniards intensified. Spain saw Georgia as an immediate threat to their continued occupation of Florida (Wright 1971). While the English made specific overtures to the Creeks for help in this struggle, the Spaniards seem to have done little except to voice concern about the situation. This lack of Seminole involvement is compounded by all the factors which then operated on the Georgia-Florida frontier. The policies of Emperor Brim which led to the Yamassee War were part of this isolation, as were the increasing ineffectiveness of Spanish colonial rule, the physical isolation of the Seminole settlements, and the aggressive trading policy of Carolinians and Georgians. All of these factors contributed to the next stage in Seminole cultural development.

SEPARATION PHASE

The period of separation, 1763–1817, developed slowly. Although 1763 also marks the beginning of the British period in Florida, the onset of the period is so dated because of the mass of documentation available rather than any connection with the transfer of sovereignty. The phase is marked by definite signs that the Florida Indians were separating themselves politically and economically from the Creek Confederacy on the lower Chattahoochee and in central Alabama. Development of a highly institutionalized British Indian policy contributed to the separation, but the process can best be understood in terms of Indian developments rather than European colonial policies.

Britain had proclaimed in 1763 a boundary demarcation beyond which the natives were to be left in relative isolation (de Vorsey 1966). Indian agents were appointed for the northern and southern departments, and a series of treaties were negotiated which, in theory, brought the independent Indian tribes under British control, defined the zones of interaction, and formalized possession of former Indian lands by the colonies. Part of this British policy is clear in letters from John Stuart, Superintendent of Indian Affairs, to various concerned persons. In reporting to General Thomas Gage on July 19, 1764, Stuart described the Alachua settlement: "About 130 Creek Families who have detached them-selves from their Nation are settled about 70 miles west of this place [St. Augustine] their village called Latchewee, and stands upon one of the Branches of the Altamaha River" (Stuart 1764a). Thus the superintendent emphasized the separation from the main Creek Nation of the Alachua settlement. It was his opinion also that the Florida Indians were not in regular communication with the rest of the nation. When he called in the Cowkeeper and his lieutenant, the Long Warrior, he reported, "Three Lower Creek Warriors who happened to be at their village when my messenger reached it. The Cowkeeper and Long Warrior expressed the warmest attachment to us. They know but little of what passes in their nation not having heard from them for several months" (Stuart 1764a).

At the beginning of the British period both the Seminole and English were aware that communications were scanty between Alachua and the centers of the Creek Confederacy. That England realized the advantages of a policy of divide and rule is indicated by Stuart's advice to Lieutenant Pampellone as he was about to take over the fort at St. Marks: "It will undoubtedly be detrimental to His Majesties service, that too strict a friendship and union subsist between the different Indian nations within this department; it is therefore incumbent upon us by all means in our power to foment any jealousy or division that may subsist between them" (Stuart 1764b).

While such a policy was in Britain's best interest, it also confirms the situation that was developing. Changed economic circumstances, distance from the nation, and different allies were evolving a separate entity of the Indians in Florida. This is illustrated in the behavior of the Cowkeeper at the Treaty of Picolata called by John Stuart in 1765. Some thirty-one chiefs of the Lower Creeks agreed to cede land east of the St. Johns to England. The more important chiefs seem to have been Secoffee, a son of Brim, and Captain Aleck. The Cowkeeper was not present, and the Long Warrior signed for him as representative of the Alachua bands. With the signing of the treaty, November 18, 1765, many gifts were distributed to the assembled Indians. On January 13, 1766, Governor James Grant wrote Gage from St. Augustine: "The Cowkeeper our nearest neighbor, has lately been here for a week with sixty attendants. He was absent from the Congress on account of the sickness of his family. He came to be made a great Medal Chief and to receive his proportion of Presents, for the Country which has been ceded and to assure me of his Friendship and good Intention" (Grant 1766).

That the Seminole leader could indulge in a charade of diplomatic illness is not surprising. British administrators in Florida were inexperienced, and it took relatively little to soothe the ruffled feelings. Whatever may have been the role of the British officials in promoting the separation of the Seminole from the Creek, it is clear that the Alachua Seminole felt the same way about the situation. The distance from the seats of the Creek Confederacy to Alachua is 242 miles from Kasita on the Chattahoochee and 303 air miles from Tukabachee in central Alabama. By twentieth-century roads, which probably approximate trail distances, the mileages are 325 and 361. No other Creek towns were so far from the central councils of the nation.

It was about this time that the Florida Indians began to be referred to as Seminoles or Siminoles in English and *Cimarrones* in Spanish documents. The word derives from the Spanish cimmarrones, applied to anything wild or untamed. The Spanish used it for the new Indian migrants to Florida because they had left their settled towns and had established themselves in wild, vacant lands. As the Muskhogean tongues have no sound corresponding to the English or Spanish "r," the Indians pronounced it "Simalones," which then changed to Seminoles. Acquisition of a separate name, as well as the other factors involved, makes this period in Seminole history one of separation and demonstrates the emergence of a new cultural entity (Fairbanks 1957).

Following the American Revolution, when Alexander McGillivray assumed leadership of the Creeks, the Florida Seminole were once again drawn temporarily into something like their original unity, which was not altogether due to McGillivray. Both the Seminole and Creek faced the common problem of acclimating to a new environment when they were also adjusting to the presence of the emerging United States. The old triune diplomacy of Emperor Brim would no longer work in this new geopolitical situation, and unification was demanded by circumstance. The period, however, saw an increasing degree of separation from the ancestral Creek polity in Georgia and Alabama. As there were no other Indian units to which the emerging Seminoles could unite, it was a time of increasing political and probably cultural independence. The Seminole were also seeking new alliances with the Spanish, even during the British occupation period in Florida (Boyd and Latorre 1953), and with the new American states.

There are abundant documentary sources and the beginnings of archeological evidence which deal with the separation phase. William Bartram described Seminole houses and Cuscowilla, a settlement in the Alachua area on the borders of a lake some ten miles south of present-day Gainesville. He describes the dependence of the Indians on herds of feral cattle, but he also records rather extensive agriculture. Cattle and horses pastured naturally on the large wet savannah. The sink-hole lakes of northern Florida are alternatively either lakes or open savannahs, according to rainfall and soil water levels. One Seminole, he wrote, had trained his dog to round up horses, surely a trait borrowed from some Scots-English trader with memories of trained highland collies. Potatoes, probably sweet, as well as melons, certainly borrowed from the Spaniards, had been added to the agricultural system. The Seminoles ate wild oranges sweetened with honey (Bartram 1958).

Trade was important as a source of guns, iron tools, cloth, ornaments, rum, and other European products that had become essential to the Indians. In exchange for these products the Seminoles offered hides—both deer and feral cattle—although the records give little precise information on the kinds of hides traded. Some other forest products such as honey and bear oil were supplementary Indian products. Trading posts were located on the St. Marys River northeast of St. Augustine, two on the St. Johns River southeast of the town, one at or near Cuscowilla, and from time to time, one at St. Marks on the Gulf coast. There was no attempt on the part of the traders to establish stores in the immediate vicinities of Seminole towns, except for Cuscowilla in the Alachua area. The traders located near good transportation routes—the St. Marys, St. Johns, and Apalachee Bay on the Wakulla River just above its junction with the St. Marks River. Water transport was of paramount importance in locating a store, and the Seminoles usually had to travel overland to reach the traders. The Seminoles apparently did not establish their communities near the stores. Limited quantities of Seminole pottery and other artifacts have been found around Spalding's Lower Store on the St. Johns (Lewis 1969). Thus Indian trade occurred in the widely dispersed posts established by the United States after the Revolution. It marked a change from the English system which located traders within Indian towns in Georgia and Alabama. Perhaps this shift was a result of the Proclamation of 1763 which established the demarcation line between Indians and Europeans, although nothing in the Proclamation or the actions of Commissioner Stuart suggests that this was a formal policy (de Vorsey 1966).

The Seminoles in this period were heavily dependent on British trade, and that it was highly profitable is indicated by the success of the traders who came down from Georgia during the time the English were in Florida. Spalding's stores seem to have operated successfully, and Panton, Leslie and Company was certainly a profitable enterprise. The general pattern of extending credit to the Indians, with payment due at the end of the following winter hunt, accumulated sizeable debts to the traders. Forbes and Company, successor to the Panton firm, was able to secure a major grant of land in settlement of these debts, but in general the trader had to resort to pressure and diplomacy to secure payment. The most effective measure was to threaten to shut off the trade unless payments were made. The Seminole, like other American Indians during this period, were heavily dependent on European trade goods. England was best able to supply these, and she used her position in the Indian trade to bolster her political objectives. With the retrocession of Florida to the Spaniards in 1783 the Indian trade was so thoroughly entrenched that Spain found that she had little experience in this business and little capacity to produce the trade goods demanded by the Indians and was forced to continue using the British trading firms until the end of the second Spanish period (Tanner 1963). Trade had become part of the Indian way of life, with the skins of deer and feral cattle as the major Indian goods. The effects of trade are seen archeologically in the quantities of iron tools, especially guns, found in sites of the period. Numerous glass bottle sherds attest to the popularity of rum, although there is no indication what impact this product was having on the Indians. Artifacts associated with women's activities show fewer influences of trade. Ceramics are little changed throughout the period, being mostly the brushed styles brought down from Georgia and Alabama. The Seminole costume was not much different from the clothing of other southeastern Indians, if one can judge by the few available drawings (Fundaburk 1958). English cloth was the major material for clothing, and the use of beads and other ornaments was common.

Settlement pattern and house form had developed systematic differences from the older styles. Bartram described quite substantial houses with a second story to catch the available breezes (Bartram 1958). It is not clear how general this form had become as no systematic excavation of a Seminole house or village has so far been attempted. It is also clear that the settlement pattern was changing radically. There is no mention of either a town square or of a council house; the conference was held in the residence of the town chief. The ancestral Creek pattern would probably have included discussions in the house of the chief, but formal deliberations would certainly have been held in either the square or the council house. As both the square and council house were also used for religious rituals, it seems likely that Seminole religious activity was being simplified. Daughter towns among the Creeks, those that budded off from major towns, often did not have these specialized community features. The town members would then be obliged to attend the feasts of their mother town. As the Seminole were far from the well-established towns and the political organization of the Creek Confederacy, they could not regularly attend these religious functions. The loss of town squares and council houses was an indication of the social and political changes taking place.

Bartram does not describe in detail the town of Cuscowilla, and archeological survey in the area around the lake has failed to reveal any evidence of a compact village. A similar situation exists at Miccosukee, east of Tallahassee. Miccosukee was one of the major Seminole settlements from early in the eighteenth century until the First Seminole War when much of it was destroyed by Andrew Jackson. In spite of its designation on several maps at the southern end of Lake Miccosukee, no concentration of midden or artifacts is visible in that area. A similar paucity of remains is characteristic of the Seminole location on the Suwannee River at Oven Hill. Considerable debris has been recovered from the bottom of the river and represents a major collection of Seminole pottery. No concentrated village site is present, however, and yet there must have been a fairly long occupation.

Seminole communities during the eighteenth century were clearly diffuse centers of settlement, without the formal arrangement of earlier southeastern Indian towns. This change in settlement pattern was a specific adaptation to their new mode of life. The pattern of agriculture combined with predation on feral cattle would almost require such a diffuse settlement. The Seminole were adopting the dispersed hamlets common to their Anglo-American neighbors. As there seems not to have been enough contact between the Seminole and Georgians or Carolinians in this period for the Indians to have borrowed it directly, it is likely that it was a case of convergent evolution. The Spaniards had a strong emphasis on nucleated towns, the *pueblo* with its square and church. Nothing that the Seminole were borrowing from the Spaniards would have influenced them to adopt a scattered settlement form. As Seminole agriculture does not seem to have differed from the ancestral Creek pattern, in spite of the introduction of Spanish crops, there is no apparent reason why their exploitation of herds of feral cattle should require such a change.

To look to political or military causes does not solve the problem of the origin of the dispersed Seminole settlement pattern. Their ancestral Creek pattern of confederation with wars for trophies was certainly a thing of the past. There were periods of tension with Spaniards, English, and other Indians, but the dispersal seems to have occurred before the formal attacks of the American forces under Jackson. Certainly the Seminole during this period had little to fear militarily from their Creek relatives or from the Spaniards. They in effect were protected from attack by more distant tribes by the powerful Creek Confederacy on their landward side, and the aboriginal Florida tribes such as the Timucua or Calusa were mere vestiges who could offer no concerted threat. The Seminole ethic of slipping away from European involvement, which had led to their removal to Florida in the first place, may have been a significant factor in their change of settlement form. It is certain that the change in village plan either reflected or was caused by changes in other aspects of the culture. Certainly the diffuse Seminole settlements of the late eighteenth century could not have supported the cohesive village political organization of the ancestral Creek culture. As Creek political organization was intimately related to the religious system, it must be concluded that religious practices were also being changed. Both Creek political and religious systems were largely in the hands of the men as officials and principal participants. It is significant that it was precisely the Seminole men who were most affected by the cultural changes brought about by the changed hunting patterns and the virtual absence of the old patterns of warfare. Whatever the causes, this diffuse settlement pattern has persisted down to the present in the scattered camps of the modern Seminoles of the Everglades. The fact of this persistence suggests that cultural factors are more important than the purely physical and environmental ones which were involved in the Seminole movement into the wet tropical savannah of southern Florida.

Pottery and other material traits can be described with some confidence for this phase. Seminole brushed pottery types seem to show a remarkable conservatism and similarity to the earlier, and later, Creek forms in central Georgia, Alabama, and even Oklahoma (Goggin 1958; Gluckman and Peebles 1974). Much of this conservatism must be related to the lesser involvement of the women in the acculturative process then going on. The only innovations that can be described lay in the differences due to clay, tempering materials, etc. At least one brushed jar from the Oven Hill site has three short legs in obvious imitation of the common cast-iron cooking pots of the period. Such experiments seem to have been rare, however, and most of the Seminole sherds could be lost in a collection of comparable Creek material. From the site of Spalding's Lower Store on the St. Johns there is a quantity of brushed sherds which suggests that either clay pots or pots containing Indian products were brought to the store for barter (Lewis 1969). Aside from ceramics, much of Seminole material culture seems to have been derived from the traders. Iron tools, including muskets, were fairly common, as were glass beads. These latter are generally a multi-faceted form of moderate size. They probably reflect the sorts available from the traders rather than any selection by the Seminole, as the same types have been found in slave cabins in the southern coastal region (Ascher and Fairbanks 1971; Fairbanks 1973).

Seminole clothing of the period clearly reflects European sources for the cloth, although the tailoring may have been Indian. Men wore long shirts or tunics of trade cloth. Leggings seem to frequently have been of buckskin as were the typically southeastern moccasins worn on most occasions. Cloth turbans with drooping ostrich plumes at the back were common. Finger-woven sashes or belts were worn around the waist or across the shoulders, and they often supported a pouch. While the waist belt is old in the southeast, the shoulder sash may be influenced by European military prototypes. Silver turban bands and crescentic silver gorgets are shown in a number of illustrations of

Seminoles at the end of this period. While much of the materials used in the male clothing was of European origin, the style developed was distinctly Indian. Seminole male dress does not seem utilitarian, and evidently it was worn for status or socio-technic purposes (Sturtevant 1967).

A few Seminole burials are known from this period. Burial of intentionally broken muskets seems to have been usual with males, although useful objects were not common in the burials of women (Goggin et al. 1959). Burials did not differ greatly from those of the Creeks of a comparable period. If a Seminole settlement such as Cuscowilla could be located and excavated it would be easier to compare archeological evidence with written documents. The Gage Papers and Bartram's journal are one means for such direct historical approach, and may solve some of the problems raised by the shift in Seminole patterns.

RESISTANCE AND REMOVAL PHASE

The phase of separation closes with the rising tensions created by the proximity of the United States in former Creek territory to the immediate north of the Seminole settlements in Florida, the impotence of Spanish authority, and the rising fervor of American land expansion. It is a period characterized as one of resistance and removal. It brought the Seminole twice into armed conflict with the United States forces, once during the second Spanish period and again later after Florida had become an American territory. Both governmental policy and the general cultural milieu under the United States differed from that under Spain. Florida was a frontier area which attracted the free-wheeling entrepreneurs eager to advance their own interests at the expense of the rest of society. The American influx brought an attitude toward blacks which was different from the relatively tolerant attitude of the Spaniards.

Florida had been a haven of refuge for runaway Negroes from late in the seventeenth century when plantation slavery had been introduced into South Carolina. Spaniards had neither held these escaped slaves in chattel slavery nor returned them to their owners. This attitude resulted from basically different Spanish attitudes toward blacks, the lack of any extensive plantation system in Florida, and Spanish hostility toward the encroaching English settlers to the north. Escaped Negroes were allowed a moderate amount of independence if they showed evidence of loyalty to the Spanish authorities. At least one small enclave of blacks was established in the vicinity of St. Augustine. Centered around Fort Mosa at the northern fringe of the town defenses, the Spanish utilized the abilities of these people as a military element, for the procurement of food, and for other services. How many other blacks were present in the remoter parts of the colony is unknown, but it was evident that many blacks were being protected by the Seminoles. The Indians had in effect adopted the Spanish attitude toward the Negroes. Perhaps the Indians felt a sense of common attitudes since they also were refugees from the abuses of the Carolinians. They had evidently not developed the antipathy of many other southeastern Indians to blacks resulting from the French and English policy of creating tension between the two groups. Thus Florida Indian-black relationships differed from those in other areas (Willis 1971). The presence of blacks is attested to by available documents and forms two patterns. The first involves individual client relationships between specific Seminoles and blacks (Porter 1945, 1946, 1951). These blacks were not held as slaves or as servants; they were regarded as advisors, particularly in matters involving whites. The second relationship involved separate settlements of blacks near or within the area of Seminole towns. Little documentary information is available, and there has been no archeological investigation of the sites of the settlements. This relationship added an element of acculturation to the Seminole, although it did not have any impact on the Seminole gene pool (Politzer 1971). The acculturational situation of the Seminole differed significantly from that of the other larger and more politically organized southeastern tribes such as the Creek. Among those tribes blacks were often held in chattel slavery by wealthy or powerful individuals and probably contributed less to the acculturation process. Trusted advisors, such as Abraham, counseled Seminole leaders on the basis of their extensive participation in plantation culture. They also often served as interpreters, and the Indians did not have to rely on the biased reporting of white bilinguals.

With the acquisition of Florida by the United States, runaway slaves became an additional source of contention between the Indians and the whites in both Florida and Georgia. The settlers considered all Negroes as the property of some white master. They were thus to be caught and returned to their rightful owners, even where title was obscure or missing. In addition, whites had developed a deep distrust of blacks as a possible source of revolt. With the constitutional prohibition of further importation of slaves, free Negroes were regarded as a highly profitable source of reward by many border people. The Seminole generally resisted slave-catching activities and seem to have felt a sense of unity with the blacks.

Even before Florida became an American territory, tensions between the Seminoles and the United States had reached a point of crisis with the First Seminole War. This hostility emerged out of the troubled border conditions that had existed in Florida for many years. In 1812, the United States went to war with Britain. There were many causes for this conflict: English actions on the high seas, the desire of the United States to round out the natural boundaries of her dominions, and the agitation of the British among the southern Indians. Governor William Claiborne had accomplished the occupation of West Florida by the tactic of "supporting local revolutions" in 1810. The following year General George Mathews began a similar coup in East Florida. Collecting recruits on both sides of the Florida border, he crossed into Florida in March 1812 and proclaimed the Territory of Florida (Patrick 1954). Easily capturing Fernandina on Amelia Island, the Patriots soon held all of the area between the St. Marys and St. Johns. Moving next on St. Augustine, Mathews managed to occupy the old Negro fort of Fort Mosa, but he was unable to take the Castillo de San Marcos. The Florida Indians seem not to have been involved in any significant way in these activites, mainly because there were no significant number of Seminoles in this area of Florida.

In June 1812, the United States declared war against Great Britain. The following month the Indians attacked the East Florida Patriots, although the battle seems to have been rather inconclusive. Mathews had sought to neutralize the Seminole threat by three conferences: two at Picolata in May and June and one at Alachua in July. Both the Spanish Governors Estrada and Kindelan had sent black emissaries to solicit Indian support. Perhaps their most effective argument was that the Americans would try to seize Indian lands. In view of Spanish attitudes towards Indian title, this was hardly a logical argument, although the Indians were familiar with the land hunger of Georgians. Certainly the Negroes were important in intensifying the Seminole hostility against the East Florida Patriots (Porter 1945:9–29). Early in February 1813, Tennessee volunteers under Colonel John Williams, adjutant general of Tennessee militia, and Major General Thomas Pinckney, former governor of South Carolina and minister to the Court of St. James, moved against the Seminoles. There was one pitched battle, two towns were destroyed, houses and crops burned, and livestock confiscated. This pretty much ended Indian resistance from the Alachua area. Their leader Payne was killed, and there was no one who could take command.

Payne carried on the lineage of Cowkeeper, and his tenure was a link between the early Alachua settlements and the later events of the First Seminole War. He had refused to participate in the Bowles affair of 1788, although he seems to have been more motivated by a desire for peace than any affection for the British. At Colerain, in 1793, he had professed friendship for the United States. His death at the battle of Newnans Lake left the Seminoles without effective or experienced leadership. His brother was Boleck, or Bowlegs, whose Indian name was *Islapao paya*, "Far away." When Colonel Thomas A. Smith attacked in the Alachua area he found the main town two miles north of present Micanopy abandoned. Smith burned it, and then moved westward and fought a battle near Bowlegs' town. His report of burning 386 houses in Bowlegs' Town apparently was an exaggeration. Few Seminole towns could have been that large (Boyd 1951:11).

Payne was succeeded by the oldest son of Solachoppo, whose wife was evidently a sister of Payne and Bowlegs, thus leaving leadership in the female line. Solachoppo's son soon died, and he was succeeded by Micanopy who moved the settlements southward to Pilaklakha and Okahumpka. Pilaklakha seems to have been a town of blacks under the protection of Micanopy who had Negro advisors (Boyd 1951:11), including the famous Abraham (Porter 1951). About the time that Micanopy moved south, Bowlegs settled at Suwannee Old Town. These events mark the first example of Seminole hostility and the role of blacks is clear, although it was not the only factor influencing Seminole attitudes. For the most part the Florida Seminoles stayed clear of involvement in the nativistic movement of the Creek War, perhaps because they felt that it was remote from their problems (United States Government 1932a:844-45). The defeat of the Alachua bands was followed by a general withdrawal of most of the East Florida Patriots.

With the collapse of Napoleon in Europe, England could devote more attention to the American campaigns and stepped up her naval activity in the Gulf of Mexico. In 1814, the English landed arms and a few men at Prospect Bluff, an installation they had built on the Apalachicola River. Two British agents, Colonel Edward Nicolls and Captain George Woodbine, were in the Pensacola area drilling troops of refugee Negroes and Indians, most of the latter probably refugees from the Creek War in Alabama. Jackson marched to Florida, captured the virtually abandoned Pensacola, and then moved on to New Orleans for the climactic battle of the war. Deprived of Pensacola, the British agents returned to Prospect Bluff where they found runaway blacks living in and around the fort. Again the Indians were largely followers of the Creek prophets in the Creek War. With the withdrawal of the British, the Indians joined forces with the Miccosukees around Tallahassee and Fort St. Marks. While some excavation has been done at the Negro Fort Prospect Bluff, no picture of cultural relationships can yet be made (Boyd 1937; Poe 1963). The artifact content of the new Creek settlement near Fort St. Marks seems indistinguishable from that of that of the Alabama Creeks and the Florida Seminole. It seems probable that the elements introduced by these Alabama refugees were more in the nature of linguistic and religious forms than any distinctive material traits.

Indians did offer resistance to the running of the boundary line between the United States and Spanish Florida. In fact, much of the line between the Apalachicola and the St. Marys rivers could not be surveyed at that time and was only determined at a later date. It is believed that the rough handling by the East Florida Patriots in addition to the influx of refugees from the Creek War stiffened the attitude of the Seminoles in resisting white encroachments. Certainly increased settlement in southern Georgia and the building of Fort Scott at the junction of the Flint and Chattahoochee rivers were regarded as security threats. The Indians and Negroes were determined to prevent supplies moving up the Apalachicola. The Americans were just as determined to have free access through Spanish territory to their southern frontier. An American gunboat under the command of Colonel Duncan L. Clinch blew up the Negro fort, killing 270 of the 340 occupants. The survivors dispersed, most to Bowlegs' Town on the Suwannee River (Porter 1946).

The troubles in Florida—the invading Patriots, the United States Army, and the British agents—warned the Seminoles of additional trouble. Perhaps there was the beginning of a movement into the south-central part of Florida by some Seminoles. By 1817, the British trader-agent Robert Ambrister had established a trading post in the Tampa Bay area to supply Indians living inland and to serve as a stepping-stone for further inroads on the Forbes trading empire. He was able shortly to establish a branch on the lower Suwannee to draw on the Seminole bands in that area who were followers of Bowlegs. Ambrister, along with a rival trader, Alexander Arbuthnot, were captured and summarily executed by Andrew Jackson at St. Marks. Certainly Seminole raids into Georgia had become more frequent during the period when Arbuthnot and Ambrister were active in Florida. While their main incentives were probably trade, they also acted as agents for British intrigue. At the same time the activities of United States soldiers, agents, and settlers along the Georgia-Florida border were ample cause for the Seminole to fear a rapid takeover of their lands by Americans.

It is difficult to assess the role of the free blacks in this rising tide of Seminole distrust, but they had much the same objectives as the Seminoles so that this was a period of intense Seminole-Negro interaction. The available archeology of the Seminole in this period fails to show any direct evidence of black material cultural elements entering the Seminole pattern. As the pattern of slave import into the New World stripped blacks of most cultural elements, the traits available in their behavior for Seminole borrowing were those of the superordinate white culture of the plantation South plus a determined resistance to being returned to slave status.

During the attacks by American forces in late 1817, it is interesting that the western towns along the Ocklockonee and Apalachicola rivers were more unified and coordinated than had been the case for the Alachua-Suwannee bands. This likely was due to the influence of refugee Red Sticks from Alabama. These men had lost the Creek War but did have experience with organized military action. Fowltown and Miccosukee were the main towns in the conflict that followed. During Jackson's raid into Florida, he claimed that he burned three hundred houses at Miccosukee, which he spoke of as "the villages." This implies that the town was in fact the diffuse settlement previously discussed (Bassett 1926). Evidently most of the Indians scattered at the approach of Jackson's army, a technique that was to be refined in later troubles with the American military. Jackson's men mainly subsisted on loot taken from the destroyed Indian towns. Captain Hugh Young in Jackson's command left a description of the area and of the Indian towns that provides information on the disposition of the Seminoles (1934-35).

In spite of the fact that Red Stick Upper Creek leaders were prominent among the Florida Indians at this time, there is little evidence of the emergence of a nativistic element among the Seminoles. Hillis Hadjo, Peter McQueen, and Homathlemico led the Red Stick movement in Alabama. Perhaps their failure to inject a nativistic religious element into Seminole resistance to Jackson was due to their disillusionment with this solution. Timothy Barnard, a long-time trader among the Georgia Creeks, reported that the Red Sticks had begun their dancing again (United States Government 1832b:683). As the frenzied dance of the Red Stick prophets was the major symbol of their power, it would indicate that they were attempting to revive the movement. Perhaps the council of older Florida residents prevailed, and they chose the tactic of flight rather than dependence on religious fervor. At any rate, the prompt appearance of Jackson's troops quickly induced the Seminole to flee rather than stand and fight. Likely Arbuthnot and Ambrister had not been able to supply the Seminole with sufficient munitions for a formal war.

Understandably a major effect of the First Seminole War was a growing distrust of the United States, and an eastward and southward shift of settlements. The former concentration along the Apalachicola was dispersed. There was also a movement away from most of the former towns. Where it is possible to define the precise location of the new settlements, they seem to have been fairly close to the old ones, generally located in inaccessible spots and of quite diffuse pattern. The aftermath of the First Seminole War must have been a severe strain on the Indians. New towns had to be located, land cleared for gardens (little if any trade was available after the execution of Arbuthnot and Ambrister), and food supplies would have been very scarce. Perhaps this accounts for the difficulty in locating Seminole settlements for this period. The Spaniards seem to have continued the pattern of gifts and limited trade with the Indians that had been established at the beginning of the second Spanish period. Available information on Seminole material culture during the closing years of the Spanish Florida era indicates a heavy dependence on many European material culture items. Guns were of major importance, of course, but more perishable things like dress items were also based on European materials. The decline of Spanish authority in Florida and the nature of Seminole relations with the Spaniards meant that little acculturation took place. The Indians had contact only with frontier ruffians interested in acquiring land, cattle, or slaves from the Seminoles so that no stable exchange of cultural elements could take place.

The First Seminole War, while it failed to damage the Seminoles to any extent, did demonstrate that Spain had a very tenuous control on Florida and that the United States was willing and able to take over the reins. With Jackson's occupation of Pensacola the intention of the United States to occupy and annex the territory was clear, and the events rapidly moved to the cession of Florida to the United States in

1821. With the establishment of the Territory of Florida some attention was paid to the so-called Indian problem. The Treaty of
Moultrie Creek in effect continued the British pattern of treating
Indian tribes as if they were sovereign nations within the territorial
confines of the larger country (United States Government 1834:429–
31).

Rising tensions created by the proximity of American settlers, dif-
ficulties in adapting to the relatively barren terrain of central Florida,
and a lack of sympathy by the territorial officials led to increased
tension. It is probable that little change in the gene pool developed
during this period (Politzer 1971). Perhaps the most significant
change to many Seminole was the inept paternalism of the Indian
agent assigned as part of the general policy of the United States. This
was in special contrast to the mere vestiges of control exercised during
the waning years of Spanish sovereignty. While there is considerable
political documentation for the phase, little archeology has been
done, largely due to the nature of Seminole settlement plans.

It seems, from available site surveys, that the Seminole were located
in diffuse groups of farm homesteads, often with the names of formal
towns. Seemingly accurate maps show rather widely spaced family
groups, probably matrilocal. Sites, such as that at the mouth of the
Suwannee River for example, must have subsisted by fishing, or
perhaps trading. Yet they have the scattered layout of the earlier
inland agricultural and herding settlements. No concentrated village
debris is present, although there is a thin scatter of brushed pottery
and such European artifacts as black bottle glass, pearlware or white-
ware sherds, and some metal artifacts. A somewhat similar situation is
found along the Apalachicola River where the site of Chief Blount's
reserve can be located through the early territorial land plats. Archeology is needed to attempt to resolve the questions of the formation of nineteenth-century Seminole settlement pattern and social organization.

Seminole population had swelled to about five thousand by the time
of the Treaty of Moultrie Creek in 1823. Much of this increase was
due to refugee Red Sticks from central Alabama who had fled from
Andrew Jackson at the end of the Creek War. Their presence was
probably a combination of persisting Creek identification with the
Seminole as well as a recognition that Florida did in fact offer a refuge
area.

At the end of treaty negotiations, the known areas of Seminole
settlement were: (1) scattered bands along the middle course of the

Apalachicola River from the Georgia border to within about fifty miles of the Gulf of Mexico; (2) from the Ocklockonee River to the Aucilla River, except for the Forbes Purchase area—This was an expanded version of the older Tallahassee-Miccosukee group and included some relatively new settlements in the area of Fort St. Marks; (3) thinly scattered groups along the approximate line of the Georgia border from Madison County eastward to the bend of the St. Marys River in Baker County—as this was mainly pine barrens, these Seminole probably lived mainly by hunting wild cattle and deer; (4) a rather thin arc of towns from the Suwannee and Santa Fe rivers eastward and southward to present Sanford and Lake Harney, then southwestward to the head of Tampa Bay; (5) one town located on Charlotte Harbor; (6) two towns on the east coast near present-day Palm Beach.

The Treaty of Moultrie Creek provided for the cession of all Seminole lands in Florida and the establishment of a reservation in the central part of the territory (Kappler 1904:203-5). This would entail the movement of the bulk of the Seminole into a restricted reserve of different resources than the environments to which they were accustomed. Military posts were to be established at Tampa Bay and near present-day Ocala, but no real provision for trade was set forth. The Everglades seems not to have been occupied, although it is believed that the Seminoles had some knowledge of the area. Much of the land within the reservation, later to be known as the "Big Scrub," was unsuitable for Indian techniques of agriculture. It did contain some game as well as the starchy zamia roots which could be used as a crisis food. Raiding for horses and cattle became a regular part of Seminole economy and served as a major factor in the increasing Indian-white tension.

It is likely that the previous scattered homestead pattern gave way to a somewhat more nucleated settlement pattern, although this is hard to confirm. The short-term nature of the Seminole occupation has left little occupational debris on the sites of Seminole communities in the Ocala area. No sites have been excavated, and few have been accurately located. Archeology would be difficult because of the short-term occupation of the towns, but might be rewarding in demonstrating cultural changes that took place following the move into a new ecological niche.

Border tensions, lack of trade, Georgian aggressions against free blacks among the Seminole, and general mismanagement by the United States Indian agent led to the inevitable outbreak of hostilities at the end of 1835. A number of first-hand accounts of the strangely Vietnam-like struggle are available (Bemrose 1966; McCall 1868; Motte 1953; Potter 1836; Simmons 1822; Smith 1836; Sprague 1848) as well as an excellent recent study (Mahon 1967). Almost all the available information concerns activities of army personnel and views Indian activities from that standpoint. Osceola, of course, seized the popular imagination at the time and has remained a major American folk figure (Goggin 1955). Some of the army posts or "forts" can be accurately located, but very little significant archeology has been done. The ephemeral nature of Seminole settlements makes it unlikely that significant remains could be recovered. These Indian settlements of the period of the Second Seminole War, however, are potentially a major source of information on material culture as well as possibly indicating useful data on social and political aspects of the rapidly changing culture. Archeology might be able to contribute in the pinpointing of settlements and perhaps even battle sites that have been located by means of documentary sources. Little anthropological knowledge can be gained from the excavation of battle sites, especially those of a guerilla type of warfare such as characterized the Second Seminole War. The war provided the national hero Osceola, who still is preserved in the memories of his people. His grave at Fort Moultrie, South Carolina, has been excavated in order to determine whether the remains had been stolen by a self-confessed looter. Excavation proved that in fact the relics claimed were not those of Osceola, and an opportunity was taken to make osteometric observations on the bones. Unfortunately the head had been removed by the physician who attended the leader in his final illness, but it seems clear that the bones found are those of Osceola.

Like the war in Vietnam, the Second Seminole War dragged on for about seven years with no conclusion, with massive relocations of population, and with an increasing unpopularity among the population who were paying in money and lives. At the end of the conflict, the American forces were simply withdrawn with the proclamation that their objectives had been accomplished. In fact the bulk of the Seminoles that had not been killed were removed to Indian territory west of the Mississippi along with at least part of the free Negroes resident among them. The most intransigent of the Indians, however, remained in Florida, mainly in the Everglades and the Big Cypress Swamp. That part of Florida was almost completely unknown to white Americans in the 1840s and access was very difficult. There a remnant, probably consisting of no more than five hundred individuals, began to develop a new phase of cultural adaptation.

WITHDRAWAL PHASE

This period, lasting until about 1880, is characterized by almost complete withdrawal by the Seminole from contact with or acculturation by the dominant Anglo-American culture. Some trade for manufactured goods was carried on as is indicated by the emergence of a characteristic Seminole clothing style during this time (Sturtevant 1967). Guns, ammunition, some foodstuffs, and perhaps other items did reach the Seminole in the process of exchanging their products for manufactured or exotic goods. What is clear is that dress, housing, an ethos of separation, and the basic features of social organization as reflected in the matrilocal camp did crystalize during this period. Little has been written about the Seminoles during this period simply because they were lost in the Everglades. Two articles by Frederick A. Ober (Beverly 1876; Ober 1875) and a few oblique references in travel books are all that is known except for inferences of their condition at the end of the period. Location of sites would be difficult due to the lack of documentation, but settlements could probably be found by intensive surface and documentary surveys. In many respects this seems to be an intensely interesting period for the archeologist as it offers a chance to see the material remains of the Seminole when they were under pressure to adapt to the new and strange environment of the Everglades and Big Cypress. The emergence of the chickee as the typical Seminole house form occurred during the withdrawal phase. Such an elaborate adaptation to subtropical and hurricane conditions must have been accompanied by other cultural changes. Whether or not these can be seen in the archeology of small isolated camps remains to be seen. In a larger, more strictly anthropological framework, the cultural changes attendant on the great reduction in Seminole population during the nineteenth century might be susceptible to archeological investigation. At the beginning of the century the group numbered nearly five thousand. At the end of the Second Seminole War and the accompanying removal to the West they numbered no more than five hundred and probably fewer than that. Many, if not most, American Indian groups suffered such losses (Dobyns 1966), but the Seminole seem to represent a special case in that they retained in isolation many previous cultural characteristics from the more populous period. This process of cultural adaptation to population decimation with retention of a cultural ethos has not been studied by a combination of ethnographic and archeologic techniques. During the 1880s the Everglades area began to be explored, and there were a few settlements along its fringes. There are a few accounts from this period (Henshall 1884; MacCauley 1887; Stephens 1883). This contact with white America begins the new phase, modern crystalization.

MODERN CRYSTALIZATION PHASE

Florida Seminole are one of the best known, but least studied of American Indian tribes. Their popularity in the eyes of the general public is due in large part to the ill-repute of the Second Seminole War, to the renown of Osceola, to their modern colorful patchwork clothing and to their location close to a major tourist area in South Florida. The lack of serious study by anthropologists is due in large part to the Indians' reluctance to speak to strangers about their tribal affairs and to the ethos of separatism which their ancestors had developed. Serious anthropological work began in the 1930s (Spoehr 1941, 1942, 1944) and has continued sporadically until the present (Capron 1953, 1956a, 1956b; Davis 1955; Freeman 1942, 1944; Gabarino 1972; Sturtevant 1954, 1955, 1956a, 1956b, 1956c, 1958). The University of Florida Indian Oral History Program is collecting tapes from both native speakers and from other knowledgeable local persons. These tapes and transcripts contain a wealth of data on the Seminole lifestyle.

Changes within the last eighty years have been many as the Seminole gradually have come to terms with the population expansion of other Florida groups. Recently the availability of funds through various federal sources has brought modern cement block housing and cattle ranching to even the most remote parts of the reservations. Seminole children attend the various county schools in the area, and there is increasing interaction with the larger community around them.

Much more ethnological work remains to be done, as many aspects of Seminole culture are imperfectly understood (Sturtevant 1958). Some linguistic studies are under way and more are contemplated. As with so many other groups, rapid cultural change means that the old ways will soon be gone and that the processes of culture change are now prime subjects for study. As more Seminoles are drawn into daily contact with the culture of twentieth-century Florida, their sense of separatism seems to be lessening, perhaps to the extent that will facilitate more studies.

No systematic archeological study of this phase of Seminole history has been done, although there has been rather frequent looting of Seminole graves. Of course little archeology of contemporary groups has been developed anywhere, but if it becomes possible, processual-oriented archeology could be rewarding. Studies directed at a better understanding of the development of modern Seminole culture as it is revealed in material objects would be intensely valuable for knowledge of culture change and to help solve the many problems of the people today. Archeology would, of course, cause considerable opposition among many segments of the present society. It is nearly certain that no systematic archeology could be done unless the direct and immediate benefits to the group could be demonstrated well in advance. There yet remains, however, more than enough work for ethnohistorians, ethnologists, and archeologists to do in the long and interesting history of these independent people.

References

Alden, John Richard.
1944. *John Stuart and the Southern Colonial Frontier, A Study of Indian Relations, War, Trade, and Land Problems in the Southern Wilderness, 1754–1775.* Ann Arbor: University of Michigan Press.

Ascher, Robert, and Charles H. Fairbanks.
1971. Excavation of a Slave Cabin: Georgia, U.S.A. *Historical Archaeology* 5:3–17.

Barcia Carballido y Zúñiga, Andrés González de.
1951. *Chronological History of the Continent of Florida.* Translated by Anthony Kerrigan from the original Spanish edition of 1723. Gainesville: University of Florida Press.

Bassett, John Spencer, ed.
1926. *Correspondence of Andrew Jackson,* vols. 1–7. Washington: Carnegie Institution of Washington.

Bartram, William.
1958. *The Travels of William Bartram.* Edited by Francis Harper from the 1791 edition. New Haven: Yale University Press.

Bemrose, John.
1966. *Reminiscences of the Second Seminole War.* Edited by John K. Mahon. Gainesville: University of Florida Press.

Beverly, Fred, pseud. [F. A. Ober].
1876. Among the Seminoles. In *Camp Life in Florida,* pp. 179–93. Edited by Charles Hallock. New York: Forest and Stream Publishing Co.

Boyd, Mark F.
1935–36. The First American Road in Florida: Pensacola–St. Augustine Highway, 1824. *Florida Historical Quarterly* 14:72–106, 138–92.

1937. Events at Prospect Bluff on the Apalachicola River, 1808–1818. *Florida Historical Quarterly* 16:55–96.

1949. Diego Peña's Expedition to Apalachee and Apalachicola in 1716. *Florida Historical Quarterly* 28:1–27.

1951. The Seminole War; Its Background and Onset. *Florida Historical Quarterly* 30:2–115.

1952. Documents Describing the Second and Third Expeditions of Lieutenant Diego Peña to Apalachee and Apalachicola in 1717 and 1718. *Florida Historical Quarterly* 31:109–39.

Boyd, Mark F., and José Navarro Latorre.

1953. Spanish Interest in British Florida, and in the Progress of the American Revolution: part 1, Relations with the Spanish Faction of the Creek Indians. *Florida Historical Quarterly* 32:92–130.

Capron, Louis.

1953. *The Medicine Bundles of the Florida Seminole and the Green Corn Dance.* Bureau of American Ethnology Bulletin 151, Anthropological Paper no. 35, pp. 155–210.

1956a. Notes on the Hunting Dance of the Cow Creek Seminole. *Florida Anthropologist* 9:67–78.

1956b. Florida's Wild Indians. *National Geographic Magazine* 110:819–40.

Cline, Howard F.

1973. *Notes on Colonial Indians and Communities in Florida, 1700–1821.* New York: Garland.

Cohen, Myer M.

1964. *Notices of Florida and the Campaigns.* Facsimile of the 1836 edition. Gainesville: University of Florida Press.

Crane, Verner W.

1956. *The Southern Frontier; 1670–1732.* Ann Arbor: University of Michigan Press.

Davis, Hilda J.

1955. The History of Seminole Clothing and its Multi-Colored Designs. *American Anthropologist* 57:974–80.

Deagan, Kathleen A.

1974. Sex, Status, and Role in the Mestizaje of Spanish Colonial Florida. Ph.D. diss., University of Florida, Gainesville.

de Vorsey, Louis, Jr.

1966. *The Indian Boundary in the Southern Colonies, 1763–1775.* Chapel Hill: University of North Carolina Press.

Dobyns, Henry F.

1966. Estimating Aboriginal American Population: An Appraisal of Techniques with a New Hemispheric Estimate. *Current Anthropology* 7:395–416.

Fairbanks, Charles H.

1957. Ethnohistorical Report of the Florida Indians. Presentation before the Indian Claims Commission, Dockets 73, 151. Stencil reproduction.

1973. The Kingsley Slave Cabins in Duval County, Florida, 1968. *Conference on Historic Site Archaeology Papers* 7:62–93.

Freeman, Ethel Cutler.

1942. We Live with the Seminoles. *Natural History* 49:226–36.

1944. The Seminole Woman of the Big Cypress and Her Influence in Modern Life. *American Indigena* 4:123–28.

Fundaburk, Emma Lila.

1958. *Southeastern Indians, Life Portraits, A Catalogue of Pictures, 1564–1860.* Luverne, Ala: E. L. Fundaburk.

Garbarino, Merwyn S.

1972. *Big Cypress: A Changing Seminole Community.* New York: Holt, Rinehart & Winston.

Gluckman, Stephen J., and Christopher S. Peebles.
   1974.   Oven Hill (Di-15), A Refuge Site in the Suwannee River. *Florida Anthropologist*
           27:21–46.
Goggin, John M.
   1955.   Osceola: Portraits, Features, and Dress. *Florida Historical Quarterly* 33:161–92.
   1958.   Seminole Pottery. In Prehistoric Pottery of the Eastern United States.
           Mimeographed. Museum of Anthropology. University of Michigan, Ann
           Arbor.
Goggin, John M.; Mary E. Godwin; Earl Hester; David Prange; and Robert
           Spangenberg.
   1959.   A Historic Indian Burial, Alachua County, Florida. *Florida Anthropologist*
           2:10–24.
Grant, James (Governor of East Florida).
   1766.   Manuscript. [Letter to General Gage, St. Augustine, January 13, 1766.] Pa-
           pers of General Thomas Gage, Clements Library, University of Michigan,
           Ann Arbor.
Henshall, James A.
   1884.   *Camping and Cruising in Florida*. Cincinnati: R. Clarke.
Kappler, Charles J.
   1904.   *Indian Affairs, Laws and Treaties*. 2d ed. Vol. 2. Washington.
Kersey, Harry A., Jr.
   1974.   The Seminole "Uprising" of 1907. *Florida Anthropologist* 27:49–58.
Lewis, Kenneth E., Jr.
   1969.   History and Archeology of Spalding's Lower Store (Pu-23), Putnam County,
           Florida. Master's thesis, University of Florida, Gainesville.
McCall, George Archibald.
   1868.   *Letters from the Frontiers*. Philadelphia: L. B. Lippincott.
MacCauley, Clay.
   1887.   *The Seminole Indians of Florida. Bureau of American Ethnology, Annual Report*, no.
           5, pp. 469–531.
Mahon, John K.
   1967.   *History of the Second Seminole War*. Gainesville: University of Florida Press.
Motte, Jacob Rhett.
   1953.   *Journey into Wilderness; An Army Surgeon's Account of Life in Camp and Field
           during the Creek and Seminole Wars, 1836–1838*. Edited by James F. Sunder-
           man. Gainesville: University of Florida Press.
Nairne, Thomas.
   1710.   *A Letter from South Carolina*. London.
Ober, Frederick A.
   1875.   Ten Days with the Seminoles. *Appleton's Journal of Literature, Science and Art*,
           vol. 14, no. 332, pp. 142–44; no. 333, pp. 171–73.
Patrick, Rembert W.
   1954.   *Florida Fiasco: Rampant Rebels on the Georgia-Florida Border, 1810–1815*.
           Athens: University of Georgia Press.
Phillip V.
   1745.   Manuscript, A.G.I. 58-1-25/147. [Royal cédula to Governor of Florida, Aran-
           juez, May 13, 1745.] Photostat, Stetson Collection, University of Florida.
Poe, Stephen R.
   1963.   Archaeological Excavations at Fort Gadsden, Florida. *Notes in Anthropology*,
           no. 8, Department of Anthropology, Florida State University, Tallahassee.
Politzer, William S.
   1971.   Physical Anthropology of Indians of the Old South. In *Red, White, and Black:
           Symposium on Indians in the Old South*, edited by Charles M. Hudson. Southern An-
           thropological Society, Proceedings, no. 5. Athens: University of Georgia Press.

Porter, Kenneth W.
  1943a. John Caesar: A Forgotten Hero of the Seminole War. *Journal of Negro History* 28:53–65.
  1943b. Florida Slaves and Free Negroes in the Seminole War. *Journal of Negro History* 28:390–421.
  1945. Negroes and the East Florida Annexation Plot, 1811–1813. *Journal of Negro History* 30:9–29.
  1946. John Caesar: Seminole Negro Partisan. *Journal of Negro History* 31:190–207.
  1949. The Founder of the "Seminole Nation": Secoffee or Cowkeeper. *Florida Historical Quarterly* 27:362–84.
  1951. Negroes and the Seminole War. *Journal of Negro History* 36:249–80.
Potter, Woodburne.
  1836. *War in Florida: Being an Exposition of its Causes and an Accurate History of the Campaigns of Generals Clinch, Gaines, and Scott.* Baltimore: Lewis and Coleman.
Simmons, William H.
  1822. *Notices of East Florida with an Account of the Seminole Nation of Indians.* Charleston: A. E. Miller.
Smith, W. W.
  1836. *Sketch of the Seminole War, and Sketches during a Campaign.* Charleston: Dan J. Dowling.
Spoehr, Alexander.
  1941. *Camp, Clan, and Kin Among the Cow Creek Seminole.* Field Museum of Natural History, Anthropological Series, vol. 33, no. 1, pp. 1–27. Chicago.
  1942. *Kinship System of the Seminole.* Field Museum of Natural History, Anthropological Series, vol. 33, no. 2, pp. 28–113. Chicago.
  1944. *The Florida Seminole Camp.* Field Museum of Natural History, Anthropological Series, vol. 33, no. 3, pp. 114–50. Chicago.
Sprague, John T.
  1848. *The Origin, Progress, and Conclusion of the Florida War.* New York: D. Appleton and Company.
Stephens, Charles A.
  1883. Iste Semole. *The Continent* 3:289–93. Philadelphia.
Stuart, John.
  1764a. Manuscript. [Letter to Thomas Gage, July 19, 1764.] Papers of General Thomas Gage, Clements Library, University of Michigan, Ann Arbor.
  1764b. Manuscript. [Letter to Lieutenant Pampellone, July 16, 1764.] Papers of General Thomas Gage, Clements Library, University of Michigan, Ann Arbor.
Sturtevant, William C.
  1954. The Medicine Bundles and Busks of the Florida Seminole. *Florida Anthropologist* 7:31–70.
  1955. Notes on Modern Seminole Traditions of Osceola. *Florida Historical Quarterly* 33:206–17.
  1956a. A Seminole Personal Document. *Tequesta* 16:55–75.
  1956b. R. H. Pratt's Report on the Seminole in 1876. *Florida Anthropologist* 9:1–24.
  1956c. Osceola's Coats? *Florida Historical Quarterly* 34:315–28.
  1958. Accomplishments and Opportunities in Florida Indian Ethnology. In *Florida Anthropology*, edited by Charles H. Fairbanks, pp. 15–55. Florida Anthropological Society, Publication no. 4.
  1967. Seminole Men's Clothing. In *Essays on Verbal and Visual Arts, Proceedings of the 1966 Annual Spring Meeting, American Ethnological Society*, edited by June Helm, pp. 160–74. Seattle: University of Washington Press.
Tanner, Helen Hornbeck.
  1963. *Zéspedes in East Florida, 1784–1790.* University of Miami, Hispanic American Studies no. 19. Coral Gables: University of Miami Press.

United States Government.
    1832a. *American State Papers,* vol. 5, class 2, *Indian Affairs,* vol. 1. Washington: Gales
        and Seaton.
    1832b. *American State Papers,* vol. 12, class 5, *Military Affairs,* vol. 1. Washington: Gales
        and Seaton.
    1834. *American State Papers,* vol. 4, class 2, *Indian Affairs* vol. 2. Washington: Gales
        and Seaton.
Wenhold, Lucy L.
    1956. The First Fort of San Marcos de Apalache. *Florida Historical Quarterly*
        34:301–14.
Willis, William S., Jr.
    1971. Divide and Rule. In *Red, White, and Black: Symposium on Indians in the Old
        South,* edited by Charles M. Hudson. Southern Anthropological Society, Pro-
        ceedings, no. 5. Athens: University of Georgia Press.
Wright, J. Leitch, Jr.
    1971. *Anglo-Spanish Rivalry in North America.* Athens: University of Georgia Press.
Young, Hugh.
    1934– A Topographic Memoire on East and West Florida with Itineraries. *Florida
    35.   Historical Quarterly* 13:16–50, 82–104, 129–64.

Taping the Indian Past: The University of Florida's Oral History Project

Samuel Proctor

THE University of Florida is one of seven universities which are part of the national Doris Duke Indian Oral History Project. To gather "Indian history from an Indian point of view" was Miss Duke's intention when she generously granted funds to a group of western and midwestern universities during the 1960s. Her goal was to create regional archives of the oral traditions of the Indian people which could be disseminated for use by Indian and non-Indian scholars and researchers.

During the latter part of the 1960s, the University of Florida had established a small oral history program, and the P. K. Yonge Library of Florida History at the university has long been interested in collecting manuscripts and books relating to Florida Indians. The university's library was an important research center for scholars working in Florida and southern history. Because of these existing programs, the University of Florida, in 1970, was invited to inaugurate an oral history program encompassing the Indians of Florida—the Seminoles and the Miccosukees. Dr. Samuel Proctor and Dr. John Mahon of the Department of History became the directors of the project. Dr. Charles Fairbanks and Dr. Paul Doughty agreed to serve as advisors. The Seminole Tribe of Florida pledged cooperation and agreed to set up the interviews and to provide interviewers. In 1971, the University of Florida's Oral History Project was broadened to include all of the forest Indians living in the Southeast, the area south of the Potomac and Ohio rivers and west from the Atlantic Ocean to the Mississippi River. Approximately eighty thousand Indians live in this area. The

Center for the Study of Southeastern Indians was created by the Board of Regents of the State University System to supervise oral history collection and related activities.

The Seminoles, the Mississippi Band of Choctaws, and the Eastern Band of Cherokees live on reservations. The other Indian groups—Creek Nation East of the Mississippi, Catawbas (South Carolina), Lumbees (North Carolina), Miccosukees, and several groups in Virginia (Western Chickahominy, Eastern Chickahominy, Mattaponi, Upper Mattaponi, and Rappahanock)—live either on state Indian reservations or on privately owned lands. Many of the southeastern Indians have become highly assimilated into the society of non-Indians and have thrown off their traditional Indian life-style. Some have broken so much with their Indian past that they have even lost their languages. Only a handful of Catawba words are still identifiable. Many, if not all, of the Virginia Indian dialects have been lost. On the other hand, the Seminoles, Choctaws, and Cherokees have rich languages which they utilize as their major means of communication, particularly the older members of the tribal communities. For many Choctaws English is a second language. Securing oral history interviews under these conditions is an interesting experience, although it does create various problems in translating and transcribing. Nonetheless, language tapes are sought, and their value to the contemporary scholar and to the researcher of the future is inestimable. Several of the tapes were used this past year in a linguistics program at the University of Florida. Others have provided the necessary source material to produce a film and radio and television scripts.

The University of Florida Indian Oral History Project has sought to use Indians as interviewers wherever possible. This is desirable, particularly for those Indians suspicious of white interviewers or uncomfortable in their presence. Where Indian interviewers are not available, the staff includes faculty members and graduate students from the University of Florida and other institutions, a few undergraduates, and some individuals who have worked with southeastern Indians and understand their life-style. Historians, anthropologists, archeologists, and journalists have been involved as interviewers.

Most of the oral history material collected is of excellent quality. During the course of the recorded conversation much extraneous material is included. Conversational flow cannot be easily channeled to fit a precise outline. It is also realized that what seems irrelevant at the moment may become very valuable data for a future researcher.

The University of Florida collection includes interviews with Indians from Florida, South Carolina, North Carolina, Virginia, Maryland, Mississippi, Alabama, and Oklahoma. To date, there are only a few interviews with the Cherokees of North Carolina, the Mississippi Choctaws, the Virginia Indians, and the Miccosukees. Most of the Choctaw tapes have emanated from a project that has developed in the Indian high school on the Choctaw Reservation at Philadelphia, Mississippi. The oral history project with the Virginia Indians is just beginning; there have been no interviews with Louisiana Indians yet. The policy of the project has been to seek information from a wide range of subjects, and interviews have been held with young and old and male and female informants.

Seminole interviews include many personal and family histories which provide insight into such subjects as economic activities, off-reservation schooling at boarding schools in Oklahoma and at Carlisle, Pennsylvania, the cattle program, religion and Indian conversion, Indian militancy, and business operations. An interview with Mrs. Frank Stranahan, long-time teacher and counselor of the Seminoles in South Florida, covers such topics as education, Indian medicine, the influence of white religion on Indians, trading practices, and federal government relations with the Indians. Louis Capron, now deceased, but for many years a friend and advisor to the Indians, describes the establishment of the Seminole reservation at Hollywood, Indian education, the Green Corn Dance, and traditional Seminole religious practices. An interview with David West, a linguist from the Wycliff Bible Society, describes lexical involvement of Indian languages and his effort to commit the Florida Indian dialects to a written language.

Several of the Seminole interviews describe the coming of Christianity to the reservations during the 1930s, the establishment of the Baptist church, and the conflict which this evangelical movement ignited. The Green Corn Dance and other traditional dances, folklore and crafts, utilization of herbs for medicinal purposes, and the role of the medicine men are some of the subjects touched on. Interviews with Indian traders reveal the methods of business transactions and the kind of goods that the Indians brought into the trading posts of South Florida in earlier years. Alligator skins, animal pelts, and bird plumes were major items traded by the Indians. The collection of interviews with Indian traders was the basis for an article by Professor Harry A. Kersey of Florida Atlantic University which appeared in the *Florida Historical Quarterly.* Professor Kersey has also written a book, *Pelts, Plumes, and Hides: White Traders among the Seminole Indians,*

1870-1930 (University Presses of Florida, 1975), based upon the University of Florida's oral history tapes. Interviews with Seminole Indian agents reveal many of the problems and controversies that have developed among the tribal leadership and the Bureau of Indian Affairs and other government agencies.

The Miccosukee Indians who live in isolated settlements along the Tamiami Trail west of Miami are very traditional and conservative. They have not responded to the request for interviews. However, Buffalo Tiger, chief of the Miccosukees, has been interviewed, and this material is part of the University of Florida collection.

The Seminole Indian interviews are supported by a collection of related documents and manuscripts from the National Archives. As time permits, the correspondence of the Indian agents who were stationed in Florida beginning in the early 1880s is being Xeroxed for the University of Florida Library. In the oral history archives there are 196 Florida Seminole tapes, representing 168 interviews and 274 hours of recordings. All of these interviews have been transcribed.

The Lumbee project is the largest in the collection. Eight interviewers—all Indian except one—have collected 255 interviews representing 376 hours of recording. The Lumbee effort to gain recognition and legitimacy is the major topic discussed. Members of this Indian community, the largest in the Southeast, argue that they have been denied many of the benefits available to reservation Indians. The Lumbees have traditionally suffered from the segregation patterns of the South and the particular area of North Carolina in which they live. The tapes contain discussions of their attempts to gain political, economic, and social rights. They have been particularly interested in preserving Old Main, the original building on Pembroke State University campus. At one time this was an Indian school, and the Lumbees take great pride in it as part of their heritage. The building was burned a few years ago, and many Lumbees charge that it was a case of arson and that the purpose was to demean them and their cause.

In the 1950s, the Lumbees were the subject of constant abuse and attack by the Ku Klux Klan. The Indians then turned the tables on the Klan and forcibly drove them out of the area. The Lumbees are very sensitive to the question of their civil rights, and this is discussed often on the tapes. One of their strongest traditions is their belief that they are the descendants of the English settlers of the sixteenth-century Lost Colony of Virginia, and they point to their name and speech patterns to verify this belief. Many have become political activists, and some support the American Indian Movement. All of these subjects are discussed on the tapes.

During World War II, a number of Lumbees migrated from North Carolina to the Washington-Baltimore area to work in the war-related factories and plants there. Economic pressures have encouraged others to continue this migration, and now there is a large settlement—perhaps as many as four thousand—living there. Most of these Lumbees are employed in industrial plants and live in the ghetto areas of Baltimore and Washington. They have become highly urbanized and are subject to all the pressures of city life. The problems of their adjustment to integrated schools, housing, and unionization and other matters are discussed in the forty-four urban Lumbee Indian interviews (representing forty-two hours of recording) that have been made. The urban Indians are very conscious of the danger of losing their heritage and make this point on the tapes. Part of the Lumbee collection includes the tapes made by Professor Adolph Dial when he was collecting material for his history of the North Carolina Lumbees.

There are four interviewers working on the Catawba Indian project at Rock Hill, South Carolina. One, Frances Wade, is a Catawba and is employed by the Catawba Nation. Major topics deal with Catawbas as members of the Mormon church, pottery making, traditional use of herbs, state and federal land management, federal aid, legal aspects of former reservation land, working conditions in the greater Rock Hill area, matters of education, public health, and welfare, and the economic conditions of the 1930s and 1940s. There is much information relating to Catawba-white relations. The Indians in South Carolina are farmers, and many work in the textile mills of the area. Labor-management problems, union activities, and discrimination are discussed on the tapes. To date, 137 interviews have been made, about 129 hours of recordings. All of the tapes have been transcribed.

There are two groups of Choctaw Indians in the Southeast that the University of Florida project is interested in. There are a handful of families living in Clay, Putnam, Bradford, and Alachua counties who claim to be descendants of a group of Choctaws who came into Florida from Alabama during the early nineteenth century. Their ancestors served as guides for Andrew Jackson when he invaded Florida during the Second Spanish Period. These people are now totally integrated into white culture, and they have no distinctive Indian characteristics or physical features. A few traditions and shreds of information have come down to them orally from their ancestors. The project has secured five interviews, approximating seven hours of recording. The tapes include a sketchy history of the Florida Choctaw tribe which cannot be documented. There is also information relating to Choctaw life and white racial conflicts, Indian-black relations, and efforts to obtain recognition for a Florida Band of Choctaw Indians.

The tribal council of the Mississippi Band of Choctaws has supported cooperation with the University of Florida's Oral History Project. Discussions are currently under way with the members of a federally funded linguistics program that is operating on the reservation with the long-range plan of developing a Choctaw dictionary. Most of the interviews are being carried on in the native language and will be translated by the linguists in Mississippi.

An oral history program has also been developed in the Choctaw high school, with tenth, eleventh, and twelfth grade students. Under the supervision of their teacher, Choctaw students have been interviewing members of the tribe. The purpose of these interviews is to secure material for articles which are published by the class in a journal titled *Nanih Waiya*. This is a development of the Georgia Foxfire Project. The tapes are being sent to the University of Florida where they are being transcribed. Thirty-four Choctaw interviews have been held, representing thirty-seven hours of recording. All of these have been transcribed. The tapes deal with a variety of subjects, including the training and education of Indian children, attitudes toward Indian-white marriage, Indian-black relationships, and discrimination toward Indians. Many Choctaws have a background of sharecrop farming, and its impact is discussed in the interviews. One tape describes a non-Christian wedding ceremony, and there is also an analysis of the role and status of women in Choctaw society. The Choctaw students have been asking questions about farming, the preserving and cooking of food, recreational interests, sports, and the making by hand of the implements which are used in these activities. For many of the Choctaws, English is a second language, and the aspects of the Choctaw language and its use in the community are discussed on two of the tapes.

Progress has been slow on the Cherokee Indian project in western North Carolina. The tribal council has indicated on several occasions that it will support the project and has appointed a member of the tribe to coordinate the interviewing. To date, there have been twelve interviews with approximately ten hours of recordings. All of this material has been transcribed. One interview with Jarret Blythe, a former

Cherokee chief, deals with efforts to gain better business opportunities and voting rights for Cherokees. Other tapes deal with
Cherokee cooking and eating habits, folklore, farming, and crafts.

The Virginia Indians retain a strong memory of and identity with
their past. In some instances, they live on tribally held land under
treaty status with the state. In spite of their acculturation, the Virginia
Indians are conscious of the ethnic boundaries between themselves
and members of the white community. When the English arrived in
what is now eastern Virginia, they found two groups of Indians: the
Iroquoian-speaking Nottoway and Meherrin, who live south of the
upper James River, and some thirty Algonquian-speaking Powhatan
tribes, who occupied the rest of the area. The Powhatan population in
1607 has been estimated at fourteen thousand. By 1800, there were
only four small reservations left in Virginia. All were state reservations established originally by treaties between the tribes and the
Colony of Virginia prior to the American Revolution. There were also
several groups who lived in seclusion without reservations, but who
kept an Indian identity among themselves. There were never any
removals in Virginia, but the Virginia Indian population continued to
decline.

In the years before the Civil War, there was an increasing amount
of antagonism toward the Virginia Indians; they were free non-whites
who resisted assimilation. The pressures against the Virginia Indians
continued during the post–Civil War years, and they were not able to
resist completely the attempted physical and cultural genocide. The
reservation and enclave populations of the Powhatan Indians have
been relatively stable since the end of the seventeenth century.

Today, the Powhatan descendants who identify themselves as Indian number approximately twelve hundred persons living in
Virginia. There are likely a few hundred more residing elsewhere
who maintain their Indian ties by occasional visits and by telephone
and letter communication. They are divided into the following
groups: Pamunkey Reservation, Mattaponi Reservation, Western
Chickahominy Tribe, Eastern Chickahominy Tribe, Upper Mattaponi
Tribe, Rappahanock Tribe, and Nansemond descendants.

The university's Oral History Project is just beginning its work with
the Virginia Indians, which will be coordinated by Dr. Helen Rountree
of Old Dominion University, Norfolk, Virginia. Contact has been
made with three of the Indian groups, and they have agreed to coop-
erate with the project. The first tapes are beginning to arrive and are

being processed. Data will be accumulated about the past and present life-styles of the Virginia Indians.

In addition to the oral history interviews, the University of Florida, through its Center for the Study of Southeastern Indians, is developing an extensive collection of documentary material on various aspects of Indian history and Indian culture. These include manuscripts, books, maps, and pictures. The documents and manuscripts have been selected from a variety of archival sources, including several thousand pages from the Bureau of Indian Affairs records in the National Archives in Washington. Several hundred pictures and slides have been added to the center's archives in recent months. These have been labeled and cataloged and are being used extensively for school programs and television and other media outlets. A slide show of Florida Indians has recently been assembled by R. T. King, a member of the university's oral history staff, and has been shown extensively. As an adjunct of the center's activities, an oral history project is being carried on at Gutiérrez Zamora, a small community in eastern Mexico on the Gulf of Mexico. Included in these interviews are a number with the Totonac Indians, who live in the area.

In the University of Florida collection, there are more than 725 interviews, and approximately 18,000 transcribed pages. There are 1,011 hours of recordings. History, anthropology, sociology, education, folklore and legend, linguistics, oral tradition, politics, economics, real estate activities, political geography, law, ethnology, genealogy, and health-related fields are some of the significant areas of investigation that are included in the collection. There is also a significant collection of tapes of Indian music. The Center for the Study of Southeastern Indians and the University of Florida's Indian Oral History Project are a tribute to the vision of Miss Doris Duke. As researchers and scholars, both Indian and non-Indian, use this material over the years, the rich story of the Indian past in the Southeast eventually will be told. Most American Indian history has been written from documents and materials compiled by non-Indians. Now Indian sources are becoming available. An increasing number of books, articles in scholarly journals, and masters' theses and doctoral dissertations related to this subject attest to the availability of primary source material on the Indians of the Southeast.

Contributors

HALE G. SMITH, a graduate of Beloit College, the University of Chicago, and the University of Michigan, was professor of anthropology at Florida State University prior to his death in 1977. He served as chairman of the department for twenty-three years, returning to teaching and research in 1972. It was under his supervision that the *Notes in Anthropology* series began publication at Florida State University. Professor Smith has been recognized both in America and abroad for his anthropological and archeological research. He has made valuable contributions to the knowledge and understanding of the archeology of Florida. His archeological work on the Arrivas House and other historic sites in St. Augustine, Fort San Carlos in Fernandina, and on Santa Rosa Island, Pensacola, have been particularly noteworthy. He was one of the authors of *Here They Once Stood: The Tragic End of the Apalachee Missions*, and he has written several monographs. His articles have appeared in major scholarly journals. He was one of the founders of the Florida Anthropological Society.

MARK GOTTLOB holds an M.A. degree from Florida State University. Anthropology was his major area of study in graduate school. He has been involved in zooarcheological research in the Southeast and is presently teaching in Shreveport, Louisiana.

CLIFFORD M. LEWIS, S.J., a member of the teaching faculty of Wheeling College, Wheeling, West Virginia, has carried out field research on the sixteenth-century Jesuit missions which were established along the lower Gulf coast of Florida. He is the co-author of *The Spanish Jesuit Mission in Virginia, 1570–1572*, published by the Virginia Historical Society.

RIPLEY P. BULLEN died on Christmas Day, 1976, while this volume was in preparation. Dr. Bullen, curator emeritus of the Florida State Museum, had a distinguished career in archeology and anthropology spanning more than thirty years. A native of New York, he first trained as a mechanical engineer at Cornell University. In 1940, Dr. Bullen joined the staff of the Robert S. Peabody Foundation for Archeology in Andover, Massachusetts, and while he was pursuing graduate studies at Harvard University, he did field excavations in New Mexico and Massachusetts. He came to the University of Florida in 1948 as assistant archeologist of the Florida Board of Parks and Historic Memorials and four years later joined the Florida State Museum as its first curator of social sciences. He helped organize the Florida Anthropological Society and started the monograph series *Contributions of the Florida State Museum, Social Sciences*. Dr. Bullen surveyed and excavated many sites in Florida and throughout the Caribbean and made major contributions to the delineation of the Florida formative period, 2,000–500 B.C. Author of more than 250 books, monographs, and articles, he also edited numerous conference proceedings and scientific journals. Dr. Bullen presented scientific papers at international meetings in Europe and throughout Latin America. The foundation of Crystal River Historical Memorial and Museum on the Gulf coast of Florida was largely due to his efforts. He received an honorary doctorate from the University of Florida in 1975.

JERALD T. MILANICH, a native of Ohio, holds his graduate degrees from the University of Florida. He is associate curator, Department of Social Sciences, Florida State Museum, and a member of the teaching faculty, Department of Anthropology, University of Florida. His special areas of interest are eastern United States archeology, North American Indians, southeastern ethnology and ethnohistory, and the colonial period in Spanish-Indian relations in the New World. He has received a number of research grants and contracts and has presented papers at state, regional, and national conferences. His articles have appeared in scholarly and professional journals, and he is editor of the *Florida Anthropologist*.

KATHLEEN A. DEAGAN, a native of Virginia and a graduate of the University of Florida, is assistant professor of anthropology at Florida State University. She has been the director of the archeological field research at St. Augustine, sponsored by the Historic St. Augustine Preservation Board, and has served as a consultant to the National Greek Orthodox Church on the restoration of the National Shrine at St. Augustine. She was the recipient of the Ripley P. Bullen Award for Outstanding Achievement in Anthropology from the Florida State Museum in 1974. Professor Deagan's book, *Archaeology at the Greek Orthodox Shrine, St. Augustine, Florida*, was published by the University Presses of Florida in the Florida State University *Notes in Anthropology* series.

LEWIS H. LARSON, JR., a graduate of the University of Michigan, is professor of anthropology at West Georgia College. He is also state archeologist for Georgia. His articles on the prehistoric and historic aborigines of the Georgia Coast have appeared in scholarly and professional journals in the Southeast and throughout the United States. His long-time research is on the Etowah archeological site in north Georgia. His book on Southeastern Indian subsistence techniques is being published by the University of Tennessee Press.

WILLIAM C. STURTEVANT is curator of North American Anthropology at the Smithsonian Institution. He holds a doctorate from Yale University, where his thesis topic was *The Mikasuki Seminole: Medical Beliefs and Practices*. He has done extensive research in ethnohistory of the Indians of eastern North America. He served at Yale University as a research associate and instructor in the Anthropology Department and was also assistant curator of anthropology at the Peabody Museum at Yale. Dr. Sturtevant was the recipient of a Fulbright Award and has lectured at the Institute of Social Anthropology, Oxford University. He is also the general editor of the forthcoming *Handbook of North American Indians*.

CHARLES H. FAIRBANKS, a graduate of the University of Chicago and the University of Michigan, is distinguished service professor of anthropology and former chairman of the Department of Anthropology at the University of Florida. His areas of specialization include southeastern archeology and ethnology, nativism, and colonial archeology. He has held three research contracts with the Indian Claims Section of the United States Department of Justice, and he has written two definitive early histories of Southeastern Indians, *Ethnohistorical Report of the Florida Indians* (Garland) and *Ethnohistorical Report on the Indians of the Central Gulf Coast* (Indian Claims Commission). He is also the author of a social history of the Seminole, *The Florida Seminole Peoples*, and his articles have appeared in many regional and national scholarly journals.

SAMUEL PROCTOR, a native Floridian, is distinguished service professor of history and social sciences at the University of Florida. He holds his graduate degrees from the University of Florida. He is editor of the *Florida Historical Quarterly*, director of the University of Florida's Oral History Project, and co-director of the Center for the Study of Southeastern Indians. He is director of the Center for Florida Studies and holds the title of Julien C. Yonge Professor of Florida History. He is the author of several books and many articles dealing with Florida and southern history.

Index